LIVES IN PROCESS: MILDLY RETARDED ADULTS IN A LARGE CITY

Robert B. Edgerton, Editor

LIVES IN PROCESS: MILDLY RETARDED ADULTS IN A LARGE CITY

Robert B. Edgerton, Editor
Mental Retardation Research Center
University of California at Los Angeles

Monographs of the American Association
on Mental Deficiency, No. 6
Series Editor, C. Edward Meyers

American Association on Mental Deficiency
1719 Kalorama Road, NW, Washington, DC 20009
1984

Published by
American Association on Mental Deficiency
1719 Kalorama Road, NW
Washington, DC 20009

No. 6, Monographs of the American Association on Mental Deficiency (ISSN 0730-7128)
Library of Congress Catalog Card Number: 84-2869
International Standard Book Number: 0-940898-13-6

Library of Congress Cataloging in Publication Data

Main entry under title:

Lives in process.

(Monographs of the American Association on Mental Deficiency, ISSN 0730-7128; no.6)
Bibliography: p.
1. Mentally handicapped—United States—Case studies. 2. Mental deficiency—Research—United States—Addresses, essays, lectures. I. Edgerton, Robert B., 1931–   . II. Series: Monograph of the American Association on Mental Deficiency; no. 6.
HV3006.A4L58   1984   305'.90826   84-2869
ISBN 0-940898-13-6

Printed in the United States of America

Dedication

This volume is dedicated to the memory of
Lesley R. Winik
student, colleague, friend

Editor's Preface

I recall the participation of a brilliant graduate student in anthropology on our research team at Pacific (now Lanterman) State Hospital, under George Tarjan and the late Harvey Dingman. Robert B. Edgerton had already participated in some third-world anthropology, gathering information first-hand by dwelling among the target groups, and he was scheduled for still more travel to exotic places. Before leaving on his subsequent trip, he applied anthropological methods to the residents at Pacific State, learning about their everyday affairs, aspirations, friendships, conflicts, and loves. He then carried his research into the community, patiently interviewing former residents of Pacific and emerging with the classic report, *The Cloak of Competence*. Later, as a professor in anthropology and psychiatry, Dr. Edgerton created the Socio-Behavioral Research Group in the UCLA Mental Retardation Research Center, the outstanding such group in our land.

This monograph is but one of several books, articles, and chapters produced by this prolific group. The papers in this volume represent the fruits of anthropological and social psychological procedures applied to an indigenous group, mildly retarded young adults in the community. The principal method was participant observation, but semi-structured interviews were also employed, and one paper depended on a quasi-experimental procedure of standardized questions to determine how people give requested geographic directions.

The editor thanks Michael J. Begab and Louis Rowitz for critical reading and helpful suggestions for revision of the manuscript, and also Marcia A. Gaston for final editing and copy editing.

C. Edward Meyers
Editor, AAMD *Monograph* Series

Acknowledgments

I want first of all to express my gratitude and that of my colleagues to Dr. C. E. Meyers for his invitation to prepare this volume. In addition to the honor he did us by his invitation, he provided continuing encouragement. His editorial contributions were also most welcome. I am also grateful to Dr. Herbert Grossman for his invitation to present preliminary versions of some of the papers in this volume at the 107th Annual Meeting of the American Association on Mental Deficiency in Dallas, Texas, June 1983.

In addition to the research grant support noted by the contributors to this volume, I gratefully acknowledge the support of the Mental Retardation Research Center, UCLA, its Director, Dr. Nathaniel Buchwald, and all members of the Socio-Behavioral Research Group of this Center. I regret that it was not possible to include papers by more of our colleagues, but their support is appreciated. I must make special mention of all those former members of the Socio-Behavioral Research Group (too numerous to acknowledge by name) whose research assistance contributed so vitally to the development of the papers collected here.

To anyone who has ever edited a volume like this, it will be obvious that much is owed to all the staff whose skills and patience converted rough drafts into polished copy. I thank Lupe Montaño, Esther Rose, Genevieve Gilbert-Rolfe, Grace Davis, and Janell Demyan. My greatest debt is to Marcia Gaston who cheerfully and competently carried out the editorial tasks that each paper required. This book owes much to her.

Finally, I thank all those many friends, parents, relatives, employers, counselors, and other concerned persons who willingly participated in our research. They were helpful in many ways. Most of all, I would like to thank the participants themselves. They allowed us to share in their lives. I hope that this volume will be accepted by them as a downpayment on the debt we all owe them.

Contents

Introduction

Robert B. Edgerton

When the earliest investigators of the social adaptation of deinstitutionalized mentally retarded persons found that the majority of these persons had apparently made a satisfactory adjustment to community life, they were surprised. Indeed, no less a figure in the field than W. E. Fernald was so surprised, when his findings indicated unexpected success, that he delayed publication of those findings for 2 years (Goldstein, 1964). The prediction had been one of failure in community adaptation, and the finding of success was jarring. By 1972, when Henry Cobb reviewed the evidence, expectations had changed so much that Cobb (1972) echoed the conventional view when he concluded, "The most consistent and outstanding finding of all follow-up studies is the high proportion of the adult retarded who achieve satisfactory adjustments, by whatever criteria are employed" (p.145).

In the decade since Cobb offered his optimistic conclusion, a great deal of research has appeared, and the pattern that emerges is anything but clear-cut (Edgerton, 1983). Success is reported here, failure there; deinstitutionalization continues, but so does reinstitutionalization. Some mentally retarded persons do very well in their adjustment to community living; others do less well. Some do well at first and encounter problems later on. Others have trouble initially but, as time passes, become more successful. Some fluctuate throughout their lives. Perhaps the most accurate appraisal that anyone can make of community adaptation is that it is a highly complex and changing phenomenon, one that we know far too little about. It is also an intensely human phenomenon, filled with joys and sorrows, boredom and excitement, fear and hope. The lives of mentally retarded persons are important—to them, to their friends and families, and to the agencies that provide services for them. All would agree, I think, that our knowledge of these lives is sorely lacking.

The contributors to this volume are members of the Socio-Behavioral Group of the Mental Retardation Research Center, University of California, Los Angeles. The work included here represents most of the approaches and a sample of the findings of the group as a whole.[1] The title of the volume, *Lives in Process,* is intended to call attention to two essential features of our approach. First, we try to study the lives of mentally retarded persons in their entirety. Everything that forms a part of those lives—dreams, fears, communication, jobs, recreation, friends, and family—is important to us, as it is to the mentally retarded persons themselves. Because these lives change in response

---

[1]For anyone wishing a broader sampling of work, including work in progress, *Working Papers of the Social-Behavioral Group* are available upon request to: K. T. Kernan, Editor, Socio-Behavioral Group, Mental Retardation Research Center, School of Medicine, University of California, Los Angeles, CA 90024.

to various environmental demands, just as they develop in reaction to maturational changes, we emphasize process not only in an effort to document change but also in a search for causal linkages. These understandings are the essentials of our perspective.

We need to say more about this perspective, how it is put to work, and how we came to adopt it. The history of research on the community adaptation of mentally retarded persons has been characterized by a search for prognostic variables: for simple, easily measured means of predicting success or failure in adjustment to community life. The current national emphasis on predicting and measuring the "progress" of mentally retarded individuals perpetuates this emphasis. These approaches have not yet been successful, as repeated reviews have noted (Brooks & Baumeister, 1977; Cobb, 1972; Haywood, 1977; McCarver & Craig, 1974; Owhaki, 1974). There are several reasons for this lack of success. One is the simplicity of the traditional variables that have been used—age, IQ, institutional history, vocational training, sensorimotor skills, and so forth; another is the failure to achieve any notable precision in the measurement of even these simplistic variables. Yet another is the failure to recognize that the dependent variable—success in adaptation—is highly changeable. Indeed, it is far less a measurable dependent variable than a multiplex process marked by change and contradiction. Some recent research has improved on the specification and the measurement of prognostic variables (Schalock & Harper, 1978; Scheerenberger & Felsenthal, 1977), but problems in conceptualizing the complex and changing dependent variable "adaptation" are still unresolved.

Although this dilemma is characteristic of work in mental retardation, it is by no means confined to this area of research. As Issac Deutscher (1966) pointed out, the social sciences in general have chosen to adopt a set of procedures that lead naturally, perhaps inevitably, to this result. The emphasis on verification of hypotheses rather than the generation of theory, with the attendant constraints of operationalism, has led many researchers into ever more objective and precise exercises in the measurement of variables that are nowhere demonstrated to be the most relevant for prediction or understanding. The result, as Glaser and Strauss (1967) have persuasively argued, is often an increasingly ritualized set of methods focused on conventional variables, on the one hand, and the absence of germinal theory on the other.

Recognition that this problem adversely affects research in mental retardation is now evident (Brooke & Baumeister, 1977; Haywood, 1977), and some empirical work that attempts to rectify matters has begun to appear (Bogdan & Taylor, 1976; Braginsky & Braginsky, 1971; Edgerton, 1967; Henschel, 1972; Lorber, 1974/1975). It is the consensus of this literature that, if we are to improve our understanding of the community adaptation of retarded persons, we must study their lives holistically, where they occur rather than in laboratories, and we must listen to these persons as they express their own views of their lives. Such a holistic and naturalistic approach to research is receiving growing acceptance in a number of disciplines (Denzin, 1971; Edgerton & Langness, 1978; Geertz, 1973; Harre & Secord, 1972; Phillips, 1973; Willems, 1967), and it has existed for many years in other fields, such as anthropology and sociology. Still, until recently, it was rarely utilized in the study of mental retardation, and it is still uncommon. In an effort to extend the use of this approach in studies of mentally retarded persons, the Socio-Behavioral Group at UCLA was organized in 1970.

The group came to include faculty, graduate students, and post-doctoral scholars from several behavioral science disciplines, bringing with them their respective concepts, theories, and methods. Anthropology, education, linguistics, psychology, and sociology have all been represented, and their diverse perspectives have proven to be invaluable. Despite our differences, from the beginning we shared a problem and an approach. Our problem was to document and explain what we could of the lives of mentally retarded persons. Our approach was centered on ethnography, employing long-term ethnographic methods based on intensive participant-observation.

Our procedures require familiarity with as many aspects of a retarded person's life as possible. Our methodological persuasion derives primarily from naturalism rather than more experimental aspects of behavioral science. Three principles are fundamental for us: (a) that phenomena be seen in their relevant context; (b) that these phenomena be seen not only through the observer's eyes, but those of the subjects as well; and (c) that reactive procedures be avoided at the same time that the investigator regards himself as a part of the phenomenon under investigation (Edgerton & Langness, 1978).

To carry out such ethnographic naturalism, we must have prolonged contact with people, and we must become, if only relatively so, a "natural" part of the lives of mentally retarded persons. When we succeed, and sometimes we do not, we eventually gain access to more than the public aspects of their lives. By virtue of our prolonged and somewhat unpredictable presence in their world, we hope to be able to see more than the obvious. We drop by, we take people away from their residences, and we sometimes stay in their residences overnight or for a week or more. We attend important events in the lives of the people (and their parents, caretakers, and friends), going to weddings, family gatherings, or weekend outings, and we introduce them to new recreational experiences. We videotape some of these encounters so that we and the participants themselves can discuss and interpret the behavior that took place (we also erase these videotapes if the people find anything in them that is objectionable). Our procedures do not "break down" all deception (efforts to deceive are, after all, part of the reality we hope to study) nor do they reduce the complexities of human life to a clear and simple truth. However, they do lessen the likelihood that an obvious deception will go unnoticed and that the contradictory complexity of a human life—even a retarded life—will be seen as simple and straightforward. The method is not intended to provide simple answers; instead, it is intended to provide the grounds for rejecting simple answers in favor of more full and accurate understanding.

Although the foundation of our approach is ethnographic, we also employ other methods when appropriate. Sometimes we observe unobtrusively, tabulating predetermined categories of behavior; sometimes we elicit life histories. We try to obtain relevant documents whenever they are available, and, occasionally, we use psychological tests or inventories. Now and then we design experimental procedures for the elicitation of data. We seldom use standardized interviews because our experience indicates that direct questions to mentally retarded persons typically not only evoke trivial or socially desirable answers, they also lead to deceptions and can seriously damage rapport. We do use such interviews with parents and other nonretarded persons, but our research with mentally retarded persons themselves depends on rapport, and any research procedure that treats retarded persons as "subjects" defeats our purposes.

We try to proceed as humanely and honestly as we can, making it clear that we are concerned with the people we study as human beings, not simply as objects of scientific scrutiny. To symbolize this attitude and to indicate that their role is an active one, we call the people in our research "participants," and, of course, in everything we write about them, including the chapters in this volume, we protect their privacy by disguising their identities. To the often lonely mentally retarded people who participate in our research, we offer interest, some companionship, and occasional diversion. If our approach sometimes alters the behavior we hope to study, we take that for granted, document the changes, and attempt to compensate for them. That is why participant-observation requires such long periods of time if it is to be effective; the role of the researcher is one focus of study, and it takes time to document and understand that role clearly. It also takes flexibility to adjust one's approach to the changing conditions one encounters. There is no catechism for our research. Nobel Laureate physicist Percy Bridgman said that there is no *one* scientific method, only "doing one's damndest" to put common sense to work. How well we have succeeded in our attempts to do this is illustrated by the work in this volume.

The first two papers report research done with a variety of persons, both mentally retarded and nonretarded, men and women, Afro-American and White, in diverse residential and working circumstances. The first paper, "Employment Experiences of Community-Based Mildly Retarded Adults" by Keith T. Kernan and Paul Koegel, focuses on the work histories and job-seeking of a sample of mildly retarded young adults. Presenting data collected by intensive ethnographic methods over a period of 30 months, Kernan and Koegel document the fluctuations in employment and the importance of strong family support in seeking and holding a job. Because Kernan and Koegel collected their data over a 30-month period, rather than at only a few points in time, they are able both to document changes throughout the period and to determine some of the reasons why they occur. Their findings significantly underscore the importance of taking a processual perspective.

In the second paper, "Getting There: Directions Given by Mildly Retarded and Nonretarded Adults," Keith Kernan and Sharon Sabsay use a novel approach to study communicative competence. Previous research has suggested that mildly retarded persons make more speech errors than nonretarded persons do, but not different kinds of errors. Still, good means for measuring communicative effectiveness have been difficult to identify, especially means that measure communication in its naturally-occurring context. Kernan and Sabsay found such a means in the course of their sociolinguistic field research. They asked both retarded and nonretarded persons to provide field researchers with telephone directions for a route to their residence. Almost all the nonretarded persons were able to give adequate directions, but over half of the mentally retarded persons were not. Kernan and Sabsay's analysis of these inadequacies is fascinating and should serve to guide other studies of social competence in various aspects of the demands of community living.

The next two papers deal with aspects of the culture of a sheltered workshop. Research in this workshop has been continuously underway for more than 7 years under the direction of Jim Turner. "Speech Etiquette in a Sheltered Workshop," by Turner, Kernan, and Susan Gelphman, describes some of the richness of this culture concerning etiquette and politeness, or as clients say, "being nice." The authors discuss ritualized salutations (introductions and the like), taboo topics and words, and deference and "normalcy fabrications," all within the overall context of workshop society where social harmony and personal self-worth are so important. Joseph Graffam and Jim Turner supplement this account with their paper, "Escape From Boredom: The Meaning of Eventfulness in the Lives of Clients at a Sheltered Workshop," which describes a variety of socially accepted means of relieving boredom or, as they put it, enhancing eventfulness. Many of these means would be seen as unacceptable, fantastic, or even pathological in other social situations, yet in the workshop they appear to be adaptive in increasing both a sense of eventfulness and self-esteem. The two papers together illustrate the subtle richness and distinctiveness of workshop life and suggest ways that workshop culture serves the needs of its various clients.

The next pair of papers deals with some important aspects of the lives of a sample of mildly retarded young adults who are living independently. Drawing from ethnographic data about these individuals, as well as interviews with their parents, Sandra Kaufman's chapter, "Friendship, Coping Systems and Community Adjustment of Mildly Retarded Adults," examines patterns of friendship among these young adults. Kaufman is able to identify four types, based on sociality and satisfaction, and shows how each type is related to social adjustment. Because her data cover an 18-month period, she is also able to discuss the process of movement from one type of adjustment to another as well as the role that parental relationships play in these adjustments. The other paper, "Self-Perspectives on Being Handicapped: Stigma and Adjustment" by Andrea Zetlin and Jim Turner, looks at the effects of parental socialization practices on the lives of these individuals. Zetlin and Turner analyze the development of personae, the experience of stigma, and the ongoing processes of strategic interaction. Like Kaufman, they propose a typology, this time of reactions to the labels of handicap or limitation. They conclude that early parental influences have very important, lasting effects.

The final pair of papers report research with samples of mildly retarded Afro-Americans, their parents, other kin, and peers. Paul Koegel and Robert Edgerton examine the lives of 12 mildly retarded Black men and women (from a larger sample) who seemed, on first encounter, to be classic examples of the six-hour retarded child pattern—labeled in school but fully competent in extra-school social living. Their paper, "Black 'Six-hour Retarded Children' as Young Adults," concludes that these 12 persons have not disappeared into the normal life of their inner-city neighborhoods. Instead, like other members of a larger sample, they are set apart from their peers, principally by the same academic limitations that troubled them in school—reading, writing, and numerical calculations. They are seen as handicapped by their parents and other nonretarded persons, and they themselves feel limited, often painfully so. The final paper, "The Social Structures of Mildly Retarded Afro-Americans: Gender

Comparisons" by Claudia Mitchell-Kernan and M. Belinda Tucker, compares the functions of kin ties in the lives of 24 young men and women. Like Koegel and Edgerton, Tucker and Mitchell-Kernan conclude that these people are not able to become accepted members of nonretarded peer groups, or "street-corner" societies; this is true especially of males, for whom peer group acceptance is quite important. In general, women also have their primary ties with other mentally retarded persons, and the sources of social support most often and reliably come from their families. Mitchell-Kernan and Tucker illustrate varying patterns of social support; they also convincingly and importantly show why women and men develop different patterns of reliance on their families and other kin. These two papers help to sketch in some detail about the lives of mentally retarded Afro-American and their kin, a previously neglected population in the literature about mental retardation.

The lives of mentally retarded persons in community settings are, like those of the rest of us, complex and changing. The papers in this volume provide no more than a glimpse of that complexity and change. What could be more pedestrian than a conclusion saying that we know too little of these lives? Only, perhaps, the assumption that we already know enough. Hopefully, readers of this volume know enough to realize that we know far too little. If "a little knowledge is a dangerous thing"—as there is no reason to doubt in this instance—then we must make the effort to learn more. This volume of papers is offered with the hope that it will contribute something to what we need to know and will help to point the way for other investigators.

References

Bogdan, R., & Taylor, S. J. (1976). *Introduction to qualitative research methods: A phenomenological approach to the social sciences*. New York: John Wiley & Sons.

Braginsky, D. D., & Braginsky, B. M. (1971). *Hansels and Gretels: Studies of children in institutions for the mentally retarded*. New York: Holt, Rinehart and Winston.

Brooks, P. H., & Baumeister, A. A. (1977). Are we making a science of missing the point? *American Journal of Mental Deficiency, 81*, 543–546.

Cobb, J. V. (1972). *The forecast of fulfillment: A review of research on predictive assessment of the adult retarded for social and vocational adjustment*. New York: Teacher's College Press, Columbia University.

Denzin, N. K. (1971). The logic of naturalistic inquiry. *Social Forces, 50*, 166–182.

Deutscher, I. (1966). Words and deeds: Social science and social policy. *Social Problems, 13*, 235–240.

Edgerton, R. B. (1967). *The cloak of competence: Stigma in the lives of the mentally retarded*. Berkeley: University of California Press.

Edgerton, R. B. (1983). Failure in community adaptation: The relativity of assessment. In K. T. Kernan, M. J. Begab, & R. B. Edgerton (Eds.), *Environments and behavior: The adaptation of mentally retarded persons* (pp. 123–143). Baltimore: University Park Press.

Edgerton, R. B., & Langness, L. L. (1978). Observing mentally retarded persons in community settings: An anthropological perspective. In G. P. Sackett (Ed.), *Observing behavior: Vol. 1. Theory and applications in mental retardation* (pp. 335–348). Baltimore: University Park Press.

Geertz, C. (1973). *The interpretation of cultures*. New York: Basic Books.

Glaser, B. G., & Strauss, A. L. (1967). *The discovery of grounded theory: Strategies for qualitative research.* Chicago: Aldine Publishing Company.

Goldstein, H. (1964). Social and occupational adjustment. In H. A. Stevens & R. Heber (Eds.), *Mental retardation: A review of research* (pp. 214–258). Chicago: University of Chicago Press.

Harre, R., & Secord, P. F. (1972). *The explanation of social behavior.* Oxford: Basil Blackwell.

Haywood, C. H. (1977). The ethics of doing research . . . and of not doing it. *American Journal of Mental Deficiency, 81,* 311–317.

Henschel, A. M. (1972). *The forgotten ones: A sociological study of Anglo and Chicano retardates.* Austin: University of Texas Press.

Lorber, M. S. (1975). Consulting the mentally retarded: An approach to the definition of mental retardation by experts. (Doctoral dissertation, University of California, Los Angeles, 1974). *Dissertation Abstracts International, 35,* 3587B.

McCarver, R., & Craig, E. (1974). Placement of the retarded in the community: Prognosis and outcome. In N. R. Ellis (Ed.), *International review of research in mental retardation* (Vol. 7, pp. 146–207). New York: Academic Press.

Owhaki, S. (1974). Behavioral characteristics of habitated retarded persons. *American Journal of Mental Deficiency, 79,* 385–390.

Phillips, D. (1973). *Abandoning method.* San Francisco: Jossey-Bass.

Schalock, R., & Harper, R. (1978). Placement from community-based mental retardation programs: How well do clients do? *American Journal of Mental Deficiency, 83,* 240–247.

Scheerenberger, R. & Felsenthal, D. (1977). Community settings for MR persons: Satisfactions and activities. *Mental Retardation, 15,* 307–308.

Willems, E. P. (1967). Toward an explicit rationale for naturalistic research methods. *Human Development, 10,* 138–154.

Employment Experiences of Community-Based Mildly Retarded Adults

Keith T. Kernan and Paul Koegel

Given the importance of work from both an individual and societal point of view, it is hardly surprising that the issue of employment has long been considered a critical one by those concerned with the successful community adjustment of mentally retarded persons. Interest in mildly retarded adults—those members of the retarded population who are most likely to succeed in the competitive sphere—has been particularly intense and is reflected in a large and multifaceted literature dating as far back as the turn of the century. The issues addressed by this literature remain alive today and especially relevant now, given the currency of normalization and deinstitutionalization as philosophies guiding the provision of services to the mentally retarded. These principles have resulted in ever growing numbers of individuals being released into the community, where their ability to adjust to employment is often taken as one of the more significant measures of their success. In addition, more individuals remain in their communities and, ideally, are being encouraged to become as self-sufficient and independent of the social delivery system as possible. Clearly, these new developments and trends further highlight the pressing need for an understanding of both the status of mentally retarded adults in the employment world and the way in which we can help make their experiences more successful.

The literature on the employment of mildly retarded persons can be divided into three basic types. The first type consists largely of follow-up studies of previously institutionalized individuals, former EMR (educable mentally retarded) students, or graduates of vocational training centers. Most of these studies are descriptive, reporting the status of their subjects, dividing them into successful and unsuccessful groups, and only occasionally trying to isolate predictors of vocational success and failure. The second group of studies is concerned with trying to isolate either single predictors of vocational success, or multiple predictors and their links to the multiple criteria seen as part of the complex phenomenon of vocational success. The third body of literature (with which we will not be concerned here) is large programmatic, reporting the relative success of procedures in the area of vocational rehabilitation.

It would be impossible in the space available here to review all of the follow-up studies that have been undertaken. Cobb (1972), however, has already done an admirable job of reviewing this literature. One of the points that clearly emerges from his work is the difficulty of comparing results from one study with the results of another. Characteristics of the sample, categories devised, criteria for placement in categories, and criteria for success differ from study to study. Sample composition ranges from those who have been institutionalized and have received little training to those who have remained in the community and have graduated from long term vocational programs, with a wide range of types lying between these two extremes. Categories range from those which fail to distinguish between competitive employment and workshop employment to those that do not directly deal with employment at all, choosing categories such as "self-supporting," "partially successful," and "unsuccessful" instead. Criteria for success on the job range from 3 months to a year of continuous employment, occasionally including a measure of job satisfaction as well.

In spite of these variations in methodological design from study to study, a consistent tendency does seem to emerge across the majority of these research efforts. Put simply, a high proportion of mentally retarded adults *do* appear to make satisfactory vocational adjustments and eventually disappear into the general population. This holds for previously institutionalized groups as well as for graduates of EMR classes and vocational programs, where unemployment rates are quoted to be as low as 10% to 38% (Brickley, Browning, & Campbell, 1982; Cobb, 1972). Indeed, the results of longitudinal studies which concurrently examine some sort of control group (Baller, Charles, & Miller, 1966; Deno, 1965; Kennedy, 1948, 1966; Richardson, 1978) confirm the impression that mildly retarded individuals, particularly in low income areas, are employed in numbers similar to their normal peers (even if at different levels of job skill).

No clear-cut message emerges from efforts to isolate variables that will predict vocational success and failure. Over the course of time, myriad variables have been tested, accepted, and rejected. It has been suggested in studies attempting to validate *isolated* variables that success on the job is predicted by personality factors (Abel, 1945; Domino & McGarty, 1972; Harold, 1955; Huber & Soferenko, 1963; Katz & Yekutiel, 1975; Kolstoe, 1961); by successful provision of rehabilitation services (Abel, 1945; Brolin, 1972); by experiences in the competitive work world (Appell, Williams, & Fishell, 1965); by the ability to render a more abstract judgment (Barrett, Relos, & Eisele, 1965); by good timekeeping skills (Collman & Newlyn, 1955); by emotional stability (Harold, 1955); and so forth. Failure has been seen as a function of inappropriate social skills (Cohen, 1960); of the presence of secondary emotional disabilities (Fulton, 1975); and of the absence of all those qualities that predict success. More recently, factor and multivariate analyses have been employed to determine the manner in which many interacting variables predict a number of different criteria (Cobb, 1972; Stephens, Peck, & Veldman, 1968). These analyses have not produced readily recognizable predictors of vocational success. "If there is one clear conclusion to be drawn from this array," remarks Cobb (1972), "it is that no simple formula for prediction is possible, that the relationships between predictors are enormously complex, and that outcomes in terms of personal, social and vocational success are the product of manifold interactive determinants" (p. 138).

Sample and Methods

As part of a general study of community adaptation, we have recently conducted research concerning the employment experiences of 48 mildly retarded, community-based individuals over a course of approximately 30 months. These individuals, ranging in age from 19 to 49 years, had all been labeled mentally retarded by the social services and/or educational delivery system but were identified by professionals as having the potential for living independently. As such, they represented that segment of the mildly retarded population which stood to gain most from community services influenced by the normalization principle. Some, in fact, were already living on their own; others were living in residential facilities or at home with their parents. Some were married; the majority were single. Many held competitive employment jobs; others worked in sheltered workshops or did not work at all. Table 1 reflects the demographics of this sample as of the beginning of the research. These numbers, however, constantly fluctuated as individual circumstances changed.

TABLE 1

DEMOGRAPHICS (N = 48)

Sex		Employment	
Males	22	Independently Employed	13
Females	26	Workshop	12
		Volunteer	1
		None or Unemployed	22
Marital Status			
Married	15	*Age*	
Single	30	18 - 22	3
Separated	3	23 - 27	24
		28 - 32	8
Residential Arrangement		33 - 37	11
Board & Care	3	38 - 42	1
Family Care	7	43 - 47	0
Independent	23	48 - 52	1
Parents	14[a]		
Residential Programs	1		

[a]One lives with in-laws

Generally speaking, intensive qualitative and naturalistic methods were employed as primary means of data collection (see Edgerton & Langness, 1978). Each sample member was visited at least twice a month by the same researcher over the course of the research project. These visits, lasting anywhere from 1 to 12 hours, took place in those settings relevant to the day-to-day lives of sample members, allowing the researcher to become intimately familiar with the places habitually frequented by these individuals and the people with whom they typically interacted. Given the constant and long-term nature of the contact, close relationships quickly developed between researchers and sample members. As researchers became valued and trusted friends, frank and open conversations became possible on topics ranging from work, leisure, feelings about family, counselors and friends, past events, and hopes for the future to more private matters such as sexuality and the stigma attached to the mental retardation label. Exposure to the significant others of these individuals and opportunities to interview them more intensively provided additional perspectives on their current and past situations. With time, a large data base, including all that people said and observations of what they actually did, yielded a rather full picture of the complex, ever-changing nature of these individuals' lives.

As a result of this intensive contact, we have a first-hand understanding of the employment activities undertaken by sample members over the duration of the research, a detailed past work history of most individuals (the nature of which varies as a function of memory and complexity), and a complete picture of individual work-related attitudes toward employment. In this report, we examine the employment status of this high-functioning group as a whole over the period of time for which data are available. Further, we compare the progress of the individuals within the group, from point of contact to 30 months later, to show how attention to careers over the interim between these two points provides a more accurate picture of these individuals' experiences than does the static approach typically found in the follow-up literature. Finally, we explore one of the factors that clearly emerges from our data as alternatively contributing to and detracting from sample members' desire to work, the extent to which they look for jobs, and the success with which they obtain them.

Documenting Employment Status: Static and Processual Perspectives

As we mentioned, our research methodology included not only the monitoring of the work experiences of our sample members for the time that each of them was visited bi-monthly but also a compilation, when possible, of their previous work lives. This retrospective record was not always complete, as our informants and their families could not always recall exact dates of employment, wages, circumstances of termination, and so on. Official work records were not always available. Our approach, therefore, was to utilize only those time periods in the lives of our informants for which we had complete and precise data. For example, if past work history was unclear, we considered only that period when the informant was being visited by our researchers. If, during a period in the past between two of the jobs on which we had complete data, another job was held but the time it was held was unclear, we eliminated the entire time period between the two well-documented periods of employment from consideration. The elimination of such periods from consideration has the effect of making our findings concerning periods of non-employment more conservative than they otherwise might be. If employment had been either long-term or in an especially desirable job, it probably would have been remembered. The fact that we have eliminated these periods from consideration strengthens the arguments concerning process that we make later in this report.

In this manner, we have been able to compile a precise and complete work history for the 48 members of our sample that covers a total time span of 2,165 months, or over 180 life years. This includes at least 2½ years for each of our sample members. During these 2,165 months, the 48 members of our sample worked a total of 1,327 months or 61% of the time. This includes time spent in competitive employment, sheltered workshops, and homemaking. Of these total life months, 30% were spent in competitive employment, 27% in sheltered workshops, and 4% in homemaking. (This represents only 3 of the 13 married women in our sample. The other 10 do not view their employment status as housewife and are either working or seeking employment.) Even if we consider homemaking to be akin to competitive employment, as the literature tends to do, it still remains the case that the members of our sample were *not* engaged in competitive employment 66% of the time. The average length of time a job was held in competitive employment was 10½ months with a range of from 1 day to 11 years.

TABLE 2
EMPLOYMENT STATUS AT TIME OF INITIAL CONTACT
AND 30 MONTHS LATER

Category	Contact		30 months later	
	No.	%	No.	%
Competitive employment				
full-time	5	10.4	11	22.9
part-time	4	8.3	7	14.6
housewife	2	4.2	3	6.2
Workshop	15	31.3	8	16.7
Actively seeking	4	8.3	2	4.2
Sporadically seeking	4	8.3	4	8.3
Not seeking at all[1]	14	29.2	13	27.1
Total	48	100.0	48	100.0

[1]We have specified a category of individuals as unemployed and not actively seeking employment. This is not a category, however, that represents the hard-core permanently unemployable nor even individuals who are not interested in finding a job in competitive employment. As is the case for all other categories we have established, membership in this category is not static but fluid and ever-changing. Of the 48 individuals in our sample, only one has never worked (except in her parent's business before they died), has never sought employment, and has never expressed an interest in or a desire to work.

At the beginning of our research, there were 14 individuals who were unemployed and not actively seeking employment. At the time of last contact, there were 13 individuals in this category. However, 5 of the original group had achieved some other status while 4 others had entered the unemployed and not actively seeking category from some other. This leaves 9 individuals who were in this category both when our research began and at present. Only 4 of these individuals remained in this category throughout the entire course of our research contact with them. These include: the woman who has never been interested in working; a woman who is attending a night school to better her chances for obtaining a job and who lives in a board and care facility where she earns spending money by cleaning the pool, paging patients for the psychiatrist, and so on; a woman who, immediately prior to our initial contact with her, had left a workshop in which she had worked for 10 years, who expresses a desire to work, and who occasionally phones her rehabilitation counselor but never follows up on any of the leads he provides; and a man who lives in a board and care facility, has had many short-term jobs in restaurants in the past, underwent serious surgery during the period of our contact with him, and currently expresses an interest only in well-paying and satisfying work.

Of the remaining 5 sample members in this category, 3 have held jobs in competitive employment between our first and last contact with them, one for a period of 17 months. Finally, the remaining 2 individuals held jobs in sheltered workshops for brief periods of time during our research contact with them.

Only 4 individuals, then, have not worked or sought employment during the course of our research and, of these, only 1 has never worked and is not interested in working.

The figures presented thus far accurately portray the performance of our sample as a group over time. They say nothing, however, about the status of individual sample members at specific points in time. Table 2 categorizes sample members in terms of their employment status both at point of initial contact and approximately 30 months later when data gathering for this report was concluded.

In comparison with published data, the percentage of people in competitive employment (22.9%, if one includes the two housewives) is remarkably low. This, however, is an artifact of our sampling procedure. Although we chose only individuals who were identified by knowledgeable delivery system personnel as being likely to lead successful lives in the community, we did want a number of types of current life circumstances represented in our sample. For this reason, our sample was stratified rather than random and was selected to include sufficient numbers of married and single people; people who were employed, unemployed, and workshop employed; people who lived with parents, in board and care facilities, family care facilities, or independently; and males and females.

Although our sampling procedure makes it impossible to compare the figures from this study to those previously reported, it *is* possible to examine the changes which the individuals in our sample made over the course of the 2½ years during which they were followed. The figures, as revealed in Table 2, suggest an improvement over time, lending the impression that a good number of individuals have "graduated" from their sheltered workshops into competitive employment, and that a few who were looking for employment were successful in their quest. While our intention is not to dispel this impression of sample improvement over time, such a static interpretation does not do justice to the fluctuation that is characteristic of this sample's experience.

Table 3 summarizes the status changes undergone by the individual sample members from the time of contact to the point at which data collection ceased. Change is most immediately apparent in the 21 individuals who find themselves in different categories at the end of data collection from the ones they were in at the start. A cursory glance at Table 3 reveals that many individuals have progressed in the expected direction—they have left workshops for competitive employment, have found competitive employment jobs after a period of searching for them, and so forth. A significant number of other individuals, however, have "regressed"—they have lost their jobs and are no longer seeking employment or have left their workshop positions and are only sporadically looking for an alternative, and so forth. If we consider the categories in Table 3 to fall in a rank order, "competitive employment (full-time)" representing the "highest" category and "unemployed, not seeking" representing the "lowest," we can characterize the changes people have made from time of contact to the present as being positive or negative on the basis of whether they have moved "upward" or "downward," and we can weight them based on the distance traveled between categories. Doing this allows us to compute the extent to which downward as opposed to upward change has taken place. The results of this procedure are summarized in Table 4. Seven individuals slipped backwards an average of 2.86 steps, but 14 people moved upward an average of 3 steps. Such improvement is consistent with previous follow-up studies which have reported increased capability and stability through time (Cobb, 1972).

TABLE 3
INDIVIDUAL STATUS CHANGES FROM INITIAL CONTACT
TO 30 MONTHS LATER

Status at time of contact	Status 30 months later	No.	%
Competitive employment (full-time) (n = 5)	Competitive employment (full-time)	3	6.2
	Sporadically seeking	1	2.1
	Not seeking	1	2.1
Competitive employment (part-time) (n = 4)	Competitive (part-time)	4	8.3
Housewife (n = 2)	Housewife	2	4.2
Workshop (n = 15)	Competitive employment (full-time)	3	6.2
	Competitive employment (part-time)	1	2.1
	Housewife	1	2.1
	Workshop	6	12.5
	Actively seeking	1	2.1
	Sporadically seeking	1	2.1
	Not seeking	2	4.2
Actively seeking (n = 4)	Competitive employment (full-time)	2	4.2
	Competitive employment (part-time)	1	2.1
	Not seeking	1	2.1
Sporadically seeking (n = 4)	Competitive employment (full-time)	1	2.1
	Competitive employment (part-time)	1	2.1
	Sporadically seeking	2	4.2
Not seeking (n = 4)	Competitive employment (full-time)	2	4.2
	Competitive employment (part-time)	1	2.1
	Workshop	2	4.2
	Not seeking	9	18.7

But what of the 27 individuals who, as represented in Table 3, fall into the same category at the end of 30 months of research as they did at the start? Is it actually the case that during the course of our research over half of this sample (56.25%) experienced no change at all? In fact, this impression of stability is not at all warranted. Of these 27 individuals, 10 either ended up in the same category in which they had started only after entering and leaving other categories in the interim period or shifted from job to job without leaving the same category. In addition, 4 individuals were not looking for employment throughout the duration of research contact—hardly a group to be commended for its stability. We are thus left with 13 individuals (27.1%) who remained stably employed throughout the course of research contact: 2 were housewives and 5 were sheltered workshop employees; in the final analysis, only 6 individuals (12.5%) held the same competitive job from time of initial contact to the end of the 30 month period, and 4 of these 6 jobs were only part time.

TABLE 4
DIRECTION AND EXTENT OF INDIVIDUAL STATUS CHANGES

Category changes	Number of people	Number of steps
Downward changes		
From competitively employed (full-time) to sporadically seeking	1	4
From competitively employed (full-time) to not seeking at all	1	5
From workshop to actively seeking	1	1
From workshop to sporadically seeking	1	2
From workshop to not seeking	2	6
From actively seeking to not seeking	1	2
Total	7	20
Upward changes		
From not seeking to competitive employment (full-time)	2	10
From not seeking to competitive employment (part-time)	1	4
From sporadically seeking to competitive employment (full-time)	1	4
From sporadically seeking to competitive employment (part-time)	1	3
From not seeking to workshop	2	6
From actively seeking to competitive employment (full-time)	2	6
From workshop to competitive employment (part-time)	1	1
From workshop to competitive employment (full-time)[a]	4	8
Total	14	42

[a]This category includes one individual who shortly after research contact left the workshop in order to devote her full energies toward keeping house and raising her three children.

A very clear message is suggested by the experiences of these 27 individuals: Figures which have been computed solely on the basis of two "slices of time" (as has consistently been done in the follow-up literature—e.g. Deno, 1965; Katz & Yekutiel, 1975; Olshansky & Beach, 1974) tell only a partial story at best and often, even if inadvertently, tell a misleading one. This is because they fail to register the variation that might have taken place in the period between those two "slices." The unique contribution provided by the intensive and consistent qualitative contact we have maintained with our informants throughout our research period of 2½ years lies precisely in documenting this interim period and in laying bare the myriad variables affecting these individuals as they struggle for stable employment. Well over one-third of the sample (37.5%) has undergone numerous category changes over the course of our research period, changes that are not all accounted for by the static view of the tables above. The interim experiences of most of these individuals further reveal the constant fluctuation characteristic of this sample and the often tenuous nature of the success of its members. Unfortunately, the detailed data that case examples provide tend to dim, although certainly not to eradicate, the impression of sample improvement over time. We offer three such case examples here as compelling reminders of the need to attend not only to static representations of employment status but to those which incorporate the flux which is so often apparent in the lives of many mildly retarded individuals.

Bobby Golden

Bobby's experiences quite clearly suggest the limitations of a static view of employment at different points of time and the need for a more intensive understanding of the overall course of employment circumstances. At initial contact, Bobby had recently lost a janitorial job, due to absenteeism, and was actively seeking work. His work history revealed numerous short-lived competitive employment jobs (janitorial work, a job as a drill press operator, etc.) and a few steadier jobs (a year as a stock clerk which ended by his choice when sporadic hours started cutting into his take-home pay, a longer period with a car rental agency which ended when negligence on his part resulted in an accident and the death of a passenger). During research contact, Bobby held six competitive employment jobs. He delivered phone books for a half a day but was fired for being too slow; delivered phone books again for 2 weeks but quit when the brakes burned out on his car; worked as a stock boy for 2 months until the taunts of co-workers led him to violently lose his temper to the point of toppling two shelving units; cleaned floors for 3 months before being fired; did janitorial work for the Department of Motor Vehicles for 3 months (after passing an orally administered county exam) until he was fired for negligence on the job; and, finally, obtained a job as a pot washer at a local university, a job which he has held for 9 months. With reference to the categories in Table 4, Bobby moved from actively seeking employment to competitive employment (full time). While this accurately summarized the direction of his progress, it hardly suggests the meandering path this progress has taken. If nothing else, Bobby's history, both before and during research contact, leads us to view his most recent job success with a certain degree of caution.

Chrissy Benny

Chrissy's experience reveals the same frenetic shift from category to category although, almost miraculously, she finds herself in the same position at present as she did at time of contact. When we first met Chrissy, she was not working and was only sporadically and halfheartedly looking for employment. She revealed that she had held a series of jobs in the past—a job as a waitress had not lasted long, a job cleaning in hospitals had been too depressing, a job working at a laundry had lasted for 7 months. In addition, she had worked at Goodwill for a year and at another workshop on three separate occasions. Yet another workshop had been her most recent employment locale. Her job there had ended as a result of pressure from her mother, her live-in boyfriend, and his mother, all of whom felt that Chrissy was too easily attracted to other men and that her experiences at work were disrupting her relationship with her partner. Shortly after research contact, and more out of boredom than anything else, Chrissy and her boyfriend applied at the workshop where she had already been employed three times (and where he had already worked once). Although both were accepted, they declined to attend until their handicapped bus passes were issued, allowing months to slip by while administrative hassles delayed the issuing of their passes. Before starting at the shop, Chrissy found a job working for the grandparents of a friend as a housekeeper and general aide. The job lasted for only 3 weeks, however. Chrissy was less than effective in her role and was told that she was no longer needed. Soon thereafter, Chrissy applied for work at the local Goodwill where she had previously worked, motivated largely by boredom in her present relationship and the lure of an old flame currently employed at that shop. Indeed, Chrissy soon married this man, leaving the shop 6 months after she started because her husband felt that work, for her, was too draining. Financial pressures led Chrissy to continue to think of working, however. Eventually she returned to the shop that she had been pressured to leave (this being some 9 months after leaving Goodwill), remaining there only 2 months. Again she looked for work sporadically, finally finding a job at a Jack-in-the-Box about 2 months later. The job lasted only a week and a half—Chrissy didn't like working in a high pressure situation—and she found herself out of work again. Recently, she has again half-heartedly talked about working but has only sporadically looked for jobs. We see then that in a 30-month period Chrissy moved from sporadically seeking competitive employment, to workshop employment again, to competitive employment again, and finally travelled full-circle back to sporadically seeking.

Elizabeth Haldeman

Elizabeth, like Chrissy, finds herself in the same category now as she did at time of contact. After encountering difficulties in finding paid competitive employment, Elizabeth volunteered at a hospital for 3 months. She then found very satisfying volunteer work teaching swimming at a Los Angeles city school for mentally and physically handicapped children. She very much wanted this position to evolve into a paying job and attempted without success to pass the exam that would have assured her a paid position. As there were funds available for hiring a TMR (trainable mentally retarded) person but not an EMR individual, the staff of the school had Elizabeth reclassified as TMR so that they could hire her. Because of her reclassification, however, school insurance regulations no longer allowed her to teach swimming. Caught in this intricate Catch-22, she withdrew from the situation, upset and despondent over her failure to secure an exciting job. She has since renewed her search for paid employment and remains committed to working with handicapped children.

Achieving Competitive Employment: The Role of Social Support

The experiences of our sample members clearly reveal that finding and maintaining suitable competitive employment is more often than not an arduous and complex endeavor. For many, the temptation is great to withdraw from the struggle to succeed in the competitive sphere and to retreat to the security of workshop employment and/or the less than luxurious life afforded by public assistance for the disabled. Our data suggest that the extent to which this happens (or, to put it in more positive terms, the extent to which sample members succeed in achieving competitive employment) is, to a large degree, a function of the support, encouragement, and help available to them. This is not to say that some individuals are not sufficiently independent and competent to locate and maintain jobs without outside help. Indeed, several sample members have done just that, in most cases providing ample evidence of the dynamic value of self-motivation. By and large, however, cohort members have depended on either/ or both of two support systems: (a) a family support system, consisting of parents and/or siblings, and (b) a service delivery support system, consisting of social workers and rehabilitation counselors. The strength of each of these support systems varies from individual to individual, ranging from those who enjoy the active aid of both family members and counselors, to those who are isolated from their families and ignored by their delivery system liaisons. A comparison of the employment status of sample members grouped on the basis of their differential support systems and a description of some of these support systems reveals the critical import of this variable.

Table 5 suggests the relationship between categories of sample member support systems and the extent to which individuals are either pursuing or maintaining competitive employment. Admittedly, these are not hard and fast categories; the line between an encouraging family support system and passive family support system is often a thin one, and decisions on category placement thus often depend on subjective judgments made on the basis of an intimate awareness of the case in question. Likewise, the question of whether someone is progressing toward competitive employment often rests on the intimate understandings that arise from our unique methodological approach. In spite of these problems, the data as summarized in Table 5 do clearly reveal certain trends that can perhaps best be explained through descriptions of some of the individuals who fall into the various categories.

For 13 (27%) of our sample members, very strong family encouragement and active family involvement in the employment process is quite evident. In some of these cases, family strategies have included the mobilization of delivery system support. Interestingly, where overt family pressure has been applied, delivery system personnel have succeeded in playing a role that they rarely play when such pressure is not brought to bear.

Almost invariably, the experiences of this group reflect the presence of their especially strong advocates. Pat, for instance, is a member of a highly achievement-oriented, intensely involved, active family. From the time of their recognition of Pat's disability, her parents have endlessly fought to help Pat attain the upper limits of her potential, enrolling her in special programs, fighting for her right to a quality education in the city schools, and consistently encouraging her in a number of ways. A younger sister and brother have been equally involved in Pat's life; one has served as an understanding confidante, the other has urged Pat to accept new challenges. Both siblings have strong feelings of responsibility for the well-being of their older sister. At time of contact, Pat was involved in a food preparation program at a local community college. Her involvement there, in fact, was a result of her mother learning of the

TABLE 5
NATURE OF SUPPORT SYSTEMS

Category description	Positive[a]	Negative[a]	Total
Clear cases of strong family/caretaker support and involvement which in many cases includes mobilization of delivery system support	12[b]	1	13
Clear cases of absent or inactive family and delivery system support insofar as effecting change in the employment area is concerned	1	14	15
Cases originally in the above category who became involved in programs that found them jobs	3	—	3
Those that fall somewhere between no support and active support:			
(a) those with family encouragement (if not involvement) and/or some active, even if erratic, delivery system help	5	1	6
(b) those largely dependent on themselves and the delivery system	1	3	4
(c) those receiving mixed messages from parents and some aid from the delivery system	—	2	2
Clear cases of negative influences inhibiting employment	—	5	5
Total			48

[a] "Positive" here is defined as remaining in the competitive employment category, if that is where the individual started out, or moving up in terms of category. "Negative" refers to staying in a category below that of competitive employment.
[b] This figure includes both Faith and Marilyn, active housewives and mothers.

program in the local paper, contacting the director to try to arrange Pat's acceptance, and arranging that special tutoring be provided for Pat through the auspices of the school. After completing 1 year of the 2-year curriculum, Pat, who was finding the academic load increasingly difficult, decided with her family that she would be happier leaving school and entering the work force. In her mind, a job in the kitchen of a place such as Goodwill was enticing— she had worked at a transitional workshop for a year and welcomed the absence of pressure. Her family, however, felt she was capable of competitive employment and their judgment prevailed. A campaign in which all family members were involved was initiated with the aim of obtaining Pat a job. With the aid of her family, Pat gathered together a resumé, complete with references and self-composed letter advising prospective employers of her desire to work, her assets, and the nature of her handicap. The Yellow Pages were combed for potential employment sites with an eye toward hospital kitchens and cafeterias. Pat and her mother both searched the daily classified ads as well, clipping out possibilities, making phone calls, and obtaining applications. An organized loose-leaf notebook contained the date resumés were sent out, the date of a follow-up phone call, the status of the job at hand, and possible leads worth exploring. Pat also enlisted the aid of the Department of Rehabilitation, bringing her counselor classified ads that she had found in the paper and having the counselor make initial phone calls so that an offer of on-the-job training could be made. Through her counselor, she also learned of various community agencies which had leads on jobs as well.

Although this strategy proved successful in finding jobs for Pat, it took a while before the "right" job was found. Pat worked a few hours at a cafeteria before being fired for being too slow, a week at a hospital before being fired for failing to adequately perform her duties, a month at a convalescent hospital before her boss decided that the job was too complex for her. These failures were devastating to Pat, and had she been given the opportunity, she would have gladly washed her hands of the competitive employment world. Her family consistently urged her on, however, even in the face of their shaken confidence in her ability to succeed. Pat finally was offered a job as a kitchen aid in a retirement apartment house and successfully adjusted to the situation, finding great satisfaction in her work and her relationships with the older people whom she served. She was again forced to search for a job some 6 months later when the food service closed due to bankruptcy, but again her family prevailed and an equally satisfying job in a senior citizens' nutrition program was found. Knowing Pat as we do, there is no doubt in our minds that without the aid of her active family she long since would have retreated to a sheltered workshop. As it is, she has consistently sought competitive jobs and is currently competitively employed.

Pat is by no means alone in the family/caretaker support she has received. Before moving into a family-care home, for instance, Ron had a history of violent anti-social behavior and a poor record at a sheltered workshop. Greg, his caretaker, an ex-marine sergeant, fully believed that Ron's behavior and attitudes had been coddled for too long and aggressively set out to change them, at times resorting to unorthodox tactics. Such tactics, however, were tempered by an unshaken faith that Ron, if given the chance, could prove his worth. Under Greg's active tutelage, Ron entered a transitional workshop where he soon began responding to Greg's persuasive tactics (e.g., warnings such as "You mess up there and you'd better give your heart and soul to God, 'cause your ass belongs to me!"). Within a year, Ron's productivity and attitudes had dramatically improved. Following through on his promise to find Ron a job if he could prove that he deserved one, Greg actively combed the area for suitable employment, urging Ron's counselors at work to do the same. Ron was finally hired by a factory where he has more than successfully worked for the last 3 years. Six months into his job, he received notification that he had been awarded the "Worker of the Year" distinction by his former workshop, and he accepted the honor from Los Angeles Mayor Tom Bradley at a dinner commemorating the event.

While almost all the sample members exposed to such support have responded positively, two individuals have, to varying degrees, succeeded in ignoring it. Sally, who was not seeking employment when we met her, did her best to avoid the badgering of her mother and siblings that she work and held herself aloof from her mother's active attempts to find her a job. She later independently decided that she was ready for work, however. After contacting a Regional Center counselor on the urging of her sister-in-law, she became involved in a training program, leaving the program after 4 of the 6 months in the belief that she was prepared. She obtained a job in a factory owned by a relative and has been employed for 9 months. Rich, however, was more successful in his efforts to turn a deaf ear to his mother's and wife's protestations that he find a job to help support his three young daughters.

Out of 13 people, the 12 success stories are closely linked to the existence of strong family support. Where an active family presence is in operation, an individual's chances for success appear to be dramatically increased. What of those individuals for whom an active family and/or service delivery support system in the area of employment is not present? Significantly, of the 15 individuals (29%) who fall into this category, 10 are not seeking employment at all, 4 are in sheltered workshops, and only 1 is competitively employed. Yet 8 of these individuals do have social workers/counselors or have had some contact with rehabilitation services; 5 have social workers *and* maintain contact with their families (indeed, 1 lives at home and 1 has regular contact with her family). Only 1 individual has neither a locally-based family nor a delivery system contact.

Currently living in a large board and care facility, Bill, for instance, has a history of marginal kitchen employment but is neither working nor interested in doing so. He has almost no contact with his family and is very seldom visited by his social worker, who has not once suggested the possibility of Bill finding work. Doug, another long-term board and care resident with no family to speak of, remembers the empty promises of many social workers affiliated with the Public Guardian's office to find him work. Ethel's parents seem quite content with her position in a sheltered workshop. Although Ethel's dissatisfactions over minimal pay could provide the foundation for a competitive employment search, neither her parents nor her seldom present social worker have latched onto this foothold, and Ethel thus remains at the shop. Hal, too, remains in a workshop despite the impression of the staff there that he is capable of competitive employment. His caretaker takes a limited view of his abilities. His social worker, who meets with the residents of his home as a group every 6 months, has far more contact with his caretaker than she does with Hal himself.

Charlie's experience is illustrative of those three individuals (6.25%) who found themselves with inactive support systems which were activated at later points in time. Comfortable at the workshop and still smarting from a previous attempt at competitive employment, Charlie made no moves toward securing a regular job. His attitude radically changed, however, when his girlfriend left the shop to find competitive employment. Charlie pressured his counselors and caretaker at that point to involve the Department of Vocational Rehabilitation in his case, and, after a period of evaluation, Rehab was successful in placing him in a private factory whose policy was to hire the handicapped at competitive rates. In a similar manner, Larry was competitively employed part time and Kay was placed in a workshop training program shortly after becoming involved in highly structured independent living programs characterized by heavy staff involvement. Neither had been working before their exposure to the program; Larry had been sporadically searching, and Kay was not looking at all. All three of these cases confirm the importance of self-motivation as well as strong support systems.

Many individuals fall somewhere between those who enjoy active encouragement and those characterized by lackluster support systems. Basically, they fall into three subgroups. A total of six individuals receive mild family encouragement, if not active involvement, and some receive active, but erratic, delivery system aid. Tom is fairly representative of this group. Tom's parents, essentially, want for Tom what he wants for himself, and thus let him run his life as he sees fit. Although such an attitude is commendable in that it overtly acknowledges Tom's autonomy, it does not take into account the fact that Tom, even after making a decision, is slow and hesitant about implementing it. Thus, although Tom was sure that he wanted to work competitively, he made no effort toward achieving it, remaining at the sheltered workshop where he was employed. Through a friend of his brother, he was finally able to find employment. When he was laid off 4 months later, however, he made no effort to find another job, and his family made no moves toward helping him. Rather, he returned to the workshop as a volunteer. After a year or so of this, the workshop's counselors became concerned that Tom was getting lethargic and dependent on his non-remunerative work. They restricted the number of days he was allowed to volunteer, hoping this would nudge him out of his inertia. Eventually, the placement counselor, a very harried man, was able to find him a job, and Tom has successfully adjusted to it. Although a positive outcome was achieved, the data suggest that had Tom had a stronger support system, the outcome would have occurred long before.

Including Tom, five individuals have either maintained or succeeded in obtaining competitive employment even in the face of this less than intense support; three of the five, however, have been unemployed for long periods during the time of our research contact. A sixth individual who falls into this support system subgroup has not been as successful. In spite of the verbal support of her mother, Elizabeth's job hunting campaign has not, in the long run, been successful.

A second subgroup of four individuals (8.33%) do not have any active family contact but depend, rather, on themselves and the fluctuating support of their social workers. Jane has managed to leave the workshop and find part time competitive employment despite the suggestion of her rehab counselor that she leave work, enroll in school, and live with him. Another three individuals have not displayed the same degree of self-initiative and find themselves in less satisfying situations. Despite the fact that Betsy has consistently suggested to her social worker that she would welcome working in a nursery program, she has been ignored. It has been far easier for Betsy's social worker to place her in workshops than to take the time from an awesome load of case management to try to find her a job. When transitional workshops did finally find Betsy competitive employment, it was not in child care but rather in cafeteria busing work. Betsy detested the job and eventually quit. She now finds herself out of work, and, although she is actively seeking the aid of local agencies, no prospects are in sight.

A third subgroup consists of two individuals (4.2%) who have received mixed messages from their parents and little more than suggestions of workshop employment from their counselors. Billy's mother, for instance, asserts her desire that he work but at the same time permits him to lie around the house and hang out in the local coffee shop. Further, she overtly acknowledges her fear that competitive employment will endanger his SSI (supplemental security income) and subtly communicates to him her belief that he is not capable of maintaining a regular job. Billy's peers only further negate the meager support provided by his parents and counselors; most of them are local toughs who remain unemployed or marginally employed. Billy's experience reflects both of these influences—he talks about work but does little, occasionally accepting short stints in the workshops suggested by his counselor.

Last, we turn to the five individuals (10.4%) for whom overtly negative influences inhibiting employment are evident. Significantly, three of these individuals remain unemployed while the other two remain in workshops despite expressed interest in competitive employment. For example, Mona's parents and husband fear that competitive employment would shatter Mona's mental stability and thus discourage her from working despite her desire to do so, encouraging her, rather, to be content with her housewife role. Katy's caretaker feels much the same, and suggests firmly to Katy that her intention to work competitively, while commendable, is far too ambitious. It is enough, the caretaker assures her, that Katy continue working at the sheltered workshop where she has been employed for the last 3 years. Again, our data indicate that had these individuals the same kind of support system that Pat has, their employment success would be much more noteworthy.

Conclusion

In examining the employment and job seeking experiences of 48 mildly retarded adults over a number of years, several important points have emerged. To begin, when we examine the long-term job histories for which we have precise and complete data, we find that the members of our sample are engaged in competitive employment only about one-third of the time. This finding contrasts rather markedly with those follow-up studies in the literature that report success rates in competitive employment ranging from 40% to 80%, with an average of approximately 60%. Although our low figures may reflect the troubled economy of recent times, they may very well be a function of differing methodological approaches, an explanation which may also account for the disparities found in published employment rates. We have already mentioned the differential criteria used to measure job success, the different populations studied, the differing criteria used to place individuals in categories, and so on.

The most significant difference between our approach and the majority of follow-up studies lies in the ability of our methodology to overcome the limitations of reporting work status at two points in time. Typically, in the follow-up literature, individuals who finish a work training program, and are placed in competitive employment, are contacted from 3 to 6 months later. The percentage of those still on the job (or on some job) is taken to be the success rate. We, on the other hand, are defining job success in our sample in a way that not only measures length of time spent on a particular job (recall that the average length of time on a competitive employment job for the members of our sample was over 10 months) but also measures the percentage of time actually spent in competitive employment over long periods of time. This procedure, we feel, gives a more accurate picture of the employment circumstances of mildly mentally retarded individuals.

A related point we hope we have made clear is that there is a highly significant amount of fluctuation in the individual employment careers of our sample members. Few people remain on the same job or even in the same employment category for any great length of time. Although the overall statistics show improvement in job success over time, the lives of individuals are characterized by instability and change. Often these changes occur due to circumstances of the employment itself. People are fired, get ill, become discouraged, fortuitously or otherwise find a job, and so on. At other times, however, work status is determined by other aspects of the lives of the individuals involved. Preoccupation with the details of moving to a new apartment, the departure of a spouse or friend from a workshop, the excitement of becoming engaged to be married, a delay in obtaining a special bus pass, and any of a myriad of other variables may affect, for better or worse, the employment status of an individual at specific points in time.

Finally, our research results clearly demonstrate the influence of an individual's support system on his or her job-seeking strategies and job success. Those individuals who have strong family support systems seek and find more jobs in competitive employment. Those who do not enjoy such a support system are far less active and successful. Moreover, although those individuals who with the help of a strong support system are constantly seeking employment may change jobs frequently and suffer many setbacks in their quest, the very fact that they are supported in the continuation of their search enhances the possibility that sooner or later they will be in the right place at the right time to find the special position that will yield them both long-term stability and a rewarding measure of job satisfaction.

References

Abel, T. M. (1945). A study of a group of mentally retarded girls successfully adjusted in industry and the community. *American Journal of Mental Deficiency, 40,* 66–72.

Appell, M. J., Williams, C. M., & Fishell, K. N. (1965). Factors in the job holding ability of the mentally retarded. *Vocational Guidance Quarterly, 13,* 127–130.

Baller, W. R., Charles, D. C., & Miller, E. L. (1966). *Mid-life attainment of the mentally retarded: A longitudinal study.* Lincoln, NE: The University of Nebraska.

Barrett, A. M., Relos, R., & Eisele, J. (1965). Vocational success and attitudes of mentally retarded toward work and money. *American Journal of Mental Deficiency, 70,* 102–107.

Brickley, M., Browning, L., & Campbell, K. (1982). Vocational histories of sheltered workshop employees placed in projects with industry and competitive jobs. *Mental Retardation, 20,* 52–57.

Brolin, D. (1972). Value of rehabilitation services and correlates of vocational success with the mentally retarded. *American Journal of Mental Deficiency, 76,* 644–651.

Cobb, H. V. (1972). *The forecast of fulfillment.* New York: Teachers College Press.

Cohen, J. S. (1960). An analysis of vocational failures of mental retardates placed in the community after a period of institutionalization. *American Journal of Mental Deficiency, 65,* 371–375.

Collman, R. D., & Newlyn, D. (1955). Employment success of educationally subnormal ex-pupils in England. *American Journal of Mental Deficiency, 60,* 733–743.

Deno, E. (1965). *Retarded youth: Their school-rehabilitation needs.* Final Report of Project VRA–RD–681. Minneapolis: Minneapolis Public Schools.

Domino, G., & McGarty, M. (1972). Personal and work adjustment of young retarded women. *American Journal of Mental Deficiency, 77,* 314–321.

Edgerton, R. B., & Langness, L. L. (1978). Observing mentally retarded persons in community settings: An anthropological perspective. In G. P. Sackett (Ed.), *Observing behavior: Vol. 1. Theory and applications in mental retardation* (pp. 335–348). Baltimore: University Park Press.

Fulton, R. W. (1975). Job retention of the mentally retarded. *Mental Retardation, 13,* 26.

Harold, E. C. (1955). Employment of patients discharged from the St. Louis State Training School. *American Journal of Mental Deficiency, 60,* 397–402.

Huber, W. G., & Soferenko, A. Z. (1963). Factors contributing to the vocational success and non-success of the institutionalized retardate. *Training School Bulletin, 60,* 43–51.

Katz, S., & Yekutiel, E. (1975). The vocational adjustment of graduates of two sheltered workshops for the mentally retarded. *British Journal of Mental Subnormality, 21* (41), 71–78.

Kennedy, R. J. (1948). *The social adjustment of morons in a Connecticut city.* Hartford: Mansfield-Southbury Training School.

Kennedy, R. J. (1966). *A Connecticut community revisited: A study of the social adjustment of a group of mentally deficient adults in 1948 and 1960.* Hartford: Connecticut State Department of Health, Office of Mental Retardation.

Kolstoe, O. P. (1961). An examination of some characteristics which discriminate between employed and non-employed mentally retarded males. *American Journal of Mental Deficiency, 66,* 472–482.

Olshansky, S., & Beach, D. (1974). A five year follow-up of mentally retarded citizens. *Rehabilitation Literature, 35,* 48–49.

Richardson, S. A. (1978). Careers of mentally retarded young persons: Services, jobs, and interpersonal relations. *American Journal of Mental Deficiency, 82,* 349–358.

Stephens, W. B., Peck, J. R., & Veldman, D. J. (1968). Personality and success profiles characteristic of young adult male retardates. *American Journal of Mental Deficiency, 73,* 405–413.

The authors are affiliated with the Socio-Behavioral Group, Mental Retardation Research Center (Neuropsychiatric Institute), UCLA. This research was supported by NICHD Grant No. HD 09474–02, The Community Context of Normalization, Robert Edgerton, Principal Investigator; by NICHD Grant No. HD 11944–03, The Community Adaptation of Mildly Retarded Adults, Robert Edgerton, Principal Investigator; and by NICHD Grant No. HD 04612, The Mental Retardation Research Center, UCLA. We are most grateful to our associates on this research project: Lorel Cornman, Robert B. Edgerton, Candy Fox-Henning, Laurel Ashley, Patti Hartmann, Cheryl Killion, L. L. Langness, Don Sutherland, Jim Turner, Lenda Walker, and Rob Whittemore.

Getting There: Directions Given by Mildly Retarded and Nonretarded Adults

Keith T. Kernan and Sharon Sabsay

It is widely recognized that successful community adaptation by mentally retarded persons is dependent, in part at least, on an ability to communicate effectively. Indeed, such an assertion is axiomatic since adaptative competence in "normalized" settings demands communicative competence. Nevertheless, little research to date has focused on the pragmatic aspects of language *use* in everyday life, concentrating instead on phonological, morphological, lexical and syntactic deficits. For these reasons, our research concentrates on those communicative tasks that mentally retarded speakers encounter as residents in the community and on their ability to perform those tasks.

In a study of narratives of personal experience told in conversation by mildly retarded adults (Kernan & Sabsay, in press), we found a number of minor "errors" of construction: grammatical or semantic errors at the sentence level, misuse of cohesive devices such as pronominalization and conjunction between sentences, and the like. Labov and Waletzky's (1967) model of the overall structure of narratives provided the most revealing framework for analyzing these narratives. Labov and Waletzky hold that narratives in their most elaborated form are constructed of six sections: abstract, orientation, complicating action, evaluation, result or resolution, and coda. Each of these sections has a specific function with respect to the narrative as a whole, and each contains a certain type of information. We found that retarded speakers often had trouble integrating narratives into ongoing conversation, work usually done in the "abstract," or first section, of a narrative. They frequently failed to apply necessary background information about circumstances surrounding or leading up to the central incidents of the narrative, the identity of participants in those incidents, and similar information usually given in the "orientation" section of narratives. Retarded speakers even omitted parts of the "complicating action" section or told incidents out of order.

In another paper (Sabsay & Kernan, 1983), we suggested that many of the problems we found in narratives could be subsumed under the heading of "communicative design" and were indicative of problems of mildly retarded speakers in all types of conversational interactions. The concept of communicative design (as we discuss in the Results and Discussion sections below) is based on conversational analysts Schegloff and Sacks' (1973) notion of "recipient design." Recipient design refers to any aspect of a speaker's utterances which is "designed" for a *specific* interlocutor (e.g., the use of the interlocutor's name, or the selection of a description in referring to someone that uniquely identifies him or her for the recipient). We found it useful, however, to have a term for those things one incorporates into one's utterances in consideration of *any* interlocutor. These include identifying a referent clearly before pronouns are used, or making decisions about what information an interlocutor already has and what he or she needs to be told in order to understand something that is going to be said later.

We maintained in both papers that the "errors" made by retarded speakers are often the same as those made by nonretarded speakers but that retarded speakers make them far more frequently, to far more serious effect. Our claim was hard to substantiate, however, because of the difficulty of evaluating the "effectiveness" or "well-formedness" of narratives objectively, particularly when one has not observed the incident(s) being reported and has no other reports from other observers or participants. Menig-Peterson and McCabe (1978) devised an interesting coding scheme for evaluating the orientation sections of narratives told by children between the ages of 3½ and 9½, but their system is not really appropriate for the far more lengthy and complex narratives of adults.

For these reasons, we chose to investigate a type of everyday speech event which lent itself more readily to objective judgments of effectivness: route directions. There is a reasonable amount of literature on the structure of directions given by adults in the United States and Germany (Klein, 1979, 1980; Psathas & Kozloff, 1976; Wunderlich & Reinert, 1979) and by American children (Bye, 1976), as well as studies utilizing the concept of "cognitive maps," or how adults deal conceptually with physical space (Lynch, 1960; Orleans, 1973).

Directions, like the descriptions of apartment layouts discussed by Linde and Labov (1975), offer an opportunity to examine the interplay of cognition, social experience, and language. In particular, the giving of route directions is an act/event:

1. whose function, as opposed to the many possible overlapping functions of narratives, is clear (i.e., the delineation of a route from one location to another in such a way that one could travel the route by following the directions);
2. that is highly listener oriented (and, therefore, encompasses an aspect of communication with which mildly retarded adults seem to have difficulty);
3. that conveys strongly prestructured information (i.e., a route);
4. that is itself highly and predictably structured;
5. that lends itself to objective criteria of effectiveness;
6. and that requires and reveals knowledge of the community environment.

Route descriptions—the actual set of directions—are always embedded in social interactions, and some part of these interactions must be considered along with the actual route descriptions as part of the speech event of "requesting and giving directions." This speech event can be divided into several sections, distinguished on the basis of the interactional work being done and the information being exchanged and by characteristic linguistic features such as the type of speech acts used.

The first section is the *Initiation and Orientation* section. In this section, an offer of directions is given or a request is made. If a request is made, then either an acceptance or a refusal will follow. In addition, certain information may, and often must, be exchanged or established in this section of the interaction: a) the destination; b) the departure and/or the starting point;[1] c) the familiarity of the recipient of the directions with the area to be traversed; and d) the mode of transportation. On the basis of this information and subsequent decisions about their ability to provide the required route information, people decide whether or not to accept the role of director and the task of giving directions. This information also influences their decisions about the form and content of the route description itself.

Before the director can begin giving the actual route description, one more important piece of "work" may need to be done. If the director is not familiar with the departure point named by the potential recipient or does not feel that he can give directions from that point but might be able to provide useful ones from some other point, he may suggest an alternate starting point. The recipient may accept this as a reasonable starting point or he may suggest another. The decision about what is a valid starting point is a particularly interesting one, involving as it does judgments and presuppositions about what areas, pathways, and landmarks interlocutors can be expected to be familiar with and which ones they cannot and, consequently, how they are to be described or referred to (e.g., Klein, 1979; Sabsay & Kernan, 1982; Schegloff, 1971).

The next section, the *Route Description,* consists primarily of route information given by the director. The interactional aspect of this section can be quite minimal, demanding only token acknowledgment from the recipient. On the other hand, the recipient is free to request elaboration or clarification of any information that he does not understand. A director constructs a route description by naming pathways (streets, freeways, etc.), connecting them with directional indicators ("turn left," "go up," etc.), and giving reference points (landmarks, intersections, etc.). Linguistically, most of this information is presented in the form of directives; Bye (1976) labels these GO- and CHANGE-directives. The director's judgments about the identifiability and/or familiarity of paths and landmarks along and by which the recipient is being oriented have considerable linguistic consequences as well (Klein, 1979).

The third section is the *Location and Description* of the destination point. This section is not mentioned by other researchers, presumably because their data consist of directions to major and, therefore, easily identifiable landmarks (Wunderlich & Reinert, 1979) or to businesses, which must be equally identifiable (Psathas & Kozloff, 1976). Our directions are primarily to residences,

---

[1]The notions of "starting point" and "orientational reference point" are taken from Psathas and Kozloff (1976). We find it necessary, however, to distinguish further between a departure point and a starting point. The departure point is the location that the recipient offers or that he supplies when asked where he is coming from (or, in the case of Klein's, 1979, and Wunderlich and Reinert's, 1979, studies, the point where the interlocutors are standing). That point may then become the starting point if the directions begin there. The directions may actually begin, however, at some location—usually a pathway—along the route (e.g., "well, you come down the San Diego Freeway"). In such cases, the director assumes that the recipient can get to the starting point from the departure point without directions. If the recipient cannot, he indicates so and an alternative starting point is negotiated.

often apartments in large complexes, and directors apparently felt that recipients required more information to be able to locate and identify their destinations. In this section, houses or apartment buildings are located on the final path ("Turn left on Raymond. It's the third building on the left hand side.") and may be described ("It's a two-story pink building." "There's a white picket fence and there'll be a white Volkswagen in the driveway."). Finally, if the entrance or apartment is difficult to find, it may be located for the recipient ("The apartment is upstairs on the left."). Note that this section is also characterized by specific linguistic items. Existential or locative constructions are used instead of directives and verbs of motion.

At the end of the Location and Description section or, if there is none, the Route Description section, the director may overtly indicate that he feels the directions are complete ("It's right there." "It's really simple, you shouldn't have any trouble."), or, if he doubts the clarity of his instructions, he may suggest something the recipient can do if he gets lost ("If you get lost, just give us a call and someone can find you."). Finally, there may be a closing section and a leave-taking, or, if the instructors have more business to attend, the interaction in which the directions are embedded will continue.

Giving directions thus is a communicative event that involves the translation of knowledge of a route into a verbal form that can be understood and acted upon by an interlocutor. Such knowledge is, of course, in large part based upon experience with the route in question, and the experience, and therefore the knowledge, that individuals will have of routes between any two particular points will vary. Experience with and knowledge of a complete particular route or with greater or smaller areas of one's physical environment is, however, only one factor in producing an adequate set of directions. Equally important is the ability to accurately encode information about a particular route in the appropriate and most effective form. Furthermore, when one agrees to give a set of directions, one is entering into a communicative contract in which the interlocutor assumes that the speaker is giving directions that the speaker himself believes to be accurate and will adequately guide a traveler along the specified route. If the speaker does not believe this, it is a part of the assumed communication contract that he must indicate so by negotiating alternative starting points, refusing to give directions at all, or through some other means indicating that the directions he gives might not work. If he does none of these, then the interlocutor—and we in our analysis—can assume that he believes the directions to be both adequate and accurate; although, in fact, they may be neither.

Method

Procedure

We have had the opportunity in the course of our research on the communicative competence of mildly mentally retarded adults to request directions to their residences from both mildly mentally retarded and nonretarded adults (parents, siblings, spouses, caretakers, and counselors). These data were collected by field researchers in the course of telephone contacts, made for other research purposes, with individuals they had never met. Researchers making such contacts were given the following instructions:

The purpose of this study is to elicit sets of directions from both retarded and nonretarded persons. In the course of the (phone) conversation setting up the first appointment with the participant, researchers should ask for directions to wherever the meeting is to take place. Directions or *any* response to the probe questions should be recorded, regardless of whether the respondent is the participant, a parent, a houseparent, and so forth. When the respondent is the participant, the response may be something like "I don't know, you'll have to ask my mother." Record such responses and then those of whomever actually gives the directions. At the appropriate point in the conversation, the researcher should ask, "Can you give me directions to your house (apartment, etc.)?" Write down everything that follows until the entire discussion about directions is completed, even researchers' questions or comments. Researchers might tape-record this portion of the conversation so that they need to record manually only the interlocutor's part of the conversation and can fill in their own part later.

These instructions produced verbal interactions between researchers and sample members that are like those produced whenever directions are requested over the phone.

Our samples consist of a total of 148 men and women. In the mentally retarded sample, there were 72 individuals: 35 men and 37 women, 16 were Black and 56 were White. All had IQs which fell within the mildly retarded range (55–69). All lacked major speech pathologies that would affect ability to talk on the phone. The nonretarded sample consisted of a total of 76 individuals: 13 men and 63 women, 31 were Black and 45 were White. The White sample members were telephoned by White researchers and the Black sample members by Black researchers. There were no noticeable differences by sex or ethnicity in the directions given, with one exception: The Black sample members more often negotiated starting points that were nearer the destination points than did White sample members.[2] In what follows, therefore, we will be concerned only with differences between the retarded and nonretarded samples.

Our two samples do differ in one important respect. Only a few of the members of the mentally retarded sample drive automobiles, while most of those in the nonretarded sample do drive. We cannot, therefore, address certain

---

[2]Orleans (1973) offers insight into how the familiarity of various groups with areas outside their own neighborhoods affects how they conceptualize their city. It may be that Black sample members gave starting points closer to the destination because they were unfamiliar with the West Los Angeles area in which UCLA is located. However, an additional contributing factor seems to be that Black respondents speaking to Black researchers assumed that the researchers were familiar with the Black neighborhood of South-Central Los Angeles where most of the respondents lived, and, therefore, assumed that no directions were required to lead the researcher into that area.

issues such as the relative contributions of IQ and experience with travel in various parts of the city to knowledge of the environment and the ability to give directions. Our samples, however, are respectable in size and representative of the actual situation: Most nonretarded adults in Los Angeles drive and most retarded adults do not. We can thus characterize the ability of these populations, as they exist in the community, to give directions, ignoring—in this study at least—the relative contributions of IQ and experience. Recall also that one of our aims in this study is to examine the *linguistic* ability of our sample members to deal appropriately with a communicative task, even if—or especially when—they have inadequate knowledge or limited experience with that task.

Scoring and Reliability

Transcripts of the conversations eliciting directions were sorted into five categories by two independent raters. These categories were:

1. *Refusals*—in which the respondent declined to attempt to give directions.
2. *Incomplete*—in which the respondent began to give directions and then either abandoned the attempt, turned the task over to someone else, or was interrupted by someone else.
3. *Maps*—in which the destination was located in terms of landmarks (usually the intersections of major streets near the destination) but no attempt was made to tell the recipient how to get there or to describe a route from the departure point.
4. *Complete/Inaccurate*—in which at least one "mistake" was made that made it impossible to follow the directions without difficulty.
5. *Complete/Accurate*—in which no mistakes were made and which, if followed, would get a traveler to the destination.

The main criterion used to determine if completed sets of directions were accurate or inaccurate was whether or not one would get from the point of departure to the destination by using the given directions. Judgments were based on what was explicitly given in the sets of directions and on the basis of indications by the researcher-recipient that he or she understood what was meant. For example, if a director said, "Come down Manchester," and the recipient responded, "Okay," then the raters assumed that the recipient know how to get to Manchester and understood what direction the director meant by "down." The raters used this knowledge as their own in evaluating the directions. All information used in judging a set of directions as accurate, then, had to be internal to the set itself, either explicitly stated by the director or clearly implied through recipient response.

Given these basic guidelines, the raters judged accuracy by attempting to trace the route given in the directions on a map. In the few cases of ambiguity on the maps, the researchers, who had been instructed to follow the directions if possible when they made actual visits scheduled during the phone call, were interviewed concerning the accuracy of the directions.

There was a high degree of agreement between the raters in sorting the responses into these categories. For the 72 sets of responses from the mentally retarded sample, there were 7 rater disagreements, giving 90% agreement. For the 76 sets of responses from the nonretarded sample, there were 6 rater disagreements, giving 94% agreement. All of the disagreements were resolved by discussion and agreement between the raters. Six individuals in the mentally retarded sample and 7 in the nonretarded sample responded to the request for directions with maps. Maps differ in structure from directions and we will not consider them further here. This leaves us with responses from 66 mentally retarded and 69 nonretarded individuals.

TABLE 1
CATEGORIES OF DIRECTION RESPONSES

	Retarded (N = 66)	Nonretarded (N = 69)
Refusals	7 (10.60%)	3 (4.35%)
Incomplete	6 (9.09%)	2 (2.89%)
Complete/Inaccurate	36 (54.55%)	10 (14.49%)
Complete/Accurate	17 (25.76%)	54 (78.27%)

The inaccurate complete sets were further analyzed to determine what types of errors accounted for their ineffectiveness. The results are given in the following section.

Results and Discussion

Let us consider first those categories in which no complete directions were actually given—refusals and incompletes. Refusals and incompleted attempts to give directions can be considered together in that they each represent—in our data—a recognition and admission on the part of the respondents of an inability to adequately describe a route between the departure and destination points. Refusals occurred at one of two points: either directly after the request for directions (signalled by comments like "Ooh, I wouldn't be able to tell you, my directions are so bad" or "I can't do that, let me ask my lady") or after the departure point was given by the researcher (greeted with comments like "I don't know much about that area" or "I don't know how to get here from *there*").

Most incompleted directions were abandoned at some point along the route, when the director got into difficulty, with comments like "Oh, I'm mixed up. Just a minute please, my husband knows," "Oh gee, I don't know. Call back this afternoon and ask my mother," or "Why don't you just call me when you get to the florist or the liquor store" (at some spot along the route unlocatable from the retarded respondent's description). In some cases in the retarded sample, directions were abandoned when the researcher asked for more information or clarification. For example, the question, "Do you know of another big street near your house?" asked in an attempt to elicit a map in the midst of directions that were becoming rather muddled, was met with "Wait a minute, I'll get my sister."

In spite of a few examples such as the suggestion that the researcher call from some unspecified florist or liquor store, there are no important differences between the two samples in the style or content of the refusals and incomplete directions. Both refusals and incompleted directions reflect a recognition on the part of speakers, often explicitly stated, of their inability to perform the requested task. If we combine the two categories, we see that 5 individuals (7%) in the nonretarded sample and 13 individuals (20%) in the retarded sample indicated that they recognized their inability to give an adequate set of directions for the requested route by either refusing to do so or by abandoning their attempt when they realized they could not complete it. Thus, although retarded individuals are slightly more likely than nonretarded individuals to be unable to give directions at all or to abandon attempts along the way, the difference is not significant and should actually be viewed positively: One-fifth of the mentally retarded sample exhibited as part of their communicative competence the recognition that they could not fulfill the communicative contract implied by an attempt to give directions. Other individuals, both retarded and nonretarded, gave complete but inaccurate directions without recognizing or acknowledging their inadequacy.

Sixty-four nonretarded and 53 retarded individuals gave complete sets of directions. Of the 64 nonretarded individuals, 54 (84%) gave accurate directions, and 10 (16%) gave inaccurate ones. Of the 53 retarded respondents, 17 (32%) gave accurate directions, while 36 (68%) gave inaccurate ones. Mildly mentally retarded respondents, then, are much more likely to give inaccurate directions. This difference is statistically significant ($x^2 = 33.24$, 1 d.f., p< .0001). What then are the reasons internal to the sets of directions for their inadequacy? Let us consider the nonretarded sample first.

Of the 10 ineffective sets given by nonretarded respondents, only one set contains more than one error. In addition to inadequately specifying an orientation point (a landmark given along a route that is given to reassure the traveler that he or she is, indeed, on track or to allow him or her to recognize a turning point), this set contained what we call a parallel gap. That is, the directions jump from one street to another parallel to it with no instructions on how to make that transition. Of the nine remaining sets:
–one gives what should be a right turn as a left turn
–two do not mention the *direction* of a turn at all
–one identifies a turning point (a freeway exit) incorrectly
–one omits a crucial turn entirely
–one gives a turn on streets that don't intersect
–one set contains a parallel gap
–two sets give unclear or confusing orientation points

There were 36 sets of inaccurate directions given by mildly retarded respondents, of which 26 contained more than 1 error. Compare this with the 10 sets of inaccurate directions given by nonretarded respondents, only 1 of which contained more than 1 error. So, not only do retarded individuals more often give inaccurate directions, their directions contain more errors per set. In 23 of the 36 inaccurate sets of directions given by retarded respondents, the errors are of the type just enumerated for the nonretarded sample. The difference for these 23 individuals, as we have argued is often the case when comparing communicative errors, mistakes, or difficulties between mildly mentally retarded individuals and nonretarded individuals, is, therefore, a matter of quantity rather than quality. There is, however, also a difference in the frequency with which certain types of errors are made. For example, 27% of the errors made by the nonretarded have to do with direction of turns, while 53% of the errors made by these 23 retarded individuals involve the direction of turns.

It would be stretching the point, we believe, to characterize these types of errors (i.e., of the same type as those in the nonretarded sample) as arising from some deficiency in communicative competence. The knowledge of the communicative contract seems apparent, as do familiarity with the route and the ability to express knowledge verbally. Mistakes are made, it is true, but they seem to be either mistakes of execution or to represent underlying cognitive deficits, such as difficulty in making right/left discrimination, rather than linguistic deficits.

These 23 sets *look* like directions, and although some of them contain multiple errors, there is enough that is correctly done in them so that the errors that are made can be identified. There are 13 inaccurate sets of directions from the mentally retarded respondents, however, that contain errors that are unlike any of those in directions given by nonretarded respondents. These errors involve aspects of communicative competence such as the knowledge of the form a set of directions should take and the types of information it should contain (e.g., GO- and CHANGE-directives), the recognition of the communicative contract that giving a set of directions implies, or errors involving what we have called communicative design. Communicative design is an aspect of communicative competence that requires the consideration of what a hearer needs to know in order to understand what is being said, the judgment of whether or not the hearer can be reasonably expected to have that information, and, if not, the ability to supply it in the appropriate form. The term thus subsumes Schegloff and Sacks' (1973) notion of recipient design, the distinction discussed by a variety of linguists between information already in the consciousness of hearers and that which they need to be given (e.g., Chafe, 1976), reference, and the like. In general, communicative design presupposes the ability to take the point of view of the hearer and to not assume that what is in one's own head is also in the head of the listener.

To illustrate the type of errors which reflect problems in communicative competence that retarded respondents make and nonretarded respondents do not, let us consider some representative sets of directions. In the first set, after a lengthy negotiation of a starting point (which incidentally is *beyond* the destination from the departure point), the directions are as follows:

D: Uh, do you know Vermont?
Researcher: Yeah.
D: Well, I guess you go on Vermont . . . now wait . . . you see a hospital, it's right there . . . you go that way. And then you turn left at the other thing.
Researcher: You turn left at what?
D: At the other thing where you see lights and stuff. Keep going and you see this thing. It's like the bus I take.
Researcher: Uh huh.
D: Keep going and you'll see a store called Diamond. It's

brick. Red brick. You just continue there. Good grief
. . . Continue until you see, oh, then you'll be in
Torrance.

Researcher: Uh huh.

D: Keep going down that way, oh, just go straight down
that road. You'll see Maple Street. Go right at Denny's.
You'll be on Hawthorne then.

Researcher: I see, uh huh. Okay, then is Phillips off of Hawthorne?

D: Oh, well just go down Hawthorne. You'll see 190th.
Make a left at the Great Western Savings Bank.

Researcher: Uh huh.

D: You'll see Inglewood and then Felton and then make a
left at Phillips.

Researcher: Okay.

D: You'll see a bar and a house and then the apartments will
be right there.

Researcher: I see.

D: There'll be a driveway right there.

Researcher: Oh, okay.

D: You'll probably see it.

Researcher: Okay, that'll be fine.

D: If you get, lost you could always ask somebody.

Researcher: Yes, that's right.

D: And then if you've got a map . . .

Researcher: Yes, I've got a good map. I don't think I'll have any
trouble.

It is clear that D is attempting to describe a route with which she is familiar but on which she rides a bus and does not drive. It is also clear that she recognizes the communicative contract and meets it by implying the directions
may not be adequate and suggesting that if the researcher has difficulty she can
ask someone or use a map. The failures that occur are ones of communicative
design, involving the assumption that she has described landmarks that are
familiar to her in such a way that they are uniquely identifiable by someone unfamiliar with the route. However, statements such as "Turn left at the other
thing," "Where you see the lights and stuff," "Keep going and you see this
thing," and "Just go straight down that road," are inadequate.

Notice also a peculiarity of this set which seems to reflect the director's
bus riding training but violates conventional practice for giving directions. On
two occasions ("You'll see Maple Street. Go right at Denny's. You'll be on
Hawthorne then," and "You'll see 190th. Make a left at the Great Western Savings Bank"), D names the street *before* the one on which a turn is made, giving
only landmarks to identify the latter. Thus, Denny's is on the corner of Hawthorne, and Great Western Savings on the corner of Artesia. The naming of the
preceding street, although usually an effective orientation device, is in this instance a source of some confusion.

The following set exhibits similar difficulties. "Straight across Manchester" and "half way down Manchester" are ineffective descriptions. In addition, the director does not recognize that his directions are inadequate ("You
can't miss me") and, therefore, do not fulfill the communicative contract.

Researcher: Can you tell me how to get to your house? I'll be taking
the Harbor Freeway going North. (Gives starting point)
W: Uhm.
Researcher: Do you know which off ramp I would exit on?
W: Do you know where Manchester and Central is? (nego-
tiates new starting point with familiarity check)
Researcher: Manchester and Central? Uh huh.
W: You come straight across Manchester.
Researcher: Going which way . . . north or south?
W: I really couldn't say.
Researcher: What other main streets are close by?
W: Uh, Firestone.
Researcher: Firestone. Well, I'll do my best to find it.
W: You get half way down Manchester and you'll see a drug
store across the street . . . You can't miss me.

Other sets of directions, though some of them are lengthy, actually give
only a minimum of information, are totally inadequate, and sometimes start
only a block or so from the destination.

Researcher: Can you give me some directions to where you live?
L: I'll try.
Researcher: Okay.
L: You got to come through Hollywood and come through
Los Angeles and come down Hollywood.
Researcher: Okay.
L: Come down to Meadow and take a right, just a little
ways from Kester.
Researcher: Okay.
L: You got my address?
Researcher: No, wait . . . just a little ways from Kester.
L: Just a minute, I'll get my address.
Researcher: Okay. (L leaves the phone for a minute or so)
L: Okay, you still there?
Researcher: Yeah.
L: My address is 1368½ Meadow. That's in Van Nuys.

Notice that L does not ask where the researcher will be coming from (departure point); therefore, the directions are totally ungrounded. Furthermore,
Los Angeles (proper) and Hollywood are areas quite distant from Van Nuys
(where Kester and Meadow are located), the actual destination, and no connection is given to indicate this. Or:

Researcher: I need to find out how to get to your place, because I
don't have that information.
G: Oh.
Researcher: Can you give me directions?
G: Yeah . . . well, it's . . . it's 411 S. Emerson . . . you
turn . . . turn right and then you see apart . . . a lot of

apartments . . . it's 411 S. Emerson . . . and it's apartment 5.

Researcher: Okay, it's apartment 5. Uhm, is there . . . can you give me any . . . uhm . . . streets before I get to Emerson that might help me out?

G: Uhm . . .

Researcher: If I'm coming from UCLA . . .

G: Let's see, uh, let's see, uh . . . let's see, uh . . . That street is called uh . . . uh . . . Oh, God, uh. I know it, but I can't, I can't think of it . . . right now . . . but when you see Emerson, you turn . . . right.

Researcher: Okay.

G: Yeah.

Researcher: And it's apartment 5?

G: Yeah.

Researcher: Is there a name of the apartment?

G: Uh, no . . . but it's 411 . . . when you see 411 you know it's the apartment.

Researcher: Okay.

G: It's white with black railings.

Researcher: Okay, and that is in Pasadena, right?

G: Yes, it is in Pasadena . . .

Again, G doesn't ask for a departure point. It is supplied quite late, by the researcher, with no improvement in the directions, which start within a block of the destination and give no actual route from the department point. And finally:

Researcher: Can you tell me how to get there?

B: You drive, you drive until you get to Robinson and then when you get to Robinson you're right there. 1920 Robinson.

Researcher: Oh, okay.

In these later examples, it is apparent that although some retarded sample members respond to the request for directions, sometimes even with great confidence, giving directions—that is, adequately describing a route from a departure point or a negotiated starting point to a destination—is not a part of their communicative competence nor, in some cases, is the knowledge of what a set of directions actually is.

It is clear that there is a large experiential component to these peoples' ability or inability to give effective sets of directions. Some of them are new to their residences and neighborhoods (e.g., those who have just entered independent living training programs). Many use buses or are entirely dependent on others for transportation and are, therefore, less likely to pay attention to or be familiar with routes even in their own neighborhood, mush less those connecting their neighborhood to distant areas of the city. This, however, has not stopped some individuals from orienting themselves and being able to direct and orient others, as indicated by the accurate sets of directions given by some retarded sample members. It is equally clear from the examples given above that there is also a large cognitive linguistic component to giving effective directions. In addition to the many sets of directions given by retarded respondents which were inadequate because of numerous errors involving absolute and relative direction (e.g., north or south, left or right), the use of unidentifiable landmarks and the like—errors also made, albeit less frequently, by nonretarded respondents—there were some sets given by retarded respondents which were inadequate solely because of problems with communicative design. That is, respondents are unable to encode known information in ways that are effective for their interlocutors. We can thus see the same problem in directions that we found in our studies of narratives: Individuals do not determine where their interlocutors are coming from so that they can provide an appropriate route; they choose inappropriate starting points and inadequately identify landmarks, streets, and turns. They do not, in other words, determine what information their interlocutor must have, decide whether or not their interlocutors have that information, and, if not, supply that information in a form that the hearer can understand.

Summary

We found, not surprisingly, that most nonretarded adults can either give accurate and adequate sets of directions to their places of residence or recognize their inability to do so and refuse to attempt to give any—86% of those in our sample. We found also that this is the case for many mentally retarded adults who reside in the community—45% of those in our sample. These individuals responded in perfectly appropriate ways to a request for directions. However, 55% of the mentally retarded sample gave inaccurate or ineffective directions. Of these, 64% made errors that differed in quantity—both in terms of total number of errors and number of errors per set of directions—but not in kind from the errors made by the nonretarded sample. This leaves 13 mildly mentally retarded individuals—20% of our total sample, 36% of those who gave inaccurate directions—who made errors that were unlike those made by nonretarded adults: errors of communicative competence that involved a lack of knowledge of the structure and function of directions or a lack of ability in communicative design.

In our studies of other everyday speech events such as narratives, we have suggested that one of the reasons for the impression interlocutors have that something is different or wrong with the way that mildly mentally retarded persons speak is that although they make the same sorts of errors that nonretarded speakers make, they make them more frequently. Because of the nature of the speech events we have studied, we have been unable to demonstrate this conclusively. However, as we pointed out at the beginning of this paper, the nature of directions is such that one can make objective judgments of accuracy and of type and number of errors. For this speech event at least, our suggestion that mildly mentally retarded speakers make errors that are like those made by nonretarded speakers but make them more frequently, is confirmed. Furthermore, we have found that difficulties with communicative design that are not usually exhibited in the speech of nonretarded persons are present not only in the narratives of mentally retarded speakers but in the directions that they give as well. Traditionally, studies of language and mental retardation have concentrated on subjects' phonological, morphological, lexical, and syntactic deficits. But for the mildly retarded, such deficits are relatively insignificant. Their greatest communicative difficulties lie, rather, in the pragmatic aspects of linguistic acts—the rules of appropriate language *use*—and in the construction of coherent multi-sentence discourse units such as narratives and directions. In addition to problems of communicative design, directions given by mildly mentally retarded speakers indicate fundamental cognitive weaknesses in utilizing spatial concepts and orientation and number. Finally, the relative lack of experience and familiarity with their environment produces refusals to give directions and contributes to difficulty in adequately identifying street names and other landmarks. Studies of discourse units such as these, then, illuminate the often stigmatizingly inappropriate speech of the mildly retarded and open new avenues for the study of the relationship between language, more broadly defined, cognition, and experience.

References

Bye, T. (1976). Aspects of the acquisition of communicative competence: The role of listener-oriented presuppositions in producing directions. (Doctoral dissertation, University of California, Los Angeles). *Dissertation Abstracts International, 37,* 2154A.

Chafe, W. (1976). Givenness, contrastiveness, definiteness, subjects, topics, and point of view. In C. N. Li (Ed.), *Subject and Topic* (pp. 27–55). New York: Academic Press.

Kernan, K. T., & Sabsay, S. (1982). Semantic deficiencies in the narratives of mildly retarded speakers. *Semiotica, 24*(2–4). (Also appears as Working Paper No. 10, Socio-Behavioral Group, Mental Retardation Research Center, University of California, Los Angeles).

Klein, W. (1979). *Local deixis in route directions.* Linguistic Agency, University of Trier, Series B, No. 41, March 1979. (Available from author, Max-Planck-Projektgruppe Nijmegen.)

Klein, W. (1980). Wegauskunfte (Route information). *Zeitschrift fur Literaturwissenschaft und Linguistik, 33,* 9–57.

Labov, W., & Waletzky, J. (1967). Narrative analysis: Oral versions of personal experience. In J. Helm (Ed.), *Essays on the verbal and visual arts* (pp. 12–44). Seattle: University of Washington Press.

Linde, C., & Labov, W. (1975). Spatial networks as a site for the study of language and thought. *Language, 51,* 924–939.

Lynch, K. (1960). *The image of the city.* Cambridge, MA: MIT Press.

Menig-Peterson, C. L., & McCabe, A. (1978). Children's orientation of a listener to the context of their narratives. *Developmental Psychology, 14,* 582–592.

Orleans, P. (1973). Differential cognition of urban residents: Effects of social scale on mapping. In R. M. Downs & D. Stea (Eds.), *Image and environment: cognitive mapping* (pp. 115–130). Chicago: Aldine Publishing Co.

Psathas, G., & Kozloff, M. (1976). The structure of directions. *Semiotica, 17,* 111–130.

Sabsay, S., & Kernan, K. T. (1983). Communicative design in the speech of mildly retarded adults. In K. T. Kernan, M. Begab, & R. B. Edgerton (Eds.), *Environments and behavior: The adaptation of mentally retarded persons* (pp. 283–294). Baltimore: University Park Press.

Sabsay, S., & Kernan, K. T. (1982). *"You can't miss me": A comparison of directions given by retarded and nonretarded individuals.* Unpublished manuscript, Socio-Behavioral Group, Mental Retardation Research Center, UCLA.

Schegloff, E. (1971). Notes on a conversational practice: Formulating place. In D. Sudnow (Ed.), *Studies in social interaction* (pp. 75–228). New York: Free Press.

Schegloff, E., & Sacks, H. (1973). Opening up closings. *Semiotica, 8,* 289–327.

Wunderlich, D., & Reinert, R. (1979). *How to get there from here.* Unpublished manuscript, University of Dusseldorf.

The authors are affiliated with the Socio-Behavioral Group, Mental Retardation Research Center (Neuropsychiatric Institute), UCLA. This article is based on a paper delivered at the 2nd Annual Meeting of the American Academy of Mental Retardation, Detroit, May, 1981. Research was supported by grants from the National Institute of Education (NIE–G–80–0016) and National Institute of Child Health and Human Development (NICHD HD 11944–02).

Speech Etiquette In A Sheltered Workshop

Jim L. Turner, Keith T. Kernan, and Susan Gelphman

The patterns of language use in any speech community reflect not only social structural variables within that community but also the concerns, values, and world view that the members of the community share (Gumperz & Hymes, 1972; Albert, 1972). The functions to which language is habitually put, the form in which things are said, whether certain topics are talked about or avoided and, if discussed, with whom, are matters that must be considered and understood in terms of such underlying and extra linguistic influences. The communicative competence of members of the speech community includes, along with an adequate knowledge of the linguistic code or codes spoken, a knowledge of these patterns of language use (Hymes, 1972).

Politeness in speaking, or speech etiquette, should especially reflect the concerns and values of the speech community, particularly those concerned with the dignity of the self and with the promotion and assurance of smooth social interaction. It is the case, for example, that in societies, such as the Japanese, that are especially concerned with the maintenance of the individual's "face," an elaborate system of honorifics that promotes that protection of self has evolved. The historical changes in the use of second person singular and plural pronouns of address in some Indo-European languages reflect shifting attitudes toward the dimensions of power and solidarity in social relationships (Brown & Gilman, 1960). Brown and Levinson (1978), in their exhaustive discussion of politeness phenomena, convincingly argue that cross-cultural variation in polite speech reflects a difference in values held by members of the cultures being compared. If language use, especially conventions of speech etiquette, reflect the values and concerns of speakers within a speech community, then it might be expected that the speech of mentally retarded individuals who interact on a regular basis would reflect the special concerns and values that they share, as a result of their handicap and similar life experiences. With this possibility as a starting point, we have examined the shared values and concerns and the speech behavior of members of a sheltered workshop for the mentally retarded. The workshop has been discussed in detail by Turner (1983) and we will describe it only briefly here.

The workshop complex is situated on 4½ acres of land and consists of the workshop itself, an activity center, a cafeteria, a swimming pool and basketball court, two kilns, a large covered patio with picnic tables and benches, and considerable open space for recreational activities. Work consists of basic light industry services: assembly, packaging, sorting, and so on. There are 200–215 client/employees at the workshop at any one time. Characteristics of the population have varied over the course of our research but are generally as follows: average age, 30 years (range, 18–55 years); average IQ, 50 (range, 29–75);

60% male, 40% female. Client turnover rate averages 48 individuals leaving and being replaced annually.

The overwhelming majority of workshop members enjoy being at the workshop and describe it as their "favorite place." Individuals who leave the workshop usually do so reluctantly and not by their own choice. For over 90% of the individuals we talked with and observed, the workshop has clearly provided the major positive reinforcing experience of their lives.

Members of the workshop interact frequently. Turner (1983) reports that, on the average, individuals interact with peers at least once every 5 minutes both at work and during free time. The great majority of these conversations do not concern work but human relationships. Friendships and romantic relationships are formed and maintained. For most of its members, the workshop provides the principal setting in which they engage in social interaction, talk, form friendships, and, in general, live their daily lives. It is, consequently, the setting in which they acquire, express, and share much of their knowledge and beliefs about social life and cultural values. It is in light of this that Turner (1983) has discussed the members of the workshop as constituting a society or subculture within the broader society. It is in view of the frequent and sustained verbal interaction, the shared rules of appropriate speech, and the values and beliefs that generate those shared rules that we consider the workshop and its members as constituting a speech community (Gumperz, 1968).

Turner (1983) has identified a number of concerns that have high salience and are of special importance in the lives of members of workshop society. We will briefly present these and other concerns and the values that are related to them. In the sections that follow, we will discuss in more detail those concerns and values that underlie conventions of speech etiquette shared by workshop members.

Turner (1983, p. 169) identifies four "focal concerns" and describes them briefly as follows:

1. *Affiliative Relationships*   Mentally retarded adults, like everyone, want a sense of community. They want to have friends and romantic involvements. They need a sense of belonging to human groups which provide access to meaningful social relations.

2. *Deviance Disavowal*   Mentally retarded adults, like everyone, want to feel good about themselves. For many, "being retarded" is the most salient aspect of their social identity. They need refuge from prevailing negative attitudes, pejorative labels, and unfavorable social comparisons.

3. *Social Harmony*   Mentally retarded adults, like everyone, want harmony and order in their own lives and the lives of those they care about. When conflict and trouble breach the social fabric, they try to repair it.

4. *Boredom*   Mentally retarded adults, like everyone, need some optimal level of novelty and stimulation. Too little stimulation and they become bored, too much stimulation and they become stressed. For their everyday lives to be positive and fulfilling, they need a satisfying level of eventfulness.

In addition to sharing these four focal concerns to varying degrees, members of workshop society adhere to a basic cultural value within the workshop, egalitarianism. All workshop members are considered of equal worth. There is, of course, recognition that some individuals are less capable than others, but this knowledge is never the basis of evaluative comparison. Any attempts to achieve even a slightly superordinate position are strongly discouraged, and, as a result, few attempts are made. In fact, people go out of their way to avoid any semblance of evaluative comparison. When, for example, a less capable worker is holding up the work on a production line, his co-workers do not comment on his slowness or attempt to help him work faster, they simply slow their pace to match his. Workshop members are also concerned with being "nice." In a discussion group in which New Year's resolutions were being made, the resolve to be nice appeared near the top of most lists. Being nice is also a characteristic of any person's "good side" and its absence marks one's "bad side."

Finally, in addition to sharing certain concerns and holding certain common values, members of workshop society have, as a result of their handicap, undergone similar experiences. Perhaps more accurately, they share a lack of experience in certain areas. Those that will concern us here are those of sex and death. Most workshop members also share, as a result of their socialization experiences, a common strategy for dealing with difficulty, trouble, or unpleasantness: They try to avoid it.

These, then, are some of the main concerns, shared experiences, and basic values of members of workshop society. Together they contribute to the world view of workshop members and underlie, to varying degrees and in multiple combinations, notions of politeness in behavior and speech. In what follows, we discuss them further and relate them to conventions of speech etiquette in workshop society.

Data were collected, field notes taken, and tape recordings made in the workshop, in the recreation areas, and in discussion groups. (See Turner, 1983, for a more complete description of the workshop setting, sample, and methodology.) Our goal is the analysis of the rules of appropriate speech in one domain in a particular society and not, it should be clear, an analysis of the linguistic deficiencies of defective speakers.

Presentation Rituals

There is in workshop society a high incidence of the forms of politeness that Goffman (1956) has termed presentation rituals. These are the prescribed acts that most readily come to mind when we think of polite speech. Goffman includes such acts as salutations, invitations, compliments, and a non-verbal ritual, minor services. We add other explicit attempts at being polite such as introductions and attempts at small talk of various types. Presentation rituals are explicit and positive attempts to be polite. They are routine and expected, and their absence is notable.

These forms of speech etiquette perform certain functions in any society or regularly interacting group. They serve to reinforce group cohension and solidarity and are a mechanism to incorporate new members into the group and to provide all group members with a sense of belonging. Brown and Levinson (1978), in their cross-cultural study of polite speech, speculate that egalitarian cultures are likely to be "positive politeness" cultures in which etiquette functions to emphasize group solidarity and harmony and to satisfy the individual's need for approval and belonging.

Presentation rituals, moreover, because they are explicit acts, afford individuals an opportunity to take the initiative and to engage in behavior that is positively valued and is considered "nice." In so doing, speakers are able not only to make other members of the group feel that they are valued and that they belong, but to feel that they themselves are appropriately fulfilling social obligations and are "being nice."

As ritual, presentations may be quite minimal in form, for example, saying hello to an acquaintance in the morning, or they may be more elaborated, such as singing Happy Birthday to a group member. In either case, they mark an event or occasion. As such, they may be elaborated or performed with unusual frequency not only to mark the significance of the event but *as* an event, an occasion of eventfulness, themselves. Such is the case, as we demonstrate below, in workshop society.

The function of creating and maintaining group cohesion, the opportunity to be nice and make others feel they belong, and the events that are marked, emphasized, or created, all combine to influence the frequency and application of presentation rituals in egalitarian workshop society. For the most part, presentation rituals in workshop society occur on the occasions and with the frequency that they would anywhere. People say "hello" to their acquaintances and friends when they arrive in the morning and "good-bye" when they leave in the afternoon, for example. There are occasions, as when a new researcher arrives, that a veritable barrage of politeness takes place. Everyone goes out of the way to greet the new arrival. "Hi's" and "hello's" are enthusiastically given, though sometimes when returned they are followed only by friendly silence. The hand of the new arrival is shaken by all and, if she is a woman, kissed by the more gallant males. Introductions are made to all present and even beyond. When one of the authors arrived at the workshop for the first time, for example, a couple she had just met insisted that she meet their counselor even though the counselor was in another room. She was asked her birthday, and, when it was discovered that it was on the same day as that of one of the greeters, this interesting coincidence was announced to all passers-by. The researchers was invited to attend the woman's wedding and to sit with her at lunch. This reception is not unusual. One's first (and lasting) impression on visiting the workshop is one of great friendliness and warmth. Such warm and elaborate receptions are not extended to all visitors, however. When groups or individuals visit or tour the workshop, they are usually treated with polite deference but are not afforded the elaborate welcome that UCLA researchers always receive. The reasons for this differential treatment are, it seems to us, clear and are embedded in the basic egalitarian nature of workshop society, in the need of workshop members for eventfulness in their lives, and in their desire to be nice to fellow members. Researchers from UCLA have been visiting the workshop for the past 7 years. One of the authors has visited the workshop and participated in discussion groups regularly one day a week for that period of time. Because the research methodology primarily has been participant observation, researchers are considered to be equal members of workshop society and, in many cases, friends of the other members. As such, they do not receive the deferential politeness given strangers or authority figures, but the positive politeness given other workshop members. The arrival of a new researcher is an event that is emphasized with elaborated presentation rituals and is also an event that may provide the opportunity for new friendships to be formed. The event thus becomes especially eventful and a new member is incorporated into the group.

Members of the workshop themselves expect to receive salutations and any breach of this expected etiquette is a matter of concern to them. One woman who feels she is not liked by the other workshop members has one constant complaint: "No one ever says 'hi' to me." The seriousness of this complaint is made clear in the following exchange originally presented in Turner (1983).

Ellen notes that she has something very important to say. She is extremely upset. Her best friend, Anne, has just returned to the workshop following 2 weeks of medical tests and Anne's ex-boyfriend Pat has been very mean and rude to her. He completely ignored her and did not even say hi. Ellen goes on and on about this—encouraging other group members to agree that it was very mean of Pat to behave in this way. Anne nods her head affirmatively each time Ellen says something bad about Pat, or about how much Pat's rudeness hurt her feelings. She remains silent, however, letting Ellen speak for her. Pat also sits quietly, a sheepish, somewhat embarrassed look on his face. Ellen continues her monologue—trying to arouse other group members to her level of indignation. Finally, Anne says, "Let's hear what he (i.e., Pat) has to say about it." Pat recounts the history of their break-up, noting how upset everyone was, since they had been going together for 3 years. Things have settled down, he has a new girlfriend and he felt it was best to "just let sleeping dogs lie." The reason he didn't greet Anne was that he didn't know how she would take it. Hal enters the discussion. There is no need for everyone to be upset. He has the solution. Pat had spoken to him and had instructed *him* to greet Anne. He had done so and had even given Anne an extra kiss on the cheek "for Pat."

From subsequent discussion it is clear that neither Anne nor Pat recall such an incident. Although neither in any way challenges Hal's story—Pat doesn't quite remember telling Hal to greet Anne for him and Anne doesn't recall receiving a kiss from Hal. Hal refreshes their memory, adding details about time and place. "It was just as you were coming to work in the morning. Right by the door. Just as you walked in. I gave you a kiss on one cheek for me and a kiss on the other cheek for Pat. That's the answer to the problem. He told me to do it for him. And I did." Another group member supports Hal, saying, "I think I remember seeing him do that. I just got off the bus. It was by the front. By the blue doors." Anne, Ellen, and Pat all seem a bit puzzled by this turn of events, but say nothing. Hal's story has absolved Pat of any rudeness or lack of consideration toward Anne. There is no longer any need for Ellen or Anne to be upset. The problem is resolved. Group discussion shifts to another topic. (p. 163)

The issue of not saying "hi" is serious enough to generate conflict. Hal's method of dealing with the conflict is especially interesting and is discussed in detail below in the section on silence and deference.

Great attention is paid in the workshop to special occasions. Birthdays, the birth of a nephew or niece, any special accomplishment, such as winning a bowling tournament, are usually announced in group meetings by someone other than the honoree. Happy Birthday is sung on members' birthdays, and on any special occasion there is applause from the group and handshakes are given the honoree. Individuals become upset if these special occasions are not announced by someone else and they are forced to do it themselves. They nevertheless do so and then happily receive the honors due them. One member of the workshop is a poet, and whenever he recites one of his poems he receives applause. In fact, any speech delivered with special fervor or skill is applauded. All of this positive politeness occurs regularly, and the absence of it is noteworthy and resented.

Members of the workshop, then, engage in presentation rituals, expect them in return, and are upset if they do not occur when it is believed they should. The only thing unusual about their use in the workshop is that they are sometimes overdone. This is the case with the greeting and introduction behavior that first-time UCLA visitors to the workshop receive. It is also the case in one of the group sessions where a certain member introduces the members to the rest of the group each time it meets. Some of the lower functioning members of the workshop overdo attempts at providing polite openings for small talk. One individual asks many times a day, "You been good? What have you been up to? What you been doing?" He listens to his interlocutor's response and appears interested but then immediately asks the question again. He and others who do the same are attempting to be polite. They know a few formulas for opening conversations but are unable to properly follow them up. Nevertheless, they, like other workshop members, value politeness and make their attempts as best they can.

Sex and Death

Sex and death are topics that involve circumspection, taboo, and careful etiquette in most societies, certainly in our own. Workshop society is no exception, but there, for a number of reasons, these topics are especially delicate or disturbing and are treated in ways that differ somewhat from the way they are treated in the broader community. The problematic nature of sex and death, and the expression of that problematic nature in the conventions of speech etiquette concerning those topics, are grounded in experiences, values, and concerns that workshop members share. Specifically, these are: the lack of information, experience, and knowledge that workshop members have concerning sex and death; the potential that sex and death have for creating trouble for workshop members, both within the workshop and outside it; and the strong desire to avoid trouble of any kind that nearly all workshop members share.

There is a lack of information regarding sex and death and little experience with sex on the part of most workshop members. The facts surrounding death have been withheld from many workshop members by protective family members so they do not know much about it. Yet they experience death. In the past few years, several workshop members have died, as have many parents, siblings, other relatives, and friends. Most of the workshop members who have died have done so unexpectedly. In some cases, the death of a close relative has not been made known to workshop members by their families, and they only learned of it from other workshop members. It is not surprising, then, that for members of workshop society, death seems mainly unpredictable. This belief combined with a lack of knowledge and a lack of any good theory about death, makes death especially frightening.

Sex too is an area about which members of the workshop have less information than do their nonretarded peers. There is, of course, a great deal of variation in how much information concerning sex members of the workshop have received from their parents. The parents as a group, however, have opposed attempts to begin sex education classes in the workshop, and sex education classes offered by other service delivery organizations have been so poorly attended that they have been discontinued. In general, the message that workshop members get from their parents is that sex is something that they are not to think or talk about, at least in the presence of parents or other authority figures. Peers in the workshop do talk about sex in non-pejorative ways, and this serves to provide a conflicting message about the appropriateness of sex as a topic. At any rate, the knowledge of workshop members regarding sexual matters is less than that of their nonretarded peers.

This is also true of their experience in sexual matters. Although some members of the workshop are married or have steady boyfriends or girlfriends, most have limited sexual experience, and many have none. Parents are concerned that their mentally retarded offspring will become pregnant, be emotionally damaged, or otherwise get into sexual trouble, and they tend to restrict the sexual activity of workshop members. The result of this restricted access to sexual knowledge and experiences is that workshop members are about as sexually sophisticated as nonretarded adolescents. Like adolescents, they regard sex as mysterious and titillating and as having the potential for creating trouble.

Death, too, causes trouble. Workshop members often have difficulty understanding, accepting, and adjusting to the death of a loved one. Frequently, the hurt and anguish will linger at a high intensity for many years. The death of a parent or other relative who provided care may work a drastic change in the life of the individual, so that their life after the death is very different from that which preceded it. Often, such a death has marked the time of family dissolution and resulted in placement of the workshop member in a foster home or board and care facility. For most, the death of a family member is a great personal loss and emotional trauma which may result in frequent visitations from the dead in dreams for many years afterward or serve as the focus of any trouble or sadness in their lives.

"Trouble" is a chief concern of workshop members. They worry about getting into trouble and the consequences of trouble. The concept of trouble is a frequent topic of conversation. Sex and death cause trouble, and talking about them causes trouble as well: sex because it is a violation of parental values that can lead to interpersonal difficulties, death because it is frightening and upsets individuals who have lost someone close to them. Moreover, the trouble that everyone wishes to avoid may spread. Friends and acquaintances may take sides in some quarrel that has arisen regarding something that has been said concerning the sexual behavior of another, for example. When someone is upset because death has been mentioned, a kind of emotional contagion is likely to spread until everyone is feeling upset, emotional, and depressed. Such trouble, like all trouble, is to be avoided.

Workshop members have been socialized to deal with any kind of problem by using avoidance and denial. They are taught that if you have trouble with someone you should stay away from him. If something upsets you, don't think about it. Avoidance and denial are the major avenues for problem resolution, staying out of trouble, and maintaining emotional well being and social harmony. Sex and death thus are topics to be avoided. Yet they are talked about. Sex, if troublesome, is also titillating and interesting. Death, if upsetting and depressing, is also puzzling, frightening, and very much a fact of life. Insufficient information and understanding of sex and death, their potential for causing trouble, the desire to avoid trouble, and the seeming inevitability of sex and death as topics are the elements that interact to form the dynamics from which conventions of speech etiquette in the workshop concerning these topics arise.

Death as a Topic

For the reasons discussed above, death is a sensitive and painful topic that is handled with care by workshop members. Knowledge of the sensitivity of the topic is part of workshop culture, and the general rule is to not talk about death or the dead. For various reasons, the topic does come up, and the reactions to it and the delicate way in which it is usually handled serve to confirm its salience and potential for pain. The attitude of workshop members toward death as a topic is demonstrated in the following exchange:

> The group has been disapprovingly discussing another workshop member who frequently talks about dead people. A researcher asks if anyone can explain why they "feel so bad about talking about people being dead."
>
> Phil: It's no good, Jim, because uh—
> Nancy: You get em upset.
> Phil: (If you) mention death, they think of their own family. You gonna cry. Someone did that to me—I gonna cry. Say something about my mother, my father, someone else—I get very upset.
> Jim: So it brings up bad memories?
> Phil: Yes, about his mother's death. He feels very bad about it. His mother died from cancer.
> Jim: So it's best just not to talk about it?
> Phil: Yes.
> Jane: Uh, Joe [another researcher], I don't wanna hear that word.
> Joe: Which one?

Jane: I can't say it.
Phil: Dead.
Jane: Dead. Yes. I don't wanna hear that word.
Joe: You don't even like the sound of the word?
Jane: No. (Joe then changes the topic).

As can be seen from this example, workshop members don't like to hear about death because it upsets them. It reminds them of the death of someone close to them and makes them sad. It is better not to talk about death and so not to be reminded. The unpleasant memories and the emotions they evoke are so close to the surface that even the word *dead* should be avoided.

This is the norm—avoidance. But, of course, neither death nor its discussion can be avoided. In workshop society, just as death as a topic is avoided for a number of reasons, it is also talked about for a number of reasons. There is a dimension that underlies most of the reasons for both the talk or the avoidance of talk about death, however, and that is a concern for the feelings of the individuals involved. Consider the following example from one of the group meetings:

Ralph: Shall we all say a prayer for Annette Williams? She came in today and told me 'Ralph, my grandmother's passed away.' When I hear that I says 'oh, no.'
Pat: Who?
Ralph: Annette's grandmother passed away this morning.
Group: Oh, no.
George: Oh, yes.
Ralph: Yes, and she won't be in Friday. She's gonna go to the funeral. After lunch, she started to cry. I knew something was bothering her. She's real upset, Joe.
Lenore: She'll be here Friday?
George: No, she won't be here Friday.
Ralph: No. We should be nice to her, right?
Lenore: Right. Be nice to Annette.
George: Bob was being mean to her.

The topic of death is introduced here because it is an important news item, and, more importantly, it announces that a fellow workshop member has suffered a loss, is upset, and that the basic positive politeness theme in the workshop, "be nice," should be especially invoked at this time. Note that the interchange begins with a request for a prayer for Annette, that it is agreed that everyone should be nice to her, and that a transgression of the basic rule has taken place. The interchange is not simply an announcement by Ralph of the death of Annette's grandmother but an expression of compassion for Annette and an affirmation of proper and caring behavior.

There are other circumstances as well, when death may be an acceptable topic for discussion. An individual may wish to talk about something that is upsetting him, and his report of his problems may include the mention of death, as in the following example:

John: Before I came here, I was in a foster home.

Ellen: Yeh.

John: (Long pause). If you guys don't mind, I like to mention one person in my real family.

Ellen: Go on.

Gordon: What? Go on.

John: My real mother died when she was really sick. (John begins to cry).

Ellen: Well, that's something else.

John: She died of a coma.

Ellen: That is something else.

John: And so she sent me down here in a foster home.

Ellen: Let's not discuss it. I know you're upset about it, so let's drop it. I don't want to hear any more. No!

Ben: I don't wanna hear about it either.

John: Okay.

Researcher: He should be allowed to talk about it if he wants to though. (The group discusses whether participants can talk about anything they wish. Finally someone says "go ahead" and John continues. His topic, however, is the foster home rather than the death of his mother).

Here John introduces a topic that is bothering him: something about his life in a foster home. After careful consideration—indicated by the long pause—he asks the permission of the group to mention a member of his real family. All the members of the group are aware that John's family is deceased, but give their permission. The mention of his mother's death causes John to cry. Members of the group then demand that the topic of death be dropped. John acquiesces, and it is only through the intervention of the discussion leader that he is allowed to continue. He discreetly drops the topic of death, however, and returns to a related topic—trouble in the foster home. Two rules of behavior are in conflict in this situation. There is the general prohibition of talk of death in the workshop, but there is also the rule of the discussion group that members can talk about whatever is bothering them. John apologetically violates the speech etiquette rule, but when he and others become upset, the rule is reinvoked. It is only through the intervention of a researcher that the group discussion rule is again given precedence and John is permitted to continue. He fortunately has the good sense not to force the issue and returns to his main topic.

As in the preceding example, death is sometimes mentioned in a discussion that is primarily concerned with some other topic. This also occurs in the exmaple that follows. Here, however, a sort of "chaining" occurs, in which death seems to become a topic in its own right. This especially upsets one member of the group and repeated attempts are made to get back to the original topic of the discussion.

The group is discussing God and religion. Mark mentions that they are all God's children and that Lent will soon be over so that they will be able to eat what they please. Ellen mentions that God brought us all into the world but, on the other hand, He also took three people "away from the workshop that we loved very much." Other speakers remind Ellen of workshop members who have died other than the three she has mentioned. This topic of conversation shifts to all the people who have died. Lucille begins to cry and Ellen says, "I think we'd better drop the subject. Lucille's crying." Phil tries saying "God is special" but then drifts into mentioning that he lost his father and girlfriend. Lucille begins to sob. Ellen says, "She's crying. C'mon that's enough. I think we'd better drop it. Phil, don't say anything more. Drop the topic." The discussion leader asks, "But doesn't it have to do with other things beside death?" Phil says that God put all the animals on earth, but Lucille continues to sob.

Ralph: What's wrong?
Ellen: Wanna sit here with us? We're gonna drop it now.
Ralph: (Said sweetly) You lost somebody in your family?
Ellen: (Sharply) That's enough!
Ralph: Is that what you're upset about? I think she lost somebody in her family.
Ellen: Oh-oh, her aunt. Drop it please.
Ralph: I don't think she wants to talk about it.
Ellen: No. No.

Lucille is hugged, people hold her hard and comfort her, and she is given a spray of Binaca. The group comes to an agreement on how they can talk about God without talking about death.

They decide they will talk about being alive and of life before they were formed inside their mothers. They have found a safe topic but still must monitor their talk to avoid any mention of death.

John: (Talking about parents and being born.) They took care of us.
Mack: Right on.
John: My *real* father—before he died . . .
Ralph: (Loudly interrupting) Ah-ah.
Jane: I don't want to hear that word.
John: *Before* he died, I mean.
Ralph: Oh, okay.

The topic of death, then, is an upsetting one. The general rule is avoidance, but it is occasionally introduced in group discussions, sometimes with legitimate reason and sometimes inadvertently and almost by accident. When the topic is introduced and people become upset, the group deals with the situation by attempting to switch the topic and by comforting those who have been upset. The general feeling is one of sympathy for the offended parties, and though speakers may be admonished to drop the subject, rarely is real anger directed at them. The feelings are different, however, toward those who constantly spread "rumors" about death:

John: He told me that Sandra told him about Elvis Presley [being dead]. (Note: This is in January, 1982.)

Fred: I don't believe that.
Lucille: She wouldn't do that. I know her too well.
Ben: That's right.
Phil: She's a grouch.
John: But why is she talking about dead?
Phil: She talk about dead because she got a big mouth.
John: You know why she's talking about dead?
Phil: Why?
John: I'll tell you why. Because she wants to bring my real family
back to . . .
Ben: She's full of baloney.
Phil: Don't talk to her. She talk about dead.
Gary: Dead people.
Phil: The dead is gone. If she still talk about death, tell her
'Forget it girl. I don't want to talk about it.'

Rumor is the term used by members of the workshop for a form of speech behavior that overlaps considerably with what might be more generally called gossip. Like gossip, it is talk between individuals concerning the affairs of some other person who is not present, and it is considered an invasion of that person's privacy. It is greatly resented and the cause of conflict when it is found out, and persons who frequently engage in "spreading rumors" are not liked. If workshop members hear, for example, that someone else has called them crazy or a baby or said that they were going to be disciplined or suspended from the workshop, they would accuse that person of spreading rumors about them. This sense of the term closely matches its more general usage and might be called either gossip or rumor in the wider speech community. Another example of rumor is talk about a married woman who had been flirting with some men in the workshop. In this case, although the woman involved would rather not have had the matter discussed, the facts of her flirtations were known to everyone in the workshop. This instance might be considered by outsiders to be one of gossip rather than rumor. Unlike gossip, however, the topic of rumor need not be something that the person being talked about wishes kept secret or something that might be considered injurious to his or her reputation. On the contrary, the topics of rumor in the workshop are often facts that would seem perfectly innocuous and are known to everyone. Topics of rumor include, for example, the fact that someone lives in a group home or rides the workshop bus to and from work. Even though this information may be generally known to all and would seem to be harmless, third party talk about it is nevertheless labeled rumor and generates much indignation and conflict.

The most potent or negatively charged topic of rumor is death. Just as talk of death upsets some participants in the discussion group, death as a topic of rumor is likely to upset and anger some, in fact most, members of the workshop. Again, it does not matter that what is said is true and is known to everyone; virtually any mention that one's parents, a friend, or even Elvis Presley is dead causes resentment, anger, and uneasiness.

Engaging in the telling of rumors, then, is a violation of speech etiquette in the workshop. It is negatively sanctioned, and people who persist in such behavior are disliked. A number of topics may be the subject of rumor, but death is among the worst and most resented.

Sex as a Topic

Within the discussion groups, which are often devoted to members' problems, sex is occasionally a topic. It is introduced by some people more often than by others. In fact, there are a number of individuals who never bring up the subject themselves, but when it is introduced, most participate in the discussion with no apparent embarrassment. The focus at these times is usually on such matters as whether or not one should engage in pre-marital sex, whether it is appropriate to find a temporary boyfriend/girlfriend when one's steady is on vacation, the belief that so-and-so is acting promiscuously, and so on. The tone is matter-of-fact, and the discussion is issue oriented. Rarely are explicit sexual matters discussed, and there is little indication of the titillation that is sometimes obvious when taboo terms are used. There are exceptions. Male members of the group may boast of a sexual conquest, for example. When this happens, it is usually done in a humorous style. On these occasions, the other members of the group may take up the fun, make jokes, and thoroughly enjoy themselves. Flirting with a risqué topic is fun and titillating, but rarely is anyone very explicit. Consider the following episode from one of the group meetings:

A researcher, Joe, asks Agnes to report to the group an incident that she had mentioned to him earlier. Agnes is embarrassed and at first pretends to not understand what Joe is talking about. She then "remembers" and looks down at the table. There is a long pause during which she is encouraged by the other members of the group to tell her story. She finally tells of an outing by a social group she had previously belonged to during which a man "had sex" with his wife on the bus in front of the group members. She says he also "had sex" with his wife before they were married, and that he "tried to do it" with a number of the girls in the group. This is met with many "oohs" and "aahs" by the discussion group. An embarrassed Agnes says, "Shut up, you guys."

In the discussion that ensues, everyone agrees that this was outrageous behavior indeed. It is the consensus, however, that such behavior should be ignored. "Everyone should stay out of it and let them do what they want."

Someone reports that her "old boyfriend, Melvin, he undid my bra strap." This is met with much laughter by the group. Another woman reports that "three boys grabbed me and took me into the garage." She ran home crying and told her mother who called the police.

This prompts Stan to blurt, "Sex is a bad thing." He encounters much disagreement from the group and amends his statement to, "People shouldn't talk about it. It's okay if they do it in private, but they shouldn't do it in public or talk about it." To this the group agrees.

The researcher, who sees in this rather free and open discussion an opportunity to explore the group members' knowledge and attitudes toward sex, asks, "What kinds of things are part of sex?" Milton is incredulous. "You mean you actually want me to explain this to you? O.K. Anybody who's very sensitive should plug their ears. Well—what it is . . ." Stan interrupts "Sex is okay. But if you want to take it and abuse it, then that's not good." To this, the group agrees. Milton continues, "But what you should do is—if people want to use it, they should wait till they get married." The group once more indicates its agreement. "Because if you do it before, it's a very serious sin. You can go and do it to somebody . . ." A researcher interrupts, "What do you mean when you say *do it?*" The group reacts with many "oohs" and "aahs" and nervous laughter. Someone suggests, "Make out. Make out." Milton accepts that explanation, "O.K. O.K. You can make out with someone," and then points out the danger of pregnancy and the trouble that might cause. Someone else stresses the possibility of contracting V.D. and warns that "doing it can be hazardous to your health and your life." Someone else says, "You can kiss, but don't do the other part." There is much group reaction to this risqué statement with many "oohs" and "aahs."

The researcher pursues his line of inquiry. "You've talked about kissing—and all the way down the line—and about the girl getting pregnant—but what about it between?" This, once again, is met by a loud group reaction. There is much excitement, embarrassment, and many overlapping comments. Someone says "naked," another mentions "touching."

A discussion of touching follows which Milton sums up, "Touching is fine, but if you're thinking of doing something other than touching, forget it. Leave it till after you're married. Touching is fine, but don't do that other stuff. Don't climb on top of the girl." The group is beside itself.

The researcher tries again. This time he asks one of the women, who is generally more preoccupied with sex than the others, what she thinks. "Well, I don't like it. My boyfriend used to keep putting his hands in my pants and my shirt all the time, and I didn't like it. No way. I kept telling him not to do it. He was caught. He asked me to lay on top of him, and I was." Much reaction from the group. "Ooh." "Ooh, you were?" "We don't allow that." "No way." "No way."

Hal discreetly steers the topic away to a lengthy discussion of touching as a form of communication.

This rather extended example is presented in detail because it illustrates some important points regarding attitudes toward sex and ways of talking about sex in the workshop. It is not a typical example since, as was pointed out above, most discussions of sex in the groups concern social relationships rather than the sex act itself. Here the researcher not only provides a receptive situation for the discussion of sex but actually attempts to push the participants beyond the bounds of what they feel to be proper. For that reason, it is instructive. It indicates not only what the boundaries are but also the attitudes toward them and the techniques employed to avoid stepping over them even when pushed.

Note that the subject is introduced by the researcher. Agnes, the narrator, is embarrassed and tries to avoid the topic. At the urging of the group members, who at this point are still unaware of what Agnes' story is about, she finally tells what happened. The language she uses is euphemistic and mild, and the reaction of the audience is typical. So too is the ensuing discussion and the consensus that "people shouldn't do it in public or talk about it." In spite of the researcher's persistent attempts to get the group to talk about what might take place between kissing and getting pregnant, he is largely unsuccessful. Those sensitive souls who may have plugged their ears at the beginning of Milton's explanation and the discussion that followed would have missed such risqué and informative descriptions as "do it," "make out," "do the other part," "naked," "touching," "that other stuff," and, finally, "climb on top of the girl," and "lay on top of him." The whole exercise is one of embarrassment, titillation, avoidance, and euphemism. It demonstrates quite clearly the delicate nature of the topic and the rules of speech etiquette that govern its discussion.

If the particularly of normal sexual behavior are to be treated with great verbal care, sexual behavior seen as deviant, especially if it involves a workshop member who is liked, is to be positively avoided. Over the course of several weeks, for example, two men in one of the groups regularly sat next to each other and petted and caressed each other. This finally culminated in mutual masturbation shielded from direct view by the table around which everyone sat. Everyone in the group, however, was perfectly aware of what was going on, and yet no one said a word. One of these men was subsequently forbidden by his parents to associate with another member of the workshop with whom he had been engaged in a homosexual relationship. He greatly bemoaned this loss of his friend in a number of group discussions and offered a variety of reasons as to why his parents had taken this action. He blamed the counselors. He suggested that the supervisors didn't like him, that others were jealous, and so on. He never mentioned his homosexual activities, and although most group members knew why his parents had interfered with the friendship, no one else mentioned it either. In fact, other group members offered evidence to corroborate his spurious reasons and offered innocuous explanations of their own. This avoidance behavior and feigned ignorance is not simply a matter of social nicety, of course, but is concerned with saving the face of a friend.

Taboo Words

The use of obscenities, or swear words in general, is considered by members of the workshop as something that is against the rules of appropriate behavior and should not be done. In fact, swearing occurs with some frequency. There are usually no sanctions applied when the violation is a matter of simply using a swear word and not an instance of cursing *at* someone. In this latter case, strong feelings are likely to be aroused. Consider the following example from a group discussion:

Lenore: She was cursing again at me.
Group: Ooh.
Lenore: I didn't like it. She was being bad.
Hal: Give her a kick in the pants.
Lenore: Herb was cussing on the bus at Milton.
Group: Oh-oh.

This bit of conversation illustrates several points. Lenore, in the context of a group discussion of the behavior of others, mentions that "she" was cussing at Lenore again. Cursing at others is often reported, and people who engage in it frequently are disliked and considered to have "big" mouths or "bad" mouths. The group reaction to both reports of "cussing" in this example is typical and indicates both the significance of the act itself and the feelings of workshop members toward it. The serious nature of the transgression is underlined by Hal's suggestion of a proper response.

Although cursing at someone is almost always reacted to in a strongly negative fashion, the response to the use of swear words in other ways may vary from outrage to mild titillation. The type of response elicited depends on a number of factors, not all of which are clear. In the following example, the reaction is relatively strong, especially given the relative lack of potency of the word that is objected to.

> Ellen has been telling a discussion group that a co-worker has a "big" mouth.
>
> Ellen: If she [Edna] can go around saying that my lead worker is a B-I-T-C-H (spells out), then she's one herself.
>
> The group responds to this with murmurs and a few quiet expressions of disapproval. Ellen goes on complaining about Edna *and* about Edna's lead worker who permits her to use such language. Ellen finally says that she will try to have Edna suspended from the workshop and that she is willing to suffer the consequences of attempting to do that: "If I am suspended, then I am suspended. But Edna is gonna get the hell outta here." Members of the group appear shocked and respond with "Oh-oh." "Bad language." "Bad language." "Bye Ellen." "Bye Ellen." Ellen is undeterred and says, "And I'll repeat it. The hell outta here." This is too much for Hal who says that he and his girlfriend, Carol, will both have to leave the group session. Carol agrees and says, "I don't wanna hear any more bad words." Ellen interprets this to mean that Carol is siding with Edna. Carol denies this and says, "I don't like bad words." Hal supports her and says, "Long as *I'm* present, no bad words are allowed in here." Ellen then accuses Hal of supporting Edna. Hal responds, "No. No. I said if you keep on saying *bad* language, that Carol and I is gonna leave." Carol supports him, and Hal closes the episode with "and please, no more."

All of this in reaction to "the hell outta here." Why this should be so is not clear. Especially when, in the context of telling of an encounter with a woman who sprayed his father's van with a garden hose, another speaker reported he such expressions as "kick the shit out of you" and "stick the hose up your ass" and got no reaction from the group at all. Perhaps Hal and Carol simply wanted to withdraw from or defuse an emotionally charged situation. Whatever their reason, they chose to accomplish it by objecting to Ellen's "bad" language. This case is, in fact, rather unusual in that the reaction to swearing is ordinarily much milder. It is presented here to demonstrate the existence of the shared rule against swearing and one end of the range of reactions to violations of the rule. The more common occurrence within the group discussion setting is that instances of "shit," "damn," or even "kissing" are met with "oohs" and "aahs" and an occasional "watch that mouth, boy." The impression one gets is that the group members consider the use of these words as against the rules but really don't object to them and, in fact, are mildly titillated when saying or hearing them. John is anxious to say, and Ben is delighted to hear, such a word in the following exchange:

> John reports that a workshop member was suspended for "touching Judy's you-know-what." A researcher notes that he had heard that the individual in question was suspended for yelling at the supervisor. John, however, sticks to his guns. "For yelling at the supervisor *and* touching." The researcher asks when it happened, and John says he didn't see it, but "my friend Bob told me that he touch a girl's you-know-what." At this point, John abandons hope that he will be asked to specify "you-know-what" and asks the discussion leader "Will you allow me to say it?"
>
> Discussion Leader: Sure, you say whatever you want.
> John: Tits.
> Group: Ooh.
> Ben: (Sitting up straight and interested) He say *tits?*

Taboo words, then, may be used in anger, for emphasis, nonchalantly, or even to amuse. Reactions to them may vary from strong disapproval to positive excitement. However, notice that all of the examples used here and, indeed, the overwhelming majority of taboo words we have heard in the workshop are quite mild. Although "bitch" was claimed to have been said in the workshop, when it was reported in the group it was spelled. Words of stronger potency such as "fuck" or "son-of-a-bitch" are seldom uttered. The rules of speech etiquette in regard to taboo words may be violated for a variety of reasons, but only slightly. Even minor violations are inappropriate for some. When a group discussion leader once said "hell," it was met not with oohs and aahs but with total silence.

The rules of speech etiquette regarding sex and death as topics or as taboo, then, are influenced by values, concerns, and experiences of members of workshop society. Death is an especially painful and little understood topic. It causes trouble when it is not avoided, by upsetting people, and a good deal of effort is devoted to avoiding the topic or, if it is introduced, to changing it. Like sex, death is a potent topic of rumor and its mention in rumor is highly resented and a serious breach of etiquette. Sex is likewise little understood and a potential source of trouble. It is also titillating, however, and so is occasionally discussed. Whether as topic or as taboo, attitudes toward sex in the workshop seem to be similar to those held by nonretarded adolescents, who have, as do workshop members, limited experience with sexual matters. When trouble arises, whether through the mention of death, the occurrence of rumor, or the use of taboo words, workshop members attempt through various means to restore the social harmony they all desire.

Silence and Deference as Etiquette

Members of workshop society, by virtue of their condition and the label that has been applied to them, are stigmatized persons. As such, many have suffered damage to their self-esteem. Although coping strategies and reactions to the stigma vary from individual to individual (Zetlin & Turner, this volume), all members of the workshop quite naturally attempt to maximize their self-esteem and sense of worth and to maintain face. In this, they are assisted by other members of workshop society. Such cooperation is the essence of etiquette (Brown & Levinson, 1978; Goffman, 1956) and is governed by the rules of etiquette shared and understood by members of the group.

We have pointed out above that social harmony and deviance disavowal are two focal concerns in workshop society. They are societal concerns, if not the personal concerns, of each and every member of the society, and, as such, they underlie certain rules of speech etiquette. Specifically, they underlie the reluctance of workshop society members to call attention to handicaps of fellow members or to challenge the attempts of fellow members to maintain their self-esteem through a strategy of self-aggrandizement. Rules of etiquette are not always followed, of course. In fact, rules may be purposely broken in order to insult or injure another, and it is often the reaction to violation of the rules that makes their salience and potency so clear.

Incompetency Insults

A topic to be avoided in a workshop for the mentally retarded is, not surprisingly, the subject of mental retardation itself. It is not a subject of discussion in the daily routine of the workshop. (On one occasion, however, a researcher did overhear two workshop members telling each other, with obvious great glee, "little moron" jokes. When they became aware they were being overheard, they were quite embarrassed and moved away.) When a researcher attempted to introduce the topic early on in the workshop society study, he was met with total silence. No one would talk about it, and, in fact, two members permanently left their group as the result of the attempt to introduce the topic. A researcher interested in workshop members' definitions of retardation, with much effort, finally persuaded a group to discuss it. The definitions they offered did not mention diminished intellectual ability but concentrated on physical handicaps, poor speech and language, and immature behavior. The examples they offered were invariably individuals who were lower functioning than themselves. Given the delicacy of the topic, it is understandable that the most serious insult that can be received in the workshop is to be called retarded or incompetent.

When someone does refer to another as retarded, it is nearly always in extreme anger and clearly meant as a pejorative. It is a marked occurrence and is reacted to strongly and negatively by those who hear it. For example, in the midst of a tirade in a group session concerning some injury Norman felt Dan had done him, Norman said, "Dan's retarded." Phil immediately and angrily responded, "Nobody likes that word." This was followed by a successful group effort to get the microphone used in tape recording the session away from Norman. A comparable insult is to call someone a baby. This implies not only childish and incompetent behavior, which is disvalued, but also functions as a euphemism for mental retardation. This insult may be delivered in a direct way, for instance, "You act like a baby," or indirectly, as in the following sample:

> Norman is once again angry with Dan. In the midst of his tirade, the researcher asks: "What's your problem with Dan?"
> Norman: He thinks its *funny*, huh? He funning me for no reason at all. Right?
> Jim: He's doing what to you?
> Norman: He thinks we're gonna beat him. We're gonna put his *diapers* on tomorrow.

Once again, the group reacted with disapproval and anger to Norman's breach of etiquette. Norman is considered a "troublemaker" by most members of the workshop, and his frequent accusations of retardation is one of the reasons.

If people are upset when someone else is called retarded or a baby, they are even more upset when the insult is directed at them. In the following case, the insult was delivered gesturally rather than verbally, not an uncommon method in the workshop. This is done by folding the arms in front of the chest as though cradling a baby and gently rocking them back and forth while looking at the intended recipient of the insult. In one group session, Jane, who was visibly upset, reported that she had a problem with Albert.

> She reports that he called her a name—*baby*—and she didn't like it. John interrupts and says that he can't believe Albert is still calling Jane a baby, noting that he has tried to prevent him from doing that in the past. After some group discussion, it is clarified that Albert did not actually call her the name but directed the sign of rocking a baby at her. Jane reiterates that she does not like it, and John agrees, "It's not very nice." Alan also agrees, "It's not very nice to say." Jane cannot bring herself to even say the word: "I not say it. I can't say it."

To say that someone is crazy is also a powerful insult. It too implies incompetence and is a direct challenge to the positive self-image of normalcy that workshop members strive hard to maintain. This is clear in the following extended example, which also includes other violations of speech etiquette and typical reactions to them. Here, the initial incident reported occurred on one of the work lines. Like the insult of "baby" described above, this insult was delivered gesturally rather than verbally. This is done in the usual manner of making circular motions with the index finger pointed at the temple.

> Ellen, who has been engaged in an ongoing feud with Ruth and Anne for some time, reports in a group discussion that Ruth, when talking with Anne, has called Ellen crazy by making the visual sign. Ellen seeks reassurance from the group by saying, "If anyone agrees with her that I am nuts, I wish I knew right now." She reiterates the problem: Ruth made the "crazy" sign. A researcher asks the group if

anyone has any ideas concerning how to deal with the problem. Nancy volunteers, "Don't listen to her, right Jim?" Ellen points out that that is difficult if you are sitting right next to her, and she persists in making signs. John says he knows what the sign means. It means "loco" and "crazy." Ellen once again seeks reassurance of her sanity and asks the researcher, "Do you think I am, Jimmy?" Jim replies, "No," but the perennial troublemaker Norman, referring to Ellen, says, "She *is* crazy." This extremely upsets Ellen who says, "That did it" and begins to cry. Norman is unrelenting and says that Ellen has a big mouth. The group then comes to Ellen's defense. John, speaking of both Ruth's and Norman's behavior, says, "That's how you hurt somebody's feelings—calling them crazy." Phil says that Norman has a big mouth.

The discussion then switches to Anne. It is agreed that she is the main cause of Ellen's problem and that she told Ruth what to do. Phil feels that, "Anne doesn't listen to nobody. She's a spoiled brat and should knock it off right now. It's not right to call people names." Ellen says she can't take it much longer, that Anne is nice to everyone else, but "when it comes to me, I'm not there. I'm just a piece of umn—alright, I'll say it." The group anticipates trouble and an attempt is made to get Ellen to stop, but she persists. "I'm just a piece of shit. To her I'm nothing but a goddamn piece of shit." The group is shocked, "Hey." "Just a minute, buddy." "Don't say that. That's very nasty." Ellen says that's how she feels—"dirty, nasty."

The researcher once again asks if anyone has any ideas. Norman says that he does: "Anne's crazy." This sets Ellen off. She interrupts Norman, screaming, "Norman, I don't wanna hear it. I don't wanna hear that word. God, I don't wanna hear that word. I don't wanna hear that word. Norman, I don't wanna hear that word from you." Tim also doesn't want to hear that word. He is angry with Norman and feels he should be quiet or get out.

The discussion returns to the original troublesome episode. John corroborates Ellen's story: "I saw her. I saw Ruth doing that thing to Ellen. I know it's not my business to butt in . . . and she should not do that. She does not have no right to hurt anybody's feelings like yours, Ellen. She does not have no right to hurt anybody's feelings like you. That makes her jealous and stubborn. I agree with Ellen. It's not her business to talk from one place to another." Ellen doubts that John really witnessed the incident and asks him when this was. John says that it was Monday, and Ellen points out it has been happening for a couple of weeks and could have happened on Monday. The topic then changes.

This example clearly demonstrates the intensity of the feelings of members of the workshop regarding violations of the rule of etiquette concerning accusations of deviancy or incompetency. Ellen is supported in her outrage and indignation by all of the group but Norman. When he agrees with Ruth's assessment of Ellen, he is chastised by others. When he tries to make up for his transgression by accusing Ellen's main tormentor of being crazy, both Ellen and Tim are extremely upset at the mere mention of the taboo word. This is similar to the reactions discussed above to the words "dead" or "death." Ellen seeks the reassurance of both the group and the discussion leader that Ruth's accusation is groundless. She is so upset that she violates the rule against the use of "bad words." The group is properly shocked. John confirms Ellen's report by stating (falsely) that he saw the incident and sums up the feelings of the members of the workshop toward such insulting behavior. Ellen accepts this support, and the incident is (temporarily) closed.

Many members of the workshop who are there as the result of having been judged by society to be incompetent deny, to themselves and others, any such incompetency. Although not employed by everyone, denial is a strategy that many use to maintain positive feelings of self-worth in the face of one of the most stigmatizing labels our society has to offer. They are in the workshop not because they are mentally retarded but because they can't read, or because they didn't finish school, or because they are physically handicapped, or for any number of reasons that are less painful than "being retarded." An implicit social contract has evolved that produces the rule of etiquette which dictates that members should be allowed to maintain their dignity by presenting a demeanor of competency. In Goffman's (1956) terms, their attempts to project the demeanor they choose should receive proper deference and should not be challenged. It is dangerous to the psyche of some and to the social harmony of all to even discuss mental retardation. Accusations of mental retardation or incompetency of any kind threaten the very fabric of workshop society. As such, they are among the most serious breeches of social etiquette and are met with outrage and with anger.

On each of the few occasions that members of the workshop have discussed the nature of mental retardation with researchers, they have stressed difficulty with speech and language as one of the principal consequences and, indeed, one of the defining features of mental retardation. The individuals they have identified as being mentally retarded are, almost without exception, individuals who have severe speech impediments, and the impediment is cited as evidence for their judgment. It must be stressed once more that workshop members are reluctant to discuss mental retardation and do so only at the request of persistent researchers. The individuals they identify as having speech impediments and, therefore, as being mentally retarded are never individuals who are present. The topic, like mental retardation itself, is in most instances taboo. It is not spontaneously discussed in the workshop. As a matter of fact, a great deal of effort is devoted to saving face for those who do have difficulty being understood. Such effort is in accord with the rule of workshop etiquette of not calling attention to incompetencies in order to preserve the positive self-image and social well-being that are so important to members of this stigmatized population. The rules may be violated, of course, if a workshop member wishes to insult someone. Unlike the use of insults such as "retarded," "crazy," and "baby," however, insults based on speech difficulties do not occur.

In face-to-face interaction with individuals who have speech problems, workshop members show great deference and studiously avoid calling attention to the problem. Such people are not avoided as interlocutors. They are treated like anyone else, and people will patiently wait, for example, while a speaker with a severe hesitation problem in his speech attempts to get his next word out. They wait for minutes to hear a message that some other speaker could deliver in a matter of seconds and do not become impatient or call attention to the matter by supplying the word the speaker is obviously attempting to say. Even in the most extreme cases, where the speech is totally incomprehensible, people patiently listen. A woman, for example, who because of a past injury cannot move her jaw except with her hand and who cannot be understood is given her turn at speaking at the lunch table she shares with others, and her speech is reacted to by her interlocutors. Not, of course, in terms of its content (since no one knows what that is), but in terms of the emotional load it seems to carry. If she appears sad, people commiserate with her. If she seems to consider what she says funny, then people laugh. Her speech is reacted to on the only level on which it can be understood. The fact that there is no comprehensible referential content is not commented upon. Some individuals, through long association, are comprehensible to fellow workers but not to newly arrived researchers. When, in such cases, the researcher shows signs of not being able to understand, someone may offer a translation or explanation. This is done matter of factly and serves to relieve the tension of the situation.

The rule of etiquette in regard to the quality and comprehensibility of the speech of others, then, is one of not calling attention to problems. One of the hallmarks of mental retardation in the view of the workshop members themselves is impaired speech and language. In order to preserve the face and the self-esteem of those so afflicted and to maintain the carefully constructed and precariously balanced claim of normal competency of workshop society in general, workshop members avoid any commentary on the impaired speech of others. The impaired speakers themselves are passive participants in this etiquette of deference and avoidance of mention. They take no active steps to present a non-stigmatized impression of themselves. They speak as they are able, and hearers are polite enough not to point out any difficulties and even to pretend to understand when they do not. A similar politeness strategy of deference, avoidance, and non-challenge is used when workshop members do take active steps to produce what they perceive to be a more positive self-image. That is, when they self-aggrandize or engage in normalcy fabrication.

Normalcy fabrications are stories created by workshop members concerning some aspect of their personal lives in which the teller claims to have had some experience that he or she has not had. It is impossible to confidently ascribe the underlying motivation for each individual presentation of a normalcy fabrication, but the content of the stories themselves is such that it presents the teller as leading a less restricted and more "normal" life than he or she actually does. A middle-aged man, for example, who has no family and who lives in a group home, has created a fictional family. He has photographs of his "wife" and "children" in his wallet which he proudly shows to co-workers and to visitors to the workshop. This is accompanied by stories and anecdotes concerning his "family" life. This particular normalcy fabrication has been ongoing for some time. Most members of the workshop know it to be false, yet it has never been challenged.

Other normalcy fabrications are more transitory. People may announce that they have been offered a job as an automobile mechanic, that they assisted the police in apprehending a purse snatcher, that they had a sexual encounter with a "high class" woman, and so on. Again, these stories are not challenged, no matter how unlikely and no matter that some individuals may tell of a new adventure each week. The tellers are permitted their pretense and the self they have chosen to present.

Normalcy fabrications are often presented by individuals following some traumatic event in their life that has threatened or damaged their self-esteem. The following selected incidents from our data on Larry are illustrative:

1. Larry was involved in a fight with another workshop member and was suspended from the workshop for a week. Larry claims it was because the other person called him a "stupid retard."
2. Larry became very indignant when a troublesome member of a discussion group asserted that the workshop is for retarded kids. Larry countered that he is not a kid and that he is not retarded. He then did not attend group discussions for a 3-week period claiming that he had too much work to do and that he needed more money.
3. Larry was taken on a weekend vacation to San Diego by his divorced father. His father brought his girlfriend along. Larry was forced to stay in a motel room and watch TV for 2 days while his father and father's girlfriend attended the horse races. Larry was quite upset when he reported this incident to one of the researchers. His arms and legs trembled and at one point he broke down and wept.
4. Larry was standing on the street outside of the workshop with a group of workshop members. Some teenagers drove by and shouted "Hey look at the retards." Larry refused to attend the workshop for the next 2 months. When he finally did return, he would often arrive late and leave late to avoid being seen with the other workshop members.

As can be seen from these incidents, Larry has even more difficulty than most other members of the workshop in dealing with the label of mental retardation. From a number of our sources of data, it is clear that Larry has a strong desire to be perceived and treated as nonretarded and that problematic behaviors often occur when his social identity as a retarded person becomes salient. Following these threats to his self-esteem, Larry's tactics to repair and maintain his self-image and self-esteem often involve normalcy fabrications. For example, after he returned to the workshop following his suspension for fighting, Larry was overheard telling a co-worker that he had spent the week "shacked up with a Black chick who had her own pool, listening to rock music and smoking pot." He claimed that he was now living in his own apartment (following incident 2) and that he was working nights as a drummer in a rock band (following incident 4). Similarly, the Monday following his trip to San Diego with his father (who has always been a major threat to Larry's self-esteem) Larry reconstructed his weekend as "having a wild time in Tijuana whorehouses with a bunch of the guys."

Normalcy fabrications, then, may function as coping tactics or even as long-term strategies when self-esteem is threatened or damaged. As such, the rule of etiquette is to not challenge them even when they are known by other workshop members to be untrue. This rule is usually followed by members of the workshop since they have a vested interest in cooperating with others to preserve self-esteem and a positive self-image for all. Members of the work-shop staff, however, may sometimes place a higher value on truthfulness and facing reality, as in the following example:

> One of the researchers was talking with Ruth, Anne, and Judy on one of the work lines. Ruth volunteered that she had been to Hawaii recently. This disclosure was apparently stimulated by the general conversation amongst the four about vacations. Ruth's story about her trip to Hawaii was basically as follows: She was down at the beach. A guy (she does not remember his name—she just called him "Honey") came up to her and asked her if she wanted to go on a date, a weekend trip to Hawaii, with him. She asked her mother, who said that she could go. They drove to the airport in the guy's Cadillac. They took a plane to Hawaii. They checked into a hotel. Their room was on the fourth floor. She discovered that all the doors had been removed inside their hotel suite. There were two bedrooms. She had to hang a sheet over the door to her bedroom. The guy tried to get her to come into his bedroom and sleep with him, but she refused. The guy asked her to marry him, but she refused. They got on the plane and came back home. The guy was 6-foot tall, had blonde hair and blue eyes.

This story also serves self-esteem maintenance and repair functions. For the previous 8 months, Ruth had a workshop boyfriend, Sam. Two weeks before, Sam had abandoned Ruth for another woman at the workshop, and Ruth had been very despondent and upset by this rejection.

Ruth had apparently told this story to Anne before, as Anne would frequently interrupt Ruth's narrative to say: "Tell Jim what he looked like. Tell Jim what kind of car he had," and so forth. As Ruth was telling this story, her supervisor came up and overheard part of it. She immediately and strongly challenged Ruth saying, "You're just making that up. That's not true." Ruth responded very emphatically and indignantly, saying that it was true and that she was not making up anything. Anne and Judy offered support for the veracity of her story and sympathy that it had been challenged.

Individuals everywhere engage in self-aggrandizement, of course, and often they go unchallenged. The workshop is not unique in that respect. In workshop society, however, the self-aggrandizement stories stand in bold relief. They are often patently false, and other members are aware that they are false. Yet they are not challenged. They are not challenged because there is a societal rule of etiquette grounded in the shared value of social harmony and the concern with deviance disavowal that prohibits their challenge and provides negative sanctions for those who violate the rule.

Occasionally, normalcy fabrications are presented not as long term strategies that function to provide an individual with the facade of a more "normal" life than he or she actually has, nor as tactics that serve to strengthen self-esteem following a damaging experience, but as rationalizations that justify apparently deviant or aberrant behavior. Tim offers such a normalcy fabrication in the following example (Turner, 1983):

John and Tim, who have been "best friends" for over 3 years, have a serious problem. John has accused Tim of "kissing boys" and no longer wants to be his friend. Various group members all agree. This is a very serious matter. Kissing boys is wrong. Boys should kiss girls, not other boys. Tim becomes increasingly distraught at this concerted attack on his behavior. His head droops to his chest, he avoids eye contact with everyone and appears on the verge of crying. Phil tries to soften the attack. "You are one of the nicest guys I know, Tim. You're one of my best friends in the whole world. But, you're not supposed to kiss boys. That's not right." Tim's hurt feelings are not relieved. He buries his head in his arms on the table. Group members remain silent. The tension level is very high. A researcher asks Tim to tell how he feels about what the others have said. Tim composes himself and begins his defense. He doesn't do it "that way." He knows it's true, a boy should not kiss boys. But he is an actor and actors sometimes have to do things that other people don't. He has pictures of actors at home in his bedroom. He writes letters to "the Fonz" and is a member of his fan club. He once won an Academy Award and has talked to Elvis Presley in person back in New York. Fred challenges the claim to an Academy Award. "I know you're a really good actor. I seen you be the Fonz and Incredible Hulk. But you didn't win no Academy Award because you weren't on TV." John comes to Tim's aid. Tim was on TV once. He was on "Bowling for Dollars." And Tim did win an award for acting. It was when he was in high school and he has a trophy at home. Joe agrees. He went to the same high school as Tim. Tim did win an acting award. He has seen the trophy himself. Various group members acknowledge Tim is a great actor. The problem about Tim "kissing boys" is forgotten. John reaches across the table and shakes Tim's hand using their "special hand shake." Both have huge grins on their faces. All is forgiven. The problem has been resolved. They are "best friends" again. (p. 156)

This interaction is especially interesting in that it exemplifies a number of techniques for resolving and avoiding conflict that workshop members frequently employ. There is, first of all, the normalcy fabrication itself. Tim, faced with the accusation that he has been kissing boys (a fact he cannot deny), with the consensus of the group that this is definitely not proper behavior, and, most importantly, with the loss of John's friendship, offers an explanation that will put the behavior in a frame (Goffman, 1974) that allows an interpretation that is non-deviant and normal. His claim of being an actor with an Academy Award is challenged, but note that the propriety of kissing boys, if one is indeed an actor, is accepted. It is necessary, therefore, to establish that Tim is a great actor who has won an award in order to make his behavior acceptable. The whole group contributes to creating this alternative reality. Even John, who initially registered the complaint and rejected Tim, contributes. Through a chain of scanty evidence and suspect logic, a new socially created reality is established, and Tim's behavior becomes understandable and acceptable.

Group creation and acceptance of an alternative reality is a common occurrence in workshop society. If a possible interpretation of the facts that will serve to resolve conflict or to soothe injured feelings can be offered, then that interpretation will be accepted. This creation and acceptance of a more forgiving truth does not, in itself, indicate an inability by workshop members to judge evidence or to employ logical reasoning. Rather, it is a result of values more strongly held in workshop society than the value of establishing the "real" truth: those of social harmony and the right to self-esteem. In this particular interaction and in the discussion in which Hal claims to have said "hi" presented above in the section on presentation rituals, the evidence is ambiguous. Tim *could* have received an award for acting, and Hal *could* have said "hi" for Pat. In the following example, however, there can be no doubt. A new reality is created and accepted.

The discussion group had grown too large and was divided in two, with each half of the group to meet on alternate weeks. Martha arrived at the group meeting and was questioned by Carol about whether she was supposed to be there. Carol suggested that it wasn't Martha's week to attend. At the next group meeting, Martha said that she was very upset and that Carol was trying to kick her out of the group. She continued to reiterate these two points concerning her feeling state and the cause of it for several minutes. Finally, Hal interrupted and proposed that it wasn't the Carol who was sitting next to him, his girlfriend, but that it was "the other Carol." At first, Martha mildly reasserted that it *was* the Carol sitting there next to him. Hal continued to offer evidence that it was indeed "the other Carol." He asked: "What bus does she ride on?" "What does she look like?" "Does she have long blonde hair?" and so on. Martha responded with silence or noncommital answers. After a few minutes of this, however, she agreed. It was "the other Carol." Martha's feelings were soothed and peace was restored.

Here there can be no ambiguity. Although other members of the group, possibly including Hal, may be unaware of the actual facts of the matter, Martha and Carol are not. They both know that it was the Carol who is present and *not* "the other Carol" who challenged Martha's presence at the group meeting. Yet, for the sake of social harmony, both accept Hal's interpretation. What is possible, if it resolves conflict, becomes what is true.

Conclusion

Workshop society, like any society, is concerned with facilitating social interaction in ways that promote group cohesion and accomplish group goals while infringing upon the rights and the self of the individual as minimally as possible. The rules and conventions of speech etiquette we have discussed function to serve these ends. The members of workshop society are, of course, members of the larger society as well, and it is not surprising that many of the features of speech etiquette in the workshop parallel or are based on features of speech etiquette in the broader society. We have not dealt with those aspects of polite speech which match those of the broader society but have directed our attention to those which are unique to workshop society and are grounded in fundamental concerns of its members.

Workshop society is an egalitarian society. As Turner (1983) has pointed out, "any verbalization, evaluative comparison, or other public behavior which asserts or implies diminished competency in others is strictly taboo" (p. 154). The ignoring of speech impediments discussed above is in part a special instance of this. It is not that members of the workshop are unaware of the diminished competency of others. Indeed, members often adapt their own speech, when communicating with lower functioning individuals, to a form that resembles "baby talk" or speech to foreigners (Ferguson, 1975). Rather, it is the mention of diminished competency that is taboo. This egalitarian value is also seen in the work behavior of workshop members. As we mentioned above, if a lower functioning member is holding up production on an assembly line, the other workers, rather than criticizing his lack of production, will simply slow down to match his pace. To mention the difficulty or to criticize the slow worker is a serious breach of etiquette and elicits accusations of being "mean" or "bossy" (Turner, 1983).

As noted earlier, egalitarian cultures emphasize group solidarity and harmony (Brown & Levinson, 1978). The egalitarian nature of workshop society, together with the high salience of the focal concerns of affiliative relationships and social harmony (Turner, 1983), are major factors underlying some of the more distinctive features of positive politeness speech etiquette that we have described. The slightly overdone presentation rituals, for example, are motivated by these concerns and with "being nice" (Zetlin & Turner, this volume).

Brown and Levinson (1978) identify avoiding disagreement as a strategy of positive politeness which functions to "claim common ground" or, in our terms, to promote group cohesion and social harmony. They specify a number of common means, such as "token agreement," "pseudo-agreement," "white lies," and "hedging opinions," for implementing this strategy. All of these are used by workshop members, as is the strategy of altercasting (Weinstein & Deutschberger, 1963) in which disagreement is preceded and softened by emphasizing positive characteristics of one's interlocutor or the nature of the relationship that exists between speaker and hearer. (Recall Phil's remarks to Tim in the "kissing boys" incident in which he prefaces his criticism with "you are one of the nicest guys I know, Tim. You are one of my best friends in the whole world. But . . . .")

Such strategies for avoiding disagreement are not unusual, and, indeed, Brown and Levinson (1978) have shown them to be commonly employed in many cultures. The resolution of conflict and the avoidance of disagreement through the social creation of a more acceptable reality is another matter, however. This is not a strategy commonly employed in the broader culture within which workshop society exists. Certainly not, at least, to the degree it is used in workshop society or to the extent that reality is reshaped, as in the examples we have presented above. The regular use of this strategy in the workshop is not, it seems to us, so much a matter of a diminished capacity to discern a true reality as it is a desire to avoid disagreement and maintain social harmony, basic values in the egalitarian workshop society. Certainly, there may be some confusion, for example, concerning whether it is really necessary and proper for even bonafide actors to practice kissing boys. Even when all participants are perfectly aware of the facts—of the "real" reality—as in the "other Carol" example, they are willing to accept an alternative reality if that reality is possible and will resolve conflict. The power of the value of social harmony is such that it takes precedence over concern for literal truth.

Although the values that both underlie and are generated by the egalitarian nature of workshop society contribute to the nature of the positive politeness that is exhibited there, another focal concern, that of deviance disavowal (Turner, 1983), has an even more powerful influence on speech etiquette in the workshop. Its influence is on what Brown and Levinson (1978) have termed "negative politeness" and what Goffman (1956), perhaps more descriptively, has called "deferential avoidance."

Some members of the workshop are afflicted with speech impediments, an identifying characteristic in workshop society of mental retardation itself. Others, in attempts to build or to maintain their self-esteem, fabricate stories that make them appear to lead more normal lives. All have been labeled mentally retarded. A fundamental and basic rule of speech etiquette in the workshop is to not call attention to these stigmata or to attempt to deny them. There is a collusion of silence, and most members cooperate. Those who do not are censured. Here, for a few short hours each working day, in the company of cooperating fellows, one's self-esteem is secure.

References

Albert, E. M. (1972). Culture patterning of speech behavior in Burundi. In J. J. Gumperz & D. Hymes (Eds.), *Directions in sociolinguistics: The ethnography of communication* (pp. 72–105). New York: Holt, Rinehart and Winston.

Brown, W., & Gilman, A. (1960). The pronouns of power and solidarity. In T. Sebeok (Ed.), *Style in language* (pp. 253–276). Cambridge, MA: MIT Press.

Brown, P., & Levinson, S. (1978). Universals in language usage: Politeness phenomena. In E. N. Goody (Ed.), *Questions and politeness: Strategies in social interaction* (pp. 56–289). Cambridge, England: Cambridge University Press.

Ferguson, C. (1975). Baby talk as a simplified register. *Stanford Papers and Reports on Child Language, 9*, 75–86.

Goffman, I. (1956). The nature of deference and demeanor. *American Anthropologist, 58*, 473–502.

Goffman, I. (1974). *Frame analysis*. New York: Harper Colophon Books.

Gumperz, J. (1968). The speech community. *International Encyclopedia of the Social Sciences, 9*, 381–386.

Gumperz, J., & Hymes, D. (Eds.) (1972). *Directions in sociolinguistics: The ethnography of communication*. New York: Holt, Rinehart and Winston.

Hymes, D. (1972). On communicative competence. In J. B. Pride & J. Holmes (Eds.), *Sociolinguistics* (pp. 269–293). Harmondsworth, Middlesex, England: Penguin.

Turner, J. L. (1983). Workshop society: Ethnographic observations in a work setting for retarded adults. In K. T. Kernan, M. J. Begab, & R. B. Edgerton (Eds.), *Environments and behavior: The adaptation of mentally retarded persons* (pp. 147–171). Baltimore: University Park Press.

Weinstein, E. A., & Deutschberger, P. (1963). Some dimensions of altercasting. *Sociometry, XXVI,* 454–466.

The authors are affiliated with the Socio-Behavioral Group, Mental Retardation Research Center (Neuropsychiatric Institute), UCLA. This research was supported by NICHD Grant HD 11944–03, The Community Adaptation of Mildly Retarded Adults, and by NIE Grant NIE–G–80–0016, Communicative Competence of Mildly Retarded Persons.

Friendship, Coping Systems and Community Adjustment of Mildly Retarded Adults

Sandra Kaufman

Although follow-up studies typically conclude that mildly mentally retarded persons achieve satisfactory adjustments to community living (Cobb, 1972), Edgerton and Bercovici (1976) point out that the measuring criteria, without exception, have been variables important to the researchers. They suggest we attune more closely to the views of mentally retarded persons themselves, particularly when considering social adaptation. Employing focused interviews and participant-observation over a 3-year period, Edgerton and Bercovici found that the mentally retarded individuals in their sample gauged social adjustment by personal satisfaction, rather than by competence or independence, and that most found their social adjustment to be more satisfactory than it was 10 years before when they were originally contacted (Edgerton, 1967).

In spite of the increased attention being paid to social adjustment, there has ben curiously little interest in friendship patterns among mildly retarded adults and the relationship of these patterns to their social adjustment. Friendship has received some attention in the literature but has rarely been studied outside of closed settings. McAndrew and Edgerton (1966) described the close friendship of two institutionalized males and found complementarity and interdependence in their relationship. Other investigators have looked at friendship among clients in sheltered workshops and community residences (Berkson & Romer, 1980; Landesman-Dwyer, Berkson, & Romer, 1979; Romer & Berkson, 1980; Turner, 1983). Several investigators have commented on the search for friends and the meaning of friendship (Birenbaum & Seiffer, 1976; Craft & Craft, 1979; Henschel, 1972; Mattinson, 1970), but no investigator has looked specifically at the friendship situations of mildly mentally retarded individuals who maintain their own households. Given the continuing emphasis on normalization, attention to this aspect of community adjustment seems worthwhile; an individual may maintain a job, be a law-abiding citizen, and stay out of debt—and yet be wretched because he has no friends.

The goal of the present study is to examine ethnographic and interview data compiled over an 18-month period to characterize the nature and degree of friendship in the lives of adult mildly retarded persons living independently in the Los Angeles area. In addition, the study examined how friendship patterns interact with other aspects of the individual and of his or her friends to affect the degree of social satisfaction experienced by members of this population. Also of interest is a conclusion by Reiter and Levi (1980), based on interviews with parents of mentally retarded adults, that having nonretarded friends is a "pressing need" for retarded individuals living in the community.

While having nonretarded friends may be defined as indicating social integration, the question remains whether the retarded persons themselves feel it is important for their well-being.

In order to examine these issues, the study was organized around the dual dimensions of sociality and satisfaction. The results of an earlier pilot study indicated the importance of these dimensions in defining the social adjustment of mildly retarded persons; some individuals appeared to be active in a wide circle of friends and to be happy, yet others in similar circumstances were discontent. Conversely, some rather solitary persons seemed to be enjoying life, while others were lonely.

For this study, we measured sociality solely on the basis of activity with friends. Satisfaction with friends, although not completely isolable from satisfaction with quality of life, was a measure of the individual's response to these interactions or to the lack of them. Various demographic variables were examined as factors possibly affecting the interaction between satisfaction and sociality: age, sex, marital status, and number of years living independently.

The Sample

The sample was one of several formed by the Socio-Behavioral Group of the Mental Retardation Research Center, UCLA, to study mildly mentally retarded adults living in the community. Those individuals chosen for the sample had to be living independently, be labeled by the delivery system as mildly mentally retarded and/or be eligible to receive funding from the network of Regional Centers for the Developmentally Disabled in the Los Angeles area, and be free from overt signs of psychosis, severe physical disabilities, or speech pathology.

TABLE 1

DEMOGRAPHICS CHARACTERISTICS OF THE SAMPLE (N = 42)[a]

Sex		Marital Status	
Male	22	Married	23
Female	20	Unmarried	17
		Widowed	1
		Consensual union	1
Age When First Contacted		Years Living Independently	
21–35	29	When First Contacted	
36–50+	13	Less than 4	24
		4–9	6
		More than 9	13

[a]Three members of the original sample (N = 46) were dropped from the friendship study because of insufficient data: One changed residence and could not be located, another moved out of the city, and the third lost interest in being contacted by the fieldworker. An additional member of the original sample was not included due to a history of psychiatric involvement.

Although the sample (N = 42) was almost equally divided by sex and marital status, most persons were under 35 years of age and had been living independently less than 4 years. All are Caucasian except for 2 individuals who, it was subsequently discovered, are primary English speakers of Mexican descent, and all but 4 persons come from middle-class homes.

Sex was predicted to have little effect on the relationship between sociality and satisfaction, in as much as Romer and Berkson (1980) found it to be a weak predictor of sociability, but marital status seemed likely to affect it; studies have reported that unmarried individuals in the larger population seem to experience loneliness more frequently than the married (Weiss, 1975). Age and the number of years spent living independently also were predicted to affect the relationship between the two dimensions. Romer and Berkson (1980) reported older mentally retarded individuals to have fewer relationships, which were just as "intense" as those of younger persons, and Weiss (1975) suggested that when social isolation has occurred over a long period of time, individuals may shrink their standards for appraising their situation and lead satisfactory lives despite the rejection they experience.

Data Collection

Four sources of information were utilized: (a) field notes accumulated by fieldworkers who engaged in naturalistic observation, (b) self-reports, (c) parent interview transcripts, and (d) summary statements made by the fieldworker on the nature and quality of each participant's relationships with peers.

Field Notes

For a period of 18 months, each of the 42 participants was visited by the same-age fieldworker assigned to him, and together they shared mundane events like home-cooked meals, bowling sessions, and trips to the doctor. Occasionally crises arose, and these were shared as well. Everything that happened during their time together was documented in the field notes which provide rich accounts of the daily activities and concerns of the participants.

The field notes are sources of information about whom the participant interacted with as well as the social dynamics of each relationship. They also proved valuable in assessing how each participant felt about his social life. Such responses might have been elicited by a formal interview, but because social desirability has been found to threaten the validity of answers on self-concept scales administered to mentally retarded persons (Zetlin, Turner, & Gallimore, 1982), a similar result might be expected with a topic as sensitive as loneliness. Instead, the notes of the fieldworker capture unguarded moments when the sample member revealed his feelings about his friends or the lack of them.

Self-Reports

An open-ended interview intended to elicit information about social support networks was administered to the participants by the fieldworkers at the end of 18 months, when rapport had been established. Included was a section containing questions about friends. The transcribed answers provide information about who the sample participant's friends were, how often interaction took place, the age of the friends, how long the relationship had existed, what they generally did together, and frequency of phone contact. The self-reports are revealing in that they document a sometimes surprising perspective on the sample members' perceptions of their friends.

Parent Interviews

Whenever possible, taped interviews were conducted with the parents of the sample members (n = 28). In some cases, parents were not available and other family members (n = 8) or a caretaker (n = 1) agreed to be interviewed. No interviews were undertaken concerning the other 5 individuals. Nevertheless, information was available on 3 of the 5 because they were in a sample studied from 1975 to 1978.[1]

The parent interviews, usually taking from 5 to 6 hours to complete in 2 or 3 sessions, were designed to cover a number of topics of interest to researchers in the Socio-Behavioral Group. The information solicited in these sessions ranged widely, but it included the son's or daughter's social history, his or her current friends, and whether the sample member seemed content with them. Background information was sometimes provided on friends reported in field notes and self-reports. In the rare cases when a parent's comments contradicted information in the other two sources of data, the fieldworker made further inquiries, but where there was still a discrepancy, the field notes and self-reports were given primacy.

Fieldworker Summaries

At the end of the 18-month period, the fieldworkers composed short summaries on a number of topics related to the psychological well-being of each of the sample members that they observed (Zetlin & Turner, this volume). Topics included perception of handicap, self-concept, and relationship with parents. Summaries were also requested on friendship, and, in these, the fieldworkers commented on the quality and nature of each participant's social life.

Data Analysis

All of the information derived from the four sources of data was condensed into a three- to four-page biography of each sample member. Each contains biographic and demographic information, as well as brief summaries of the individual's social history, current relationship with family members, personality, adaptive behavior, extent of involvement with the delivery system, and recreational outlets. In addition, there is also material on sociality and satisfaction. A description is provided of the person's current friends and spouse, if there is one, and the nuances of each relationship—where they met, their activities together, how frequently they see each other, the attitudes of the

[1]That research was supported by NICHD Grant HD 09474–02, the Community Context of Normalization, and by NICHD Grant HD 04612.

sample member toward the friend/spouse, and so forth. Each of the completed summaries was read by the fieldworker assigned to the sample member, and any discrepancies or errors were appended at the end of the summary.

These summaries were used to rank the sample members on the dimensions of sociality and satisfaction. Whereas the individuals who fell at the extremes of each dimension were easily identified, problems arose in ranking the others, for interactions varied widely in quantity and quality. Sorting out this diversity was initially a task of making distinctions between "friends" and "acquaintances." As a result, the following decisions were made. (a) Casual contacts such as chats with strangers in shopping malls or on the street were not considered friendships, nor were ritual courtesy greetings exchanged with neighbors. A friendship, therefore, required continuing contact. (b) Friendship also meant that the friendly encounters be in person; people known only over the phone or by letter whom the participant rarely or never saw were not considered friends. (c) Fieldworkers, although named by four sample members, were not counted as friends, although other delivery system personnel were when named by the participants. (d) Individuals seen only in a work setting were included as friends if they were described as such in the self-reports. (e) If a relationship had ended by the time of the self-reports and the sample member did not list it as a friendship, it was counted anyway if the interaction had lasted more than 6 months or if it had existed less than that time but was intense. (f) Occasionally conflicts arose between a participant's account and the views of the fieldworker. For example, one woman stated that she had only three friends, yet the fieldworker knew that nearly every weekend she socialized at bars and brought people back to her apartment to "party." Conversely, another sample member talked constantly of three women who competed for his attention, but other evidence had convinced the fieldworker that the man was fantasizing. In cases like these, the fieldworker's assessments were accepted as more credible.

After these guidelines had been completed, the next task was the development of criteria for ranking each individual on the first dimension, sociality. An analysis of the data indicated that the criteria most relevant for members of this sample were the number of friends, the frequency of interaction with them, and the degree of the participant's involvement in specific settings. Of these, the number of friends seemed most capable of explaining the variation. The next most important was the frequency of interaction. It was gauged directly and indirectly. In many cases, the biographical summaries stated how often friends saw each other. When this information was not available, indirect estimates were made in one of two ways. One was the degree of reciprocity in a friendship; non-reciprocal friends tended to see each other less frequently on a social basis than reciprocal friends. A reciprocal friendship was based on mutuality, with the participants regarding each other as equals, but a non-reciprocal or "receptive" friendship was based on superior and inferior positions with one partner primarily receiving from the other (Reisman, 1979). Many of the friendships the retarded individuals had with nonretarded persons were one-sided in this manner, and, as a consequence, social interaction tended to be less frequent. If any doubt existed whether a relationship was reciprocal or not, it was designated as non-reciprocal. Marital status was the other index of interaction frequency, for it was assumed that couples saw each other frequently.

Among the sample members, even a boyfriend/girlfriend relationship appeared to indicate frequency of get-togethers. To ensure that it did for purposes of ranking on sociality, a decision was made that partners were not considered to be romantically involved unless they were seeing each other at least once a month. This last rule was arbitrary; it affected only one woman who expressed romantic interest in a male friend seen every 4 weeks.

The final measures of sociality dealt with settings. Although an individual who attended a sheltered workshop or who became involved in a church or synagogue could be considered more social than a person who did neither, someone whose interactions with friends were confined to these settings was deemed less social than another individual who interacted with friends outside of those settings.

The next task was to rank the sample members on satisfaction, a dimension defined in relative terms because sample members knew rejection by the larger community, and some were experiencing it from their families as well. This finding was not surprising; we might expect to find social isolation among those who are socially stigmatized because of handicaps (Weiss, 1975). Satisfaction had to include the full range from overt pleasure to acceptance of, even resignation to, one's situation. Ranking on this dimension was made simpler when relationships with friends were examined separately from those with spouses. Dissatisfaction was said to be present when the sample member was experiencing one or more of the following conditions: being unhappy with one's associates, liking someone and receiving inadequate reciprocation, not seeing or interacting with someone as often as one would like, or not having enough friends. Marital dissatisfaction, on the other hand, meant simply that the spouse was displeased by his/her partner.

TABLE 2
OUTCOME OF RANK ORDERING ON SATISFACTION

High Satisfaction	Happily married and satisfying friends (n = 6)
	Unmarried and satisfying friends (n = 9)
	Happily married and unsatisfying friends (n = 5)
	Unhappily married and satisfying friends (n = 6)
	Unhappily married and unsatisfying friends (n = 6)
Low Satisfaction	Unmarried and unsatisfying friends (n = 10)

With the ranking on both dimensions completed, a decision was made to divide the sample members into four groups based on high/low sociality and high/low satisfaction. Collapsing into groups has proven useful in qualitative work (Turner, 1983; Zetlin, Turner, & Gallimore, 1982); even though a loss of statistical power occurs, it is counterbalanced by the gain in clarity of exposition.

The first step in forming the groups was to designate the first 21 persons as high in sociality and the second 21 as low. As a reliability check, a rater with no prior knowledge of the sample members completed independent rankings. The general purposes of the research were briefly explained to the rater (a Doctor of Business Administration). He was then instructed to read the biographical summaries, the guidelines for distinguishing between friends and acquaintances, and the criteria for ranking. He was advised that the task required, most of all, a global assessment. Then, without knowledge of the first rank ordering, he was asked to place each of the participants in one of two groups, high social or low social; 75% of his ratings concorded with those in the first ranking. The concordance would have been higher had I remembered to state in the guidelines another rule I was using without being aware of it, that of categorizing as "high social" those individuals who seem to be loners by inclination yet who are living with gregarious spouses or roommates. The second rater labeled them as "low social" (n = 3). Also, only 41 of the sample members were rated on sociality because the rater accidentally overlooked one.

TABLE 3
OUTCOME OF RANK ORDERING ON SOCIALITY

High Social	Married plus a number of reciprocal friends (n = 6)
	Unmarried plus a number of reciprocal friends and a romantic involvement (n = 7)
	Married plus 4 reciprocal friends (n = 4)
	Married plus 3 reciprocal friends (n = 2)
	Unmarried plus 4 or more reciprocal friends and no romantic involvement (n = 2)
	Married plus 2 reciprocal friends (n = 3)
	Married plus 1 reciprocal friend (n = 1)
	Married plus 1 non-reciprocal friend and involvement in church (n = 1)
	Unmarried plus 3 reciprocal friends and a romantic involvement (n = 1)
	Unmarried plus 2 reciprocal friends and no romantic involvement (n = 1)
	Unmarried plus 1 reciprocal friend and no romantic involvement (n = 3)
	Married plus 2 non-reciprocal friends (n = 3)
	Married plus 3 non-reciprocal friends seen only in work setting (n = 1)
	Unmarried plus reciprocal friends seen only in work setting and no romantic involvement (n = 1)
	Married plus 1 reciprocal friend in work setting only (n = 2)
	Married and no friends (n = 1)
Low Social	Unmarried plus 4 non-reciprocal friends and no romantic involvement (n = 1)

The second rater was similarly asked to categorize each of the sample members as either high or low in satisfaction, following the procedure described for independent ranking of sociability. At the conclusion of his ratings, 73% of his designations were in accordance with those in the first rating. It should be noted, however, that he completed the ratings for only 19 of the 42 individuals.

Working only with the first ratings, I placed the individuals who fell in the high category on both dimensions in a group labeled "high social/high satisfaction." The remaining persons in the high social group had already been designated as low satisfaction, and they formed the "high social/low satisfaction" group. In a similar fashion, the persons who were in the low social category were placed in "low social/high satisfaction" and "low social/low satisfaction" groups. Using this process, four groups based on the two dimensions were formed.

Results

The results of the data analysis are presented in two sections, quantitative and qualitative. In the first section, the statistical findings are briefly described (see Table 4). In the second section, composite portraits in which the statistical

TABLE 4

RELATIONSHIPS BETWEEN CHARACTERISTICS

OF THE SAMPLE AND SATISFACTION

Group	(High Social) Social Bees	(Low Social) Recluses	(High Social) Rebels	(Low Social) Victims
n	13	10	7	12
X Age***	35.84	39.7	28.71	33.42
X Years living independently**	9.42	10.65	3.57	4.08
Sex Male	(6) 46%	(5) 50%	(4) 57%	(7) 58%
Female	(7) 54	(5) 50	(3) 53	(5) 42
Married	(7) 54	(8) 80	(4) 57	(5) 42
Low/No emotional dependence on parents/caretakers*	(8) 62	(8) 80	(1) 14	(7) 58
Employed competitively or attending workshop**	(9) 70	(7) 70	(1) 14	(8) 67
Types of friendships with retarded	(11) 84	(8) 80	(7) 100	(8) 67
with non-reciprocal normal***	(2) 15	(6) 60	(1) 14	(7) 58
with reciprocal normal****	(10) 77	(5) 50	(3) 43	(1) 8
with normal non-reciprocal and reciprocal	(11) 84	(7) 70	(4) 57	(7) 58

Note: Numbers in parentheses are frequencies

*$p<.10$

**$p<.05$

***$p<.02$

****$p<.01$

material reappears are drawn for each of the four groups, and representative individuals are described.

Quantitative Analysis

The four groups were found to be virtually identical in terms of sex and marital status: Approximately equal numbers of males and females were distributed in each group, and a Fisher Test established that any between-group differences in the number of married and unmarried individuals were not significant.

Age proved to be associated with high satisfaction (Mann Whitney approximation of the $z = 1.97$, $p < .025$). As age correlated highly with the number of years living independently (Spearman rho (40) = .634, $t = 5.85$, $p < .001$), it was not surprising that the number of years living independently was also associated with high satisfaction (Mann Whiney approximation of the $z = 2.20$, $p < .05$). Thus, significantly more older persons with greater experience living in the community were found in the two high satisfaction groups than in the two low satisfaction groups. In other words, older people who had been living independently longer tended to be more satisfied than younger individuals just starting out, regardless of sociality. These results tend to support Edgerton and Bercovici's (1976) finding that the passage of time most mentally retarded individuals are more satisfied with their social adjustment.

Two other variables, employment and emotional dependence on parents/caretakers (caretakers were family members in all but two cases), also distinguished among the sociality/satisfaction groups. These variables suggested themselves after I had examined each group for the types of individuals it contained. By emotional dependence was meant an apparent need to be in frequent communication with parents/caretakers, not so much for instrumental help as for emotional support; this was gauged by the frequency of phone calls initiated by the participant as well as the number of in-person interactions. (No distinction was made at this point in the analysis between congenial versus conflict-ridden relationships.) The high social/low satisfaction group contained a markedly lower percentage of persons who were employed (14%) compared to an average of nearly 70% employed for each of the remaining three groups (Fisher Test, $p < .05$). An interaction appeared to be in effect among sociality, satisfaction, and emotional dependence on parents/caretakers, although it only approached significant levels (Fisher Exact Probability < .087). The complicated relationship is best seen by examining the low social/high satisfaction group and its opposite, the high social/low satisfaction group, both of which exhibit extremes; the former being low in dependence (20% dependent) and the latter being high (86% dependent).

In summary, although sex and marital status did not differentiate among the four groups, age and years living independently did, with the oldest, most experienced individuals tending to cluster in the two high satisfaction groups. In addition, the persons in the high sociality/low satisfaction group were found to exhibit a low rate of employment and a high rate of emotional dependence on parents/caretakers, while the individuals in the opposite, low sociality/high satisfaction group, were discovered not to be emotionally dependent on parents/caretakers.

Tests for association of friend types with any group or groups were also performed. The initial distinction between reciprocal and non-reciprocal friends was expanded to include three types: retarded, reciprocal normal, and non-reciprocal normal. (The term "normal" is used to refer to any person who appears to be of normal intelligence. It is used because it is less awkward than "non-retarded.") The three types of friends differ in a number of ways:

(1) *Retarded friends.* Retarded friends were encountered in social clubs for the developmentally disabled, group therapy sessions, college classes for the handicapped, sheltered workshops, and board and care homes where the sample member had lived previously or where he knew a resident and through him or her met other residents. Friends also came from previously attended high school special education classes, or they were met through friends. In all of these relationships, the partners acted as peers.

(2) *Reciprocal normal friends.* Normal persons who were reciprocal friends similarly interacted with the sample member on a peer basis, but initial contact usually came about under quite different circumstances. To be sure, a few were met within the delivery system. Mentally ill and learning disabled individuals who failed to measure as psychometrically retarded were occasionally permitted to participate in social clubs or independent living programs. However, the overwhelming majority of reciprocal normal companions were encountered casually in places like bars or parks or the local donut shop. Casual arrangements with neighbors, particularly elderly ones, also sometimes turned into reciprocal friendships, and, as with any type of friend, a few normal people who became reciprocal friends were introduced through other friends.

In two cases, idiosyncratic interests provided an opportunity for reciprocal friendships with normal people. A man in the high social/high satisfaction group was absorbed by trains, and he joined other aficionados on jaunts to train junctions and yards. Through his interest, he was able not only to find a social niche in the nonretarded world, he also found part time employment in a model train shop where he was consulted for his knowledge and expertise. Another man, in the low satisfaction/low social group, had a hobby that reflected his poor social adjustment. Barricading himself behind elaborate phone gear, he sat in his apartment manipulating his equipment and talking with other "phone freaks," as he termed them. The phone freaks proved not to be very satisfying, but he found the interactions better than being alone day after day. He was too fearful of rejection to risk meeting these people in person, but after years of therapy, he has finally begun to venture out.

(3) *Non-reciprocal normal friends.* Non-reciprocal normal friends are distinguished from both retarded and reciprocal normal friends by the inequality in the relationship. The sample member was usually very aware that he must not "bother" these people too much or he would lose them as friends. Non-reciprocal normal friends were friends of the family, neighbors, fellow employees or supervisors at competitive places of work, members or staff personnel of a church or synagogue attended by the participant, and professionals in the delivery system, particularly counselors.

Each of these types of friends was examined for its possible relationship with any of the four groups (see Table 4). Individuals who had one or more mentally retarded friends were distributed randomly, but possession of one or more non-reciprocal normal friends was found to be significantly associated with low sociality (χ^2 for two independent samples, $p = 6.25 < .02$, $df = 1$) and that of one or more reciprocal normal friends with high satisfaction (χ^2 for two independent samples, $p = 6.37 < .01$, $df = 1$). The finding that satisfaction seems to go with having reciprocal normal friends gives weight to Reiter and Levi's (1980) assertion that mentally retarded people in the community have a compelling need for normal friends. Nevertheless, the two investigators failed to distinguish between reciprocal and non-reciprocal normal friendships. When the two were combined, equal numbers were found in each of the four groups (Fisher Exact Probability = .135). It appears, therefore, that the present data supports Reiter and Levi's claim only as far as reciprocal normal friends are concerned.

Qualitative Analysis

Each of the four groups will be considered separately. A composite portrait is drawn which includes a review of the quantitative findings relevant to each group, and representative individuals are described. Discussion of the two high satisfaction groups is organized around the types of adaptations individuals have fashioned in coping with the problem of finding and maintaining friendships, whereas consideration of the low satisfaction groups centers around the factors that seem to hinder the process of making and keeping friends.

The Social Bees (High Social/High Satisfaction) N = 13. Statistically, the Social Bees have more reciprocal friends, are older, and have been living independently longer than the individuals in the low satisfaction groups. Nevertheless, 5 of the 13 had been out of the family home less than 3 years when first contacted. Also, most of the Social Bees, bolstered by a strong work ethic, work competitively. In general, they are assertive, outgoing, sociable people. Nonetheless, they exhibit a variety of social adaptations: the "conformers," the "passive socializers," the "self-appointed father figures," and the "non-conformers."

The "conformers" are a number of women who follow conventional norms in their social arrangements. Each has a circle of either mentally retarded friends or normal friends met within handicapped networks with whom they enjoy socially approved pastimes—going to the movies, eating out, bowling, window shopping in the malls, and the like. All are either married or have boyfriends whom they plan to marry one day, and all are neat in their appearance and generally keep tidy apartments. All but one have been independent for less than 2 years, and all interact frequently with parents or siblings. It appears that these women have accepted, at least for the time being, the middle-class values of their families.

"Passive socializers," on the other hand, are more retiring persons who lead active social lives because they have attached themselves to gregarious spouses or roommates. Bud Zigler, a taciturn man, 46 years of age, has been married to Penny for 22 years. Until a year ago, the Ziglers lived an uneventful existence with Bud working all day, Penny volunteering at a child care center part time, and both extensively volunteering at their synagogue. As they were not included in social activities outside the temple, the couple was lonely. Bud was fairly content to arrive home, shower, eat supper in silence, and settle down with the TV for the evening, but Penny decided she had had enough. In the past year, with the encouragement of a counselor, she deliberately set out to do something about it. Meeting with success, their apartment has begun to buzz with the conversation and laughter of a small group of retarded friends. Bud feels a bit of an outsider on these occasions, and he performs his duties as host rather perfunctorily, but on the whole he seems to prefer having people around chatting with Penny than returning to the lonely existence they knew before.

Very much the opposite of the passive socializers are two married men, both "self-appointed father figures," who each rule over a cohort of friends by force of their aggressive personalities and their prestige as owners of audio-visual equipment. Their homes are magnets to admiring associates. For example, Barry Carter, 30, amid an array of tape recorders, stereo components, television sets, and even a phone with programmed numbers, takes charge of any and all under "his" roof. His wife and their housemate chafe under Barry's frequently demeaning remarks and pontifications, but association with Barry has its rewards because so many peers—particularly residents of the nearby board and care home where Barry used to live—drop by to socialize. Barry has tested his limits with his father and mother; he and his companions enjoyed outings at a local pornography theater, until his parents found out and declared the night club off-limits. Life with Barry can be eventful, interesting, and entertaining.

Two other Social Bees care little about parental restrictions or the norms of the larger society. Having had little contact with family members for years, each of these "non-conformers," one male and one female, has slipped into a casual way of life within run-down sections of Los Angeles where they interact only with normal people. Fred, for instance, is a gentle man who covers his softness with a blustering, irreverent facade. He thoroughly delights in shocking the sensibilities of conventional folk in public places by detailing in stentorian tones his latest sexual activities with his girlfriend/prostitute, June. She comes to visit him two to three times a week in his hotel room which is so crammed with junk that it is difficult to turn around, let alone get to the bed. Even though Fred pays June $5 each time she comes, June is genuinely fond of him and has been faithfully arriving at his room for 5 or 6 years. The indignity of increasing impotence weighs heavily on Fred, however, and he occasionally faults June. "I'm just ready to come and here she is, talk, talk, talk, talk . . . takes my mind off what I'm thinkin' about. I pulled the sonofabitch out and says 'forget it. You got the five bucks . . . go.' I just smoke my goddamn cigar say 'hell with you, sombitch,'" cackles Fred.

Because he lives in the skid-row section of the central city, Fred has become extremely "street-wise"; he knows exactly who and what situations to avoid. Even so, his room has been burglarized frequently, and he has been robbed while working in a liquor store and laundromat. A friend who has moved to a safer neighborhood has urged Fred to join him, but Fred fears his friends would not be able to visit him there. These friends have been picked carefully, and Fred is devoted to them. He quietly brings groceries to elderly shut-ins, lends companions money at the end of the month while scolding them for getting drunk because it leaves them so vulnerable on the street, and worries about same-age peers who are unable to find employment because they are over 50.

The Recluses (Low Sociality/High Satisfaction) N = 10. Statistically, the Recluses share some characteristics with the Social Bees. Both are generally older and have been living independently longer than their high satisfaction counterparts. Also, like the Social Bees, the Recluses are employed, although they are more likely to be clients of workshops. Other characteristics emerged during the statistical analysis. The Recluses are the least emotionally dependent on parents/caretakers; in some measure, this quality is due to being older and parents being deceased. Also, as one of the two low social groups, they tend to have more non-reciprocal normal friends than the high social people. Looked at more holistically, the Recluses are fairly solitary people who seem to have found contentment with one or two associates, one of whom may well be a spouse. Most lead routine lives in which faithful attendance at their place of employment assumes high priority. Weiss (1975) points out that having an in-flexible routine is a good way to ward off loneliness, and Turner (1983) notes that workshops provide social opportunities for people who otherwise have to fill long, uneventful days.

The married couples could be referred to as "cocooners" (Mattinson, 1970) in the sense that spouses fill most of the need for companionship. This is true of Jeff, 39, and Rhoda, 45, who had been married for 3 years when first contacted. Their socializing is limited to one or two mentally retarded friends seen irregularly and selected staff members at UCLA visited once a week.

Although neither Jeff nor Rhoda is working at present, they apparently find many activities to occupy their time. Their apartment is cluttered with ac-quisitions related to their interests. Jeff tends the hamsters, fish, and birds which reside in tanks and cages sprawled on the dining table. He also enjoys jokes and riddles out of books and completing paint-by-number pictures while Rhoda sits nearby knitting or finishing needlework items from kits. These cre-ations are often given to their friends at UCLA, some of whom they have known for over 10 years. Every Tuesday they pile into a city bus with paper-bags full of "things," including sandwiches and, perhaps, handmade gifts, and they travel to UCLA where they make their social rounds for the week. After dropping by the research office to say hello to their fieldworker and other staff members they have come to know, they saunter over to visit Rhoda's former occupational therapist. While there, Rhoda also solicits help with her knitting from the therapist's secretary. That done, a visit to a doctor at the medical center might be in order; Rhoda usually has an ailment that needs looking after. Gifts may be presented to any of these individuals, and Rhoda and Jeff bask in the warm thanks they receive for their thoughtfulness. The day is capped by attending a group therapy session for retarded couples, where they sit holding hands, and after the session, they board the bus for home.

"Loners" are unmarried individuals who seem to prefer being alone. Shirley Feldman, 58, was wed at 18 to a normal man and spent the last 11 years of her 22-year marriage caring for her invalid husband and her paralyzed mother. When they passed away, she did not attend the funerals. Today she lives in one section of the family home with tenants. Prior to being enrolled in a sheltered workshop by her sister/caretaker, she had had no contact with men-tally retarded people, and at first she did not like them. However, she had been so lonely and had found talking with normal neighbors and family friends so difficult that she soon welcomed going to the workshop. Shirley's adjustment was helped by her move into a position slightly above that of the other workers as a liaison between staff and clients. Over time, she has become an informal peer counselor whom the other employees consult at lunch hour about their personal and work problems. Shirley is well-liked by peers and staff and she, in turn, enjoys going to work so much that she always arrives an hour early and has perfect attendance. Three of the older women clients have become her particular friends, but she does not see them outside the workshop. She says she likes her routine and does not want it disturbed; she goes to work, comes home, cleans her room, makes the next day's lunch, watches TV, and goes to bed. "My life is in this house here, and I mind my own business and don't let anyone bother me," she states emphatically.

The Rebels (High Social/Low Satisfaction) N = 7. Of all the groups, the Rebels are the youngest, the least experienced in independent living, and the most emotionally dependent on their parents. They seem to be very insecure about themselves and exhibit it in a dependency/resentment syndrome in which they turn constantly to their parents for emotional as well as instrumental support, while simultaneously complaining about their parents' restrictions. With one exception, none is employed, and all lack motivation to seek work. Although they interact with a number of people, they have difficulty keeping friends. Either the persons they know do not measure up to what they are looking for, or their associates tire of their erratic behavior, complaints, or ill-considered plans; sometimes both occur simultaneously. The problem of measuring up to expectations particularly aggravates the marriages in this group. It has contributed heavily to two divorces being filed (and then withdrawn) and one wife suffering a nervous breakdown. Blame displacement is also characteristic of the Rebels, as will be typified in the following example.

Without informing his parents, Donald Sanders, 26, married a nonretarded but psychotic woman named Janice one afternoon while two friends, a married couple, acted as witnesses. Marital problems began immediately, and through them all, Donald maintained that his wife was at fault, not he. His expectations were clearly stated: "I got married because I wanted a wife to come home to and who would cook for me and clean house so I don't have to do nothing, 'cause I did that for quite a few years." Janice, however, had her own needs which she felt were not being met. The resulting fights were so intense that the young people were evicted from their first apartment. The married couple who had acted as witnesses at the wedding took Janice in and even allowed Donald to stay for a few days, but the scenes were so explosive that the newlyweds were not only told to leave, they were denied permission to phone.

Donald filed for divorce and entered an independent living training facility. Janice was admitted to a psychiatric hospital. Donald's new roommate, Richard, delighted Donald, and he entertained hopes of living with Richard when they graduated. However, Richard soon tired of Donald's selfishness and perpetual state of agitation. The final scene occurred when Donald suddenly decided to reconcile with Janice. Retrieving her from the hospital one afternoon, he brought her back to the apartment, which was against the program rules, and Richard was caught up in the resulting fracas as Donald tried to outwit and outshout the staff. Program administrators were not to be deterred, however, and Donald and Janice were out on the street again. Throughout all of these events, Donald repeatedly begged his parents to help him, yet whenever they entered the picture, he screamed that they were preventing him from being independent. Now homeless, he could not take Janice to his parent's house because his father and mother were exhausted by his crises, and he could no longer turn to his longtime friend, David, because David's parents, distressed by Donald's and Janice's behavior, had forbidden their son to see Donald. In sum, during the present study, Donald's social adjustment deterioriated. He wore out his welcome with both his own parents and his roommate, incurred the displeasure of David's gate-keeping parents, and his marriage was in total disarray.

   The Victims (Low Social/Low Satisfaction) N = 12. The appellation of Victim seems appropriate for this group because its members seem the most hapless of the sample. Discussion could become mired in the controversy over the victim's role in his own predicament, but that issue is not germane. My purpose is merely to describe what is seen at this point in the lives of these people, whatever the etiology of their situations. The victims appear to be acted upon rather than having control over events, yet it is questionable whether they see themselves in this light, for, unlike the complaining, perpetually miserable Rebels, they use denial as an active part of their coping repertoire. Statistically, they are younger with fewer years living independently than individuals in the high satisfaction groups, and, like the Recluses, more of them have non-reciprocal normal friends than do the members of the high social groups.

   Unlike the Rebels, some of the younger Victims have warm, close relationships with their parents, but the parents' very benevolence seems to stifle incentive to develop an independent social life. Mark Foster, 26, is quite content to be taken care of by his parents, who are fully prepared to do so; they have even groomed Mark's sister to take over when they are unable to continue. Mark calls his parents a minimum of twice a day, spends every weekend with them, and would not mind moving home again. He is lonely, yet denies it by constantly fabricating stories about women who fight over his attentions and by self-aggrandizement, mainly tales of how he always trounces Charlie, a friend he sees occasionally to play basketball. Although Mark very much wants more friends, he finds it easier to call or go home than to seek out and sustain relationships with peers.

   Other Victims have become trapped in stressful marriages. One couple's marriage has been traumatized by the arrival of children.[2] When Rich Williams, 40, proposed to 34-year-old Marilyn 6 years ago, she jumped at the chance, sensing that it might be her last opportunity to have a husband and children. Rich, too, wanted children. He envied his sisters with their youngsters, and his father says Rich, who has suffered a great deal of rejection in his life, always told him he wanted to have children so he could have someone to play with.

   The arrival of three little girls in 3 years (Rich was prevailed upon to get a vasectomy after the last child was born) at first boosted their self-esteem, for as parents they could take their places in Mormon church activities. However, the daily demands of living with active youngsters has put a severe strain on the parents, even though they live with Rich's mother who provides a great deal of support. Lacking even rudimentary parenting skills, the couple copes

---

[2]Recent research on a sample of 10 Black and 3 White retarded parental units indicates that some function quite well, at least when the children are pre-schoolers. The critical ingredients seem to be acceptance and support by the extended family and the presence of only one infant at a time (Zetlin, Weisner, & Gallimore, 1982).

ineffectively. Marilyn alternates between ignoring the children's cries and exploding, and Rich, wanting them to do as he says and finding they have their own agendas, is driven to such distraction that he responds by striking them and/or leaving the house. As the problems mount, the marriage is deteriorating.

The older members of the low social/low satisfaction group have been victimized by rejecting families and an indifferent society. Roy Carver, 60, was relinquished for adoption as an infant because his parents had no money to take care of a sickly baby born with a crippled leg. Little is known about his past other than that he was institutionalized by his brother at age 22, an act that still makes Roy angry. Released when he was 37, he lived in a series of board and care homes until he began living independently 11 years ago. His life is monotonous. Emerging from his dingy apartment each weekday, he takes a bus to the sheltered workshop where he has worked for over 20 years. His sister says he is very conscientious about his attendance: "He has walked many miles with that leg just to get to work when the buses didn't go." Returning home each evening, he dines in the same restaurant, watches the same TV programs, and routinely calls his sister who lives in a nearby town. Once every few months he takes a bus to visit her, but each weekend he takes a trip with Samuel, his same-age friend who lives close by. Their favorite destination is Knotts Berry Farm, but some weekends they bus to the zoo or a Dodger game or the beach. Roy has no other friends. When he was asked how his life would be different if Samuel suddenly moved away, Roy was startled. "I won't have nobody . . . I'd be blank," he finally decided.

Roy appears to belong with the Recluses more than with the Victims, for he leads much the same kind of routine life, with an emphasis on workshop attendance, as Shirley Feldman. The difference is that Shirley has made it quite clear she wants to be left alone, while Roy states he wishes he had more friends. Roy never complains, however, and he never seems to feel sorry for himself.

Lastly, there are those individuals who are Victims of their own attitudes. Elizabeth McGregor, 29, is lonely because she rejects her mentally retarded peers. Peer rejection may, like the low self-esteem of the Rebels, be related to parental attitudes. The association is, however, unclear. Although Elizabeth feels abandoned by her family, and another peer rejector, the young man who hides behind the telephone equipment, has had a stormy relationship with his father who appears to have entertained unrealistic ambitions for his handicapped son, a third peer rejector, a woman, seems to have a pair of loving, supportive parents. Elizabeth initially gave the fieldworker the impression of being very busy and socially very active with non-handicapped people; she spoke constantly of her participation in college classes, in a young peoples' group as well as a Bible study group at her church, and in the choir. Over time, however, the fieldworker sensed a note of desperation in her chattering about how she was "improving" herself through these activities. During the summer when many of them ceased, time hung heavy. "Why doesn't someone come over here and do something with me," she asked, "or I gotta find myself something to do, but there really isn't anything to do." She maintained social contact by eating in a coffee shop where she was known and by "goofing off" in markets and stores. She said she frequents them because there "might be" something to look for "to see ahead of time if I'd like to buy it." While there, she asks questions of employees like which potato she should buy.

Part way through the study, Elizabeth moved into an independent living training program where she was thrown into daily contact with mentally retarded individuals, and her fieldworker was struck by how differently Elizabeth responded to the staff members versus her peers. At a Halloween party which Elizabeth gave, she directed her conversation almost entirely to her counselors and was courteous and deferential toward them. By contrast, she condescendingly referred to her peers as "kids" and ordered them about. Craving acceptance and not finding it, Elizabeth states, "I'm really normal inside and I don't know how to get that out."

Discussion

In the present study, the heterogeneity in social adaptation exhibited by a sample of independently living, mildly mentally retarded individuals was reduced to a four-group typology based on two dimensions, sociality and satisfaction.[3] It is important to remember that these are model types, useful heuristically. The individuals in each group are not completely homogeneous, and the types are not named or recognized by any of the actors. In addition, the category membership is frequently temporary. Even during the relatively short period of the study, some individuals changed from one mode of adaptation to another. The Ziglers, for example, started out as Victims, but after Penny established a social circle, she and Bud moved to the Social Bee category. The Williamses reversed the process; until the arrival of the second child, they were Social Bees because of Marilyn's many friends, but the presence of the three babies has catapulted them into the Victim group. Another Social Bee, Randall Goss, had a fairly lively and happy social life until a few months into the study when he suffered a series of reverses: friends moved away, he was evicted from his lodgings, and the minister of his church, whom he believed was a friend, humiliated him. As a result, Randall became a Victim. Even Elizabeth McGregory, one of the Victims, appears to be moving, although her destination is unclear at this time; recent contact reveals that she is engaged to be married. In sum, the friendship situations of these people are changeable. Edgerton comments that "social adjustment, particularly among mentally retarded persons, may sometimes fluctuate markedly, not only from year to year, but from month to month or even week to week" (Edgerton and Bercovici, 1976, p. 495).

Nevertheless, a few general conclusions may be made about factors which differentiate between dissatisfied and satisfied individuals. The principal one is the passage of time: The satisfied Social Bees and Recluses were found to be

---

[3]Turner (1983) recently developed a similar typology using a sheltered workshop population. Although he, too, looked at sociality, his other dimension is high/low work rather than satisfaction. There are other differences as well: his sample members are mostly moderately retarded, few live independently, and his observations are limited to a closed setting. Yet the portraits of his four groups are enough like mine to provide some validity to both.

significantly older and more experienced in living independently than the discontented Rebels and Victims. In addition, four other variables also were found to play a part in the attainment of social satisfaction. First, employment, whether competitive or workshop, provides structure to daily existence and tasks to fill otherwise endless days. Although competitive employment carries higher prestige, and for some individuals this factor outweighs all others, from the viewpoint of social opportunities, a workshop is more functional. Reciprocal friends and romantic partners are difficult to find in competitive places of employment, but a pool of both are readily available in a sheltered facility. Second, a willingness to consider other mentally retarded people as potential friends also seems to help. Social opportunities are narrowed when a young person refuses to attend workshops or social clubs for the developmentally disabled, or if he does attend them, feels uncomfortable about his associates. And third, whereas marriage can either facilitate or impede a satisfactory social adjustment, the arrival of the children, particularly more than one, hinders it. A final factor which contributes to satisfactory social adjustment is a healthy sense of self-esteem which, at least in part, is a result of the individual's relationship with his or her parents. Reisman (1979), citing research on the social relations of normal children, states that while it would be incorrect to say that parental attitudes alone determine the success children have in relating to others, they contribute heavily: Neglectful, rejecting, or anxious/neurotic parents tend to produce insecure children who have difficulty making friends. Recent research indicates that mentally retarded children may be subject to even greater risk. Zetlin and Turner (this volume) suggest that parents pass on to the mentally retarded child more of their attitudes concerning the child's handicap than has been realized, and the child's self-concept and subsequent social adjustment reflect these attitudes. The present study seems to indicate that troubled parent/offspring relationships and the child's resulting insecurity may extend into adulthood where they can continue to create problems. In general, the Social Bees and the Recluses had harmonious relationships with their parents. By contrast, the unhappy Rebels were generally in conflict with their parents, and most of the Victims either felt abandoned or their parents were deceased.

Clearly, social adjustment is not a construct which can be measured in either simple or uniform terms. It assumes a variety of shapes and forms and is conditioned by such factors as age, experience, relationship with one's family of origin, and occasionally by less pervasive factors such as employment status, attitude toward one's peers, and the presence or absence of offspring. Prescriptions for normalizing the lives of these adult mildly retarded individuals can only be made once the characteristic forms of adaptation which these people have made are better understood. Sociality and satisfaction, seen from the perspective of the mentally retarded adults themselves, would seem to be appropriate organizing concepts for describing and assessing these adaptations.

References

Berkson, G., & Romer, D. (1980). Social ecology of supervised communal facilities for mentally disabled adults. 1. Introduction. *American Journal of Mental Deficiency,* *85,* 219–228.

Birenbaum, A., & Seiffer, S. (1976). *Resettling retarded adults in a managed community.* New York: Praeger.

Cobb, H. (1972). *The forecast of fulfillment: A review of research on predictive assessment of the adult retarded for social and vocational adjustment.* New York: Teachers College Press.

Craft, A., & Craft, M. (1979). *Handicapped married couples: A Welsh study of couples handicapped from birth by mental, physical or personality disorder.* London: Routledge & Kegan Paul.

Edgerton, R. B. (1967). *The cloak of competence: Stigma in the lives of the mentally retarded.* Berkeley: University of California Press.

Edgerton, R. B., & Bercovici, S. (1976). The cloak of competence: Years later. *American Journal of Mental Deficiency, 80,* 485–497.

Henschel, A. M. (1972). *The forgotten ones: A sociological study of Anglo and Chicano retardates.* Austin: University of Texas Press.

Koegel, P. (1982). Rethinking support systems: A qualitative investigation into the nature of social support (Doctoral dissertation, University of California, Los Angeles). *Dissertation Abstracts International, 43,* 1214–A.

Landesman-Dwyer, S., Berkson, G., & Romer, D. (1979). Affiliation and friendship of mentally retarded residents in group homes. *American Journal of Mental Deficiency, 83,* 571–580.

Mattinson, J. (1970). *Marriage and mental handicap.* London: Gerald Duckworth and Company, Ltd.

MacAndrew, C., & Edgerton, R. (1966). On the possibility of friendship. *American Journal of Mental Deficiency, 70,* 25–30.

Reisman, J. M. (1979). *Anatomy of friendship.* Lexington: The Lewis Publishing Co., Inc.

Reiter, S., & Levi, A. M. (1980). Factors affecting social integration of noninstitutionalized mentally retarded adults. *American Journal of Mental Deficiency, 85,* 25–30.

Romer, D., & Berkson, G. (1980). Social ecology of supervised communal facilities for mentally disabled adults: 2. Predictors of affiliation. *American Journal of Mental Deficiency, 85,* 229–242.

Turner, J. (1983). Workshop society: Ethnographic observations in a work setting for retarded adults. In K. Kernan, M. Begab, & R. Edgerton (Eds.), *Environments and behavior: The adaptation of mentally retarded persons* (pp. 147–171). Baltimore: University Park Press.

Weiss, R. S. (1975). *Loneliness: The experience of emotional and social isolation.* Cambridge: The MIT Press.

Zetlin, A., Turner, J., & Gallimore, R. (1981). *The meaning of self-concept in a sheltered workshop.* Paper presented at the annual conference of the American Psychological Association, Los Angeles.

Zetlin, A., Weisner, R., & Gallimore, R. (1982). *Diversity, shared functioning, and the role of benefactors: A study of parenting by retarded parents.* Paper presented at the Society for Research in Child Development Study Group on Children of Handicapped Parents: Research and Perspective, Temple University, Philadelphia.

The author is affiliated with the Socio-Behavioral Group, Mental Retardation Research Center (Neuropsychiatric Institute), UCLA. This study was part of a larger investigation of the personal and social adjustment of retarded persons living in community settings (directed by J. Turner, A. Zetlin, & R. Gallimore). Funding for the collection of ethnographic materials in this study was provided by NICHD Grant HD 11944–03, The Community Adaptation of Mildly Retarded Persons. This chapter is a revision of my thesis completed for a Master's degree in Education, 1982. The original is on file in the College Library, UCLA. Special thanks is extended to my Committee members, Carollee Howes and Ron Gallimore, and to my Committee Chairman, Harold Levine. Grateful acknowledgement is also given to Jim Turner, Andrea Zetlin, and Lesley Winik. I am also deeply indebted to the fieldworkers: Marsha Bollinger, Tom Brauner, Melody Davidson, Pauline Hayashigawa, Linda Hubbard, Dave Tillipman, and Thom Ward. Paul Koegel generously shared the data from his study of social networks (Koegel, 1982) and provided helpful suggestions in the course of the research.

Self-Perspectives on Being Handicapped: Stigma and Adjustment

Andrea G. Zetlin and Jim L. Turner

The consequences of conferring the label "mentally retarded" on an individual has been a topic of much debate (Dexter, 1964; Edgerton & Sabagh, 1962; Farber, 1968). Although some scholars argue that recognition of one's inferior status cuts to the core of selfhood (Edgerton, 1967; Mercer, 1973; Wright, 1960), others find little evidence to support the idea that labeling one as mentally deficient has long-lasting and devastating effects (MacMillan, Jones, & Aloia, 1974). Regardless of one's position, however, the complexity of assessing the effects of being labeled mentally retarded on the "life career" of the individual is universally recognized (Guskin, 1978; Hobbs, 1975; MacMillan, 1977).

Goffman (1963) contends that the individual must first become personally aware of society's disdain for its members who possess a particular form of "differentness" (i.e., mental retardation) and then recognize that he or she is considered a member of the stigmatized group. The individual's reaction to being associated with a negatively perceived group is then dependent on a number of factors, including: the family's attitude, which directly affects how they transmit the message of their child's handicap to the child; the visibility and severity of the handicap; and the local community's response to the handicap.

Self-reports by individuals who have been labeled mentally retarded often indicate that they fell and fear the stigma associated with their socially inferior statuses (Bogdan & Taylor, 1976, 1982; Valpey, 1982). Jones (1972) interviewed 23 high school students assigned to special classes and found that they concealed information about their placement and coursework to avoid ridicule from regular class students. In addition, some claimed that labeling and/or placement had changed their friendships, made it more difficult to keep a girlfriend, or had a negative effect on opportunities for post-school placement. Similarly, follow-up studies of former special class students also revealed feelings of degradation associated with special class placement (Gonzali, 1972; Jones, 1972). Reports from formerly institutionalized persons indicate that "an admission of mental retardation was unacceptable—totally and without exception . . . They employed almost any other excuse, from epilepsy to 'craziness'—excuses that were themselves highly stigmatizing. Never was mental retardation admitted" (Edgerton, 1967, p. 207).

Guskin, Bartel, and MacMillan (1975) suggest that the humiliation these individuals feel is derived from their desire to be members of the larger "normal" group, juxtaposed with awareness of their assignment to a group with inferior status and the negative attributes imputed to them as members of that

93

group. Although it is acknowledged that they experience feelings of humiliation and are sensitive to the status designated them, the question remains: To what extent does the social stigma of the disability affect the individual's sense of self-worth?

Edgerton (1967) found that, in the early years following their release from the state hospital, the stigma of mental retardation dominated every aspect of the lives of the ex-patients he followed. All 48 individuals expended a great deal of effort denying their mental incompetence and employed the self-protective adaptive processes of denial and "passing" to invoke nonretarded personal identities. Turner and Gallimore (1979) studied a cohort of mildly retarded adults residing in the community and found that they too actively employed adaptive techniques to defend the integrity of their self-concepts. Moreover, there appeared to be some relationship between the nature of the coping strategies invoked and the individual's attitude toward his or her handicap. Turner and Gallimore identified four such strategies: the "acceptors," who accepted "being handicapped" but enhanced their self-esteem by characteristically stratifying other mentally retarded persons according to functioning capacity and comparing their own abilities and accomplishments to lower functioning individuals, and the "deniers," "avoiders," and "redefiners," who used various forms of strategic self-presentation to protect nonretarded self-conceptions. Deniers tended to view the world in conspiratorial terms, attributing their limitations or failures to the prejudicial attitudes of others, who never gave them a chance (i.e., blame attribution). Avoiders seemed content to assume they were passing as normal and saw the lack of challenge to that status as confirmation. Lastly, redefiners attributed their difficulties in life to other incapacities that they perceived as less stigmatizing than mental deficiency (e.g., nervousness, poor vision, speech problems), and they then used these to justify eliciting assistance from others (i.e., tactical dependency).

Some individuals seem to respond to being labeled mentally retarded by rejecting the characterization and producing self-esteem maintenance strategies to protect somewhat fragile, nonretarded definitions of self. Moreover, these self-presentation tactics, such as denial, passing, blame attribution, and tactical dependency, are often used by individuals with histories of degrading treatment by others. For example, Edgerton (1967) notes that by attributing their relative incompetence to the depriving experience of institutionalization, while at the same time insisting that their releases were confirmation of the original erroneous placements, ex-patients have an excuse available that sustains self-esteem in the face of constant challenges in the community.

There is some indication that the need to sustain these forms of strategic self-presentation decreases over time. Edgerton and Bercovici (1976) report that, after 12 years of living independently in the community, the ex-patients' concern with stigma and passing seemed to have faded to relative insignificance. In contrast, however, Turner and Gallimore (1979) found that for almost half their sample members deviance disavowal was a continuing concern, requiring some form of strategic self-presentation to get by as nonretarded. This was also true for mentally retarded adults working in a sheltered workshop (Turner, 1983). Almost half of the clients studied over a period of 6 years were highly sensitive to their mentally retarded statuses and saw the workshop setting as a haven from the pejorative label. Just how long-lasting the effects of labeling are, however, still remains unresolved.

American society has undergone many changes since Edgerton's (1967) study. New social policies have been implemented which appear to have had significant effects on the lives of mentally retarded persons. Most mildly retarded individuals are now reared in their family homes and the threat of institutionalization no longer hangs over them. Instead, needed services are procured through an extensive community care system whose use, however, places the retarded individual in a double bind. In order to be the recipient of services, such as on-going case management, occupational and vocational training, psychological counseling, or tutoring, one needs to identify himself or herself as handicapped; reluctance to admit to a handicapping condition may result in denial of needed support or failure to seek it. This report continues the study of stigma by examining how a sample of mildly retarded adults (most of whom have never been institutionalized) have adapted to being labeled mentally retarded given this new social climate. More specifically, we will focus on the attitudes of mildly retarded adults toward their social identities as handicapped persons and the relationship of those attitudes to other indices of personal and social adjustment.

Method

Subjects

Over an 18-month period, beginning in July 1980, 46 mildly mentally retarded adults living independently in the greater Los Angeles area were followed and intensely studied. These sample members ranged in age from 22 to 60 years (mean = 35.35; s.d. = 10.08). There were 25 males and 21 females; 44 were Anglo and 2 were of Mexican descent. All 46 sample members were specifically selected to be free from major behavioral or emotional problems; it was later learned, however, that 1 sample member did have a history of psychological disturbance.

Most sample members spent their childhood years living at home with family members; however, 7 spent some time in a state institution (one was admitted at age 12 and stayed for 18 years, and another spent as little as 10 months at age 9), 5 attended private special education residential schools for various periods of time, and 3 resided in foster care or board and care homes from very young ages. Although the socioeconomic status (SES) of the families of the sample members was not a controlled variable, the parents of all but 4 individuals were middle class; the remaining 4 sample members were from lower SES families.

During the period of observation, all individuals resided in their own apartments in the community, either alone, with roommates, or with spouses. Of these individuals, 22 had been involved in independent living training programs before venturing out on their own, and another 5 had lived in board and care facilities for a short period before their move to independence. At the time of contact, 27 sample members had been living independently for less than 4 years, 7 had been on their own between 4 and 9 years, and 12 had lived independently for 10 or more years. Twenty-three of the sample members were married; in all except one case, both members of these relationships had been identified as mentally retarded. Two of the couples had children—one couple had 1 child and the other had 3 children. Another sample member had been married for 21 years when widowed.

Twenty sample members were competitively employed either full or part time, 9 were clients at sheltered workshops, and 17 were unemployed. Of those unemployed, 2 were caring for their children, 1 was suffering from a terminal illness, some took classes at junior colleges, some performed volunteer work, others sought employment, and some were content to remain unemployed. Thirty-two of the sample members received supplemental security income (SSI), and 35 were California Regional Center clients currently receiving ongoing services.

Although IQ data were not available for all of the sample members, all were individuals who had been classified as mentally retarded at some point in their developments by a component of the service delivery system. All except 4 sample members had been placed in special education classes during their school years and remained there until they graduated or dropped out. Of the 4 who were not enrolled in special education, 1 attended regular classes in a Catholic school until 7th grade and then remained at home, 2—identical twins—spent one month in a special class until their parents discovered that much of the day was spent coloring and had them transferred back to the regular class, and the fourth had been expelled from a series of kindergartens at the age of 6 because of an uncontrollable seizure condition and was never re-enrolled.

In only 24% of the cases, however, did the schools encounter parents who failed to suspect any problems in their children's developments prior to contact with the school system. In 38% of the cases, parents were concerned with their children's developments during the early childhood years (i.e., slowness, excessive crying, hyperactivity) and sought medical advice. For some this had occurred as early as 6 months, for others at the toddler stage, and for others at 3 or 4 years when comparisons with peers made their children's "differentness" very apparent. For another 13% of the sample members, it was evident from birth that they would be disabled; for 6%, traumas to the head were experienced at some point during childhood resulting in brain damage and significantly impairing performance; in another 4%, major seizures occurred during the childhood years without any prior symptoms. For the remaining 15% of the sample, no information was available.

Procedure

Sample members were located through a variety of sources, including California Regional Centers for the Developmentally Disabled, residential facilities, sheltered workshops, social groups, and training programs. Various agencies identified a pool of potential sample members and approached them for permission to be contacted by our researchers. Once a potential sample member agreed to become involved in the research, participant-observation began.

In addition to the participant-observation described in the Introduction to this volume, field researchers also undertook more focused data collection on the topic of handicap. Researchers were instructed to use opportunities which either occurred naturally during the course of a visit (e.g., when comments were made concerning receipt of SSI or other services designated for the handicapped) or could be eased into through indirect questioning (e.g., probes concerning school memories) to discuss the sample members' feelings concerning their limitations and their statuses as handicapped persons. Tape recordings of conversations and the researcher's notes were then used to construct a detailed narrative account of each contact. The resulting field notes provide a record of everyday concerns, behaviors, and skills, and because they are extremely detailed, they allowed us to examine a number of features of the sample members' lives, including their modal attitudes toward being mentally retarded. At approximately 6- and 18-month intervals, field researchers were asked to summarize their knowledge of each of the sample members they had followed. Three major areas of concern were included in the structured format provided for their comments: the saliency of being mentally retarded to the sample member's identity and everyday life, current relationships with family members and peers, and characteristic ways the sample member handled problems which confronted him or her.

In addition, structured interviews were conducted with parents or other close family members of 37 sample members to obtain information on past and current issues in the lives of these individuals. Family contacts were initiated by field researchers, and, in total, 120 questions were asked, typically requiring 2 or 3 interview sessions and 7 to 9 hours for completion. Topics covered included: the impact of the mentally retarded child on family members' lives, the developmental history of the child, and school, social, residential, and work histories. For the other 9 sample members, such information was unavailable because family members were either deceased or for other reasons inaccessible (e.g., in very poor health, living out of state).

Results

The author and another researcher, both familiar with the three sources of data discussed above, made independent judgments as to the modal attitude each sample member held toward his or her condition. We identified four distinct attitudes based on sample members' willingness/reluctance to discuss their handicaps, the tension and anxiety related to the acknowledgement of having problems, the salience they assigned their handicaps in day-to-day living, and the strategies they invoked for coping with their limitations. The four attitudes identified are: (a) *acceptance* (e.g., "I'm retarded, it means there's a lot of things I can do on my own and a lot I can't, but I do what I feel I can do."), (b) *qualification* (e.g., "I'm slow in learning but not retarded."), (c) *vacillation* (e.g., "I may have trouble reading and doing math but I don't consider myself a handicap."), and (d) *denial* (e.g., "I don't have any problems, I have no problems."). Inter-rater agreement averaged 81% across all subjects. Note, however, that although modal attitudes could be reliably identified, many sample members vary their presentations of self depending on the circumstances. For example, qualifiers and vacillators were the most difficult to characterize because they were the least willing to discuss their handicaps openly, and they invoked various forms of strategic self-presentation until intimacy and trust had developed with their field researchers. In fact, two-thirds of the inter-rater disagreements involved sample members who were eventually characterized as qualifiers or vacillators.

Some sample members appear to be gradually redefining their attitudes toward their handicaps over time. Indeed, we have found that most mildly retarded adults subscribe to the belief that being mentally retarded is not a permanent, irrevocable condition. Rather, many maintain that one can outgrow one's handicap (e.g., "I used to be retarded, but I'm not anymore.") and that normative accomplishments, such as living independently, getting married, obtaining competitive employment, and so forth, have removed them from "being retarded" as a social identity and status.

Once sample members' modal attitudes toward their handicaps had been classified, the data were analyzed to determine the corresponding relationships with other indices of socioemotional adjustment, including: strategic goals, peer relations, involvement with the delivery system, employment record, socialization history, and well-being. The results of the analysis are presented below. A series of Kruskal-Wallis One Way Analysis of Variance of basic demographic variables (see Table 1) revealed that members of the four attitude

TABLE 1
MEAN PROPORTIONS OF DEMOGRAPHIC CHARACTERISTICS
FOR EACH ATTITUDE GROUP

	Acceptors (n = 10) (7 males, 3 females)	Qualifiers (n = 13) (6 males, 7 females)	Vacillators (n = 10) (6 males, 4 females)	Deniers (n = 13) (6 males, 7 females)
Chronological Age[a]	37 (8.3)	31 (5)	32 (9)	41 (12.6)
Years of Independent Living[a]	11 (11)	4 (3.3)	7 (8.2)	12 (11.3)
Marital Status	.60	.62	.50	.38
Competitive Employment	.70	.38	.50	.23
Sheltered workshop employment	0	.15	.10	.46
Unemployed	.30	.46	.40	.31
Regional Center Clients	.70	1.00	.90	.85
SSI Recipients	.80	.62	.80	.62
Department of Rehabilitation Clients	.30	.62	.50	.31
Graduates of Independent Living Training Program	.40	.46	.60	.38

[a]Mean number of years, standard deviations in parenthesis

groups do not differ from one another with respect to age, sex, number of persons married, or number of years of independent living. However, when a Mann-Whitney U test of significance was performed comparing the two oldest groups, acceptors/deniers, with the two youngest groups, qualifiers/vacillators, significant differences were found in terms of age ($z = 2.42$; $p < .01$) and number of years of independent living ($z = 2.63$; $p < .01$).

Acceptors

Ten of our sample members appear to have accepted the diagnosis of mental retardation and include it in their self-definitions (See Table 2). For the most part, these individuals have few reservations about referring to themselves as mentally retarded and do so in a matter-of-fact manner. One man views himself as "mostly normal with slight retardation." Another man describes himself as "a little handicapped, a little arthritis, a little mentally retarded . . . it means that I'm a little slow." A third man characterizes himself and his wife as "slow learners which is a kind of mental retardation." Although it is evident that being retarded has had a significant impact on the life careers of these people (for example, two men were institutionalized during their adolescent years, one man is married to a Down's syndrome woman and has all handicapped friends), their comments and everyday life behaviors indicate that most assign little importance to their handicapped statuses with respect to their day-to-day lives. One man stated, "We're (referring to himself and his wife) both slow at learning. If somebody tells us to do something, we might not know how to go about doing it, but if they show us once or twice then it's done. We're just on the borderline, retarded or not retarded." Similarly, another man noted, "I don't learn things fast as other people do, but I learn 'em."

Four individuals noted that they had had problems with neighborhood kids teasing them, and another man stated that "mental retardation is a handicapping condition only a few people in a million have, most people have the gift you have (referring to the field researcher)." All members of this group seem aware that being labeled mentally retarded is stigmatizing; however, the label or condition does not seem to be a salient feature in their self-evaluations or general sense of self-worth. Instead, most emphasize their accomplishments and take pride in the lifestyles they have achieved. Their independence, acquiring material possessions, managing their own homes, holding down jobs, and being married, all serve to help them feel good about themselves. One woman proudly recited that she had a job, paid the bills, supported herself, and had an apartment—"this handicap, yes, I've got it, but look what I've done." Another sample member stated, "If my mom (deceased) could understand where I am, I'm married and settled, she'd be so proud of me. I've come so far, nobody would ever believe I've come so far."

These sample members possess, as do all individuals, images centered around the way they believe adult life is supposed to be. The components of these images, such as independence and self-sufficiency, have been emphasized by their parents and others as essential to a normal adult lifestyle. At this point in their lives, their personal achievements are viewed as confirmation of mastery over the demands of adult life and as evidence that the image of the successful adult has been largely realized. More specific achievements, such as the

TABLE 2
SUMMARY OF DESCRIPTIVE CHARACTERISTICS
FOR EACH ATTITUDE GROUP

Sample Members' Attitude Toward Handicap:	Acceptance	Qualification	Vacillation	Denial
Willingness to discuss handicap	open/casual	casual/guarded	reluctant	very reluctant/avoid topic
Parental attitude toward handicap	acceptance	acceptance/qualification	ambivalence/avoidance	ambivalence/avoidance
Parental practices	promotion of self-sufficiency	promotion of self-sufficiency	overprotection	overprotection/overregulation
Sample members' focal concerns/strategic goals	normative/accomplishment	progress/growth	deviance disavowal	routinization
Current attitude toward parental & agency dependence	positive	positive	negative	negative
Past use of programs/services (based on parent report)	low use	high use	high use	low use
Affiliative relationships	prefer nonhandicapped; nurturant or authoritative toward handicapped peers	prefer mildly handicapped; warm relationships; reject severely handicapped	prefer mildly handicapped or non-handicapped; shallow, unstable relationships; reject severely handicapped	few or no peers; prefer family relationships

Well-being/quality of life (self-report)	Content	Content	Miserable	Content
Reference group	Positive reference group—normals	Negative reference group—severely handicapped	Negative reference group—severely handicapped	Positive reference group—normals

ability to get around the city by bus, skill at managing monthly budgetary demands, and the capacity to remember appointments and memorable dates, intensify this belief. Moreover, most characteristically describe themselves to others in terms of their normative accomplishments (e.g., "You know, I keep busy, I have my job, my wife to come home to, we go out and do things . . ."). Their presentations of self are thus rarely defensive or blatantly self-aggrandizing.

Although acceptors view their "normal" lifestyles as probably their most significant achievements, most see nothing troublesome about their reliance on others when times are difficult. They seem capable of juggling their independent statuses with a willingness to accept the assistance of a parent, sibling, or spouse when problems are encountered. For example, one man who is illiterate relies on his wife to read for him; one woman always defers to her husband when questioned during conversations to conceal her lack of comprehension; another man admits that he wouldn't have initially made it on his own without relying heavily on his dad and roommate for help. Similarly, most have no qualms about accepting services specifically designated for the handicapped. Eight of the 10 receive SSI payments, and 7 are Regional Center clients. Although these sample members attempt to manage most everyday problems on their own and, for the most part, do so adequately, when confronted with difficult problems—for example, SSI foul-ups, running short of money at the end of the month, difficulty getting the landlord to do repairs—they seek help from family members or delivery system personnel. This situation-specific, limited reliance on others appears to be a comfortable coping strategy for these sample members.

Of the seven acceptors for whom background information is available, all but two came from families who seem to have been accepting and open about their children's retardation from the start. Parents offered clarifying explanations to assist their children's understanding of their conditions—"Everyone has unequal abilities," "No two people are alike"—and provided extra time and special attention so their children would experience a sense of accomplishment. They made concerted efforts to employ growth-promoting practices and thus to foster independence and self-maintenance skills. One mother, for example, boasted of how she taught her son to use the bus system. She described how she would specify which number bus to board and where to get off and then would drive behind the bus to make sure he did not miss the stop. Another parent arranged for a teacher from her son's high school to live with the boy for a year, during which time he learned independent living skills. One father described being informed by the doctor that his son would not be able to ride a bicycle because of his poor depth perception. However, the image of his son running alongside his friends as they peddled along on their bikes was too much for the father, and he went out and bought his son a bicycle. Within a short time, he had taught his son to ride and from that day on decided he would never set limits for the boy. His son now has a job, is married, and drives his own car, accomplishments even the father admits were beyond his expectations. These parents' encouragement of the development of new skills was especially striking given the relatively few support services available at the time their children were growing up. However, all of them were driven by the concern that their children be self-sufficient because the parents "weren't going to be around forever."

The families of the other two sample members, although aware that their children were "slow," chose to ignore the condition, preferring instead to over-protect and indulge their children. In both cases, other family members (an aunt and uncle in one case and an older sister and brother-in-law in the other), alarmed at how little was being done to foster self-maintenance and independence skills, took over the care of the children and promoted acceptance of their handicaps and self-sufficiency.

For all these individuals, family encouragement to strive for normal life-styles has resulted in some problems in social relationships. They either display an arrogant or nurturant dominance over their mentally retarded peers or spouses, whom they view as inferior, or show less interest in associating with mentally retarded peers and more interest in maintaining relationships with non-retarded individuals. One man usually accompanies his wife and her mentally retarded friends but is quick to identify them as his wife's associates. His "I-don't-have-much-in-common-with-them" attitude is reinforced by his mother's assertion that "he likes winners and people he can learn from." He seems to prefer his volunteer work at the church and his casual associations with the other (nonretarded) volunteers, who appear tolerant of him. Another man, al-though dependent on his wife to read for him and to help with the budgeting, never misses an opportunity to criticize her or impose his will on her. He pre-fers to spend all his free time fostering relationships with people he has met through his model train hobby, either helping them out in their train hobby shops or accompanying them on weekend excursions to various train yards throughout California (leaving his wife home alone). A third sample member describes herself as "in-between two worlds, that of the disabled and that of the normal, fitting in neither one." She exhibits a markedly different approach in her dealings with the two groups, displaying a condescending, oppressive at-titude toward her mentally retarded peers and assuming a non-authoritarian, peer-like stance with her nonretarded associates (mostly counselors and church members). Although preferring her associations with nonretarded peers, re-peated rebuffs by these individuals has forced her to reconcile her attitude to-ward her disabled peers. She now assumes the role of leader and helper of dis-abled people (thus elevating her status within her own mind) and sees it as her mission to rescue some of her disabled friends from their own foibles.

Not all of the individuals in this group have always held attitudes of ac-ceptance toward their handicaps. For some, there appears to have been a de-velopmental progression, a working their way into acceptance. At least four de-nied their retardation at earlier points in time. One parent recounted that for years she and her husband would say to their son: "You have to admit that you're retarded." However, the mere mention of the term "retarded" would send him into a rage until "one day when he got older, it just came to him that he was and he accepted it."

Two sample members still seem to be in the process of coming to terms with their handicaps. Although willing to admit to being mentally retarded and open about their conditions, they continue to dwell on the impact, both past and present, on all spheres of their lives. One sample member was angered by his parents' use of an "unfair" double standard in their differing treatment of him and his nonretarded sister. He saw their refusal to allow him to ride his bike to school, to buy a motorcycle or scooter, and to watch violent movies and TV shows as a form of "babying" him which he considered unjust. The other sample member felt her family was uncomfortable in dealing with her as a child, "as they didn't know what my abilities and limitations were." She would have preferred them to be more open in discussing her condition with her because "a handicap doesn't affect just one member of the family, it involves the whole family."

Comments by both sample members indicate their sensitivity to the stigma associated with being labeled mentally retarded. They have each noted that some employers do not want to hire mentally retarded workers and that non-retarded persons sometimes feel awkward around retarded individuals. The woman described being transferred to another high school because schoolmates would tease her, causing her to come home crying each day. The man noted that sometimes "older people relate to me from adult to child." Both would prefer to socialize with nonretarded peers because "retarded friends tend to make you more retarded." However, they have each experienced rejection by "normals" during their attempts to mix. Both seem eager to be thought of as normal adults and as achievers of normal adult lifestyles. The woman has remarked, "I'm really normal inside, but I don't know how to get that out," and the man noted, "I've been working hard quite some time to normalize myself." Over the past 18 months of research contact, they have each made gains toward reconciling their handicaps with their lifestyles. The woman has recently become engaged to a mentally retarded man with cerebral palsy and is quite content with the match and their prospects for the future. The man is now willing to admit that "I wish I didn't have a handicap . . . it would be nice if I could hold down a regular job rather than work on a crew for the handicapped . . . I wish I could drive a car rather than having to depend on buses . . . I wish I was never in programs for the mentally disabled . . . I wish I was normal like you (referring to the field researcher), but there's not much I can do about it, so there's no point in feeling sorry for myself about it, because its not going to solve anything."

Qualifiers

The 13 qualifiers are similar to acceptors in their unwillingness to admit having limitations (See Table 2). However, they reject the label "mentally retarded," which they contend connotes severe problems, and prefer terms like slow learner, brain damaged, and mildly handicapped. References to their conditions are usually qualified, such as "a slight amount of brain damage," "it's not severe, it's just mildly," or "not retarded but below average for my age." In many cases, parents have reinforced these qualifications. One mother, for example, assured her daughter that she only has "little problems here and there," and another sample member noted, "my dad said I don't have it very bad."

Qualifiers are generally more preoccupied with their limitations than the acceptors. Although matter of fact about referring to themselves as mildly handicapped, they view their disabilities as affecting the quality of their lives. They describe trouble with budgeting, slowness at learning new things, and difficulty handling pressure on the job as problems they must contend with because of their handicaps. One unemployed woman painfully noted that she couldn't read the cards at the state unemployment office to find out what jobs were available. Another unemployed man complained that employers should have patience with his slow pace and be willing to train him. A third sample member reported that he was unable to work on the aerospace contract at his workshop (a highly desirable assignment) because of inadequate math skills. Most manage, however, to maintain a delicate balance between recognizing and admitting specific limitations, without relying extensively on their handicaps as an excuse for not being able to do things or engaging in self-deprecation.

As a group, qualifiers appear to be more aware of the stigma associated with being mentally retarded than the acceptors. Many recall having been teased and taunted at school, having been nicknamed "Retardo" and such by neighborhood children, having felt uneasy about younger siblings' accomplishments. One sample member said he was "looked upon as though I was nothing" because of his special class placement. As adults, four sample members claimed they had been denied jobs because of their handicaps. One woman, who had been a volunteer at a child-care center for 4 years, was dismissed shortly after becoming a paid employee because of her seizure condition. She is currently contesting the layoff with the help of her father and a counselor from the Department of Rehabilitation. A number of sample members voiced concern about giving birth to handicapped children. One, the parent of a 1-year-old boy, had him tested to make certain he was developing normally. Three others decided to undergo voluntary sterilization, fearful that, as one stated, "the kid would turn out worse than me . . . instead of being handicapped he would turn out retarded."

There is a striking similarity between the attitudes of these sample members toward their handicaps and those of their parents. When asked to describe their children's handicaps, almost all of the 12 parents interviewed began by minimizing their conditions. One parent referred to her child as "a borderline case who always performed at the top of the special class." She wondered if "they had pushed her and kept her in regular classes, would she have gone further than by being with children who were lower than her." Another parent described her son as "an in-between kid," noting that "he didn't belong in the really handicapped class but couldn't make it in a regular class." A third parent explained that her daughter was "in that crack where you're not capable and yet you're too capable." All but one of these parents described themselves as strongly committed to their children's forward progress and repeatedly asserted that they wanted their sons or daughters to "achieve the most they could." Most actively sought out every special program or service available at the time. Because the qualifiers are significantly younger than the acceptors and the deniers (who will be discussed below), more of these training programs were in fact available. As a result, all qualifiers attended special education school programs; some were sent to private day schools, others to residential schools, and the remainder to public school special education classes. One mother commuted many miles so her son could attend a special education class, the only one that had an opening. Another parent, frustrated by the lack of appropriate programs available for her child ("he was too high functioning for one program and too low functioning for another"), was instrumental in organizing a local program especially designed for her son and others like him. Many of these parents worked as volunteers in special education classes; a number of parents joined organizations to learn from professionals and other parents what they could do for their children; some enrolled in university courses or read books about the exceptional child.

Most salient was the belief these parents held that their handicapped children could achieve significantly if helped. One mother explained that she "never understood what mental retardation meant" so her daughter was always treated as normal with a constant emphasis on trying. Another parent recalled that "no one told me my daughter wasn't going to progress, no one knew her upward potential. So, being an optimist, it was a question of being patient and working and seeing where it went." One qualifier's parents were the exception. They appear to have rejected their son from an early age. They describe him as a very difficult child and, from the age of 7, moved him in and out of board and care facilities. As a result, his current qualified attitude may be more related to experiences and influences outside the home; for example, his closest friends are themselves qualifiers.

Most parents of qualifiers remain heavily involved in their children's everyday lives. One sample member sees her mother almost daily and telephones her two or three times a day. She is grateful for the close relationship she has with her mother and commented, "I don't know what I'd do without her." Her mother chauffeurs her and her 1-year-old son to the market, budgets their money, subsidizes the apartment rent, and is there for advice and counsel. Her mother has insisted that she abort two previous pregnancies, and she is presently trying to discourage a threatened marriage separation. Another sample member still relies on her mother to pick out which clothes she should buy. Because her parents are the nearest source of assistance, she calls them if she is having trouble reading a piece of mail or if she needs a ride somewhere at night.

These parents also recognize the need for their children to be more self-sufficient and most continue to push their sons or daughters toward increasing independence. One woman's parents noted that they are careful not to have their daughter come home too often. They intentionally keep her at a distance so that she continues her progress toward greater self-reliance. Another mother insisted, "I plan to be around until I'm 100. So I think there's enough time for my son to get himself together. There's a lot more potential in him that he's ever realized or put forth . . . the ability is there." Most of these parents, however, do not expect their children to ever attain completely autonomous life styles. Although they see their sons or daughters as being capable of developing the skills needed to handle routine self-maintenance, they expect them to require assistance when out-of-the-ordinary problems arise. As preparation for the future, they encourage their children to strengthen relationships with counselors and support agencies. One mother who recently suffered a minor stroke requested that Regional Center assign her daughter a new counselor so that she would begin to rely more on the counselor and less on her mother. One father wanted to make himself less accessible to his daughter so he refused to give her his new home telephone number. She is now able to contact him only when he is at work and must seek support from her counselors or rely on herself at other times.

Given this parental orientation, it is not surprising that qualifiers' self-descriptions emphasize the progress they are making toward independent lifestyles. One woman contrasted her present job and independent living situation with her life a few years before. At that time, although in her late twenties, she was still living at home with her parents and working in a sheltered workshop. She proudly acknowledges that neither she nor her parents ever dreamed that she would accomplish as much as she has. Another sample member stated that his growing awareness of his capabilities through group therapy has allowed him to obtain a clerical job and to begin thinking about "getting off" SSI which he views as degrading. These qualifiers' focus on accomplishment and growth allows them to project favorable images of themselves, as well as to indirectly emphasize the difference between themselves and the more severely disabled. Although the qualifiers have experienced a pattern of socialization similar to that of the acceptors, who use the qualities of normal adults for social comparison, the qualifiers refer to the severely handicapped to establish what they are not. Given the age difference between the acceptors and qualifiers, it is possible that these individuals may be at an early stage of a developmental progression which will eventually lead them to assume the identities of acceptors. Similarly, their extensive dependence on parents and siblings may eventually decrease to that of limited situation-specific reliance, as is true of the acceptors.

Being younger than the acceptors (and the deniers) has affected them in another way that over time may influence their attitudes toward their handicaps. All of these individuals have been dependent since childhood on programs and services specifically designated for the mentally retarded, services which were not necessarily available for the acceptors when they were younger. All of the qualifiers are clients of local service agencies for the developmentally disabled: six are recipients of SSI, seven have received vocational services through the Department of Rehabilitation, six are graduates of independent living training program, and at least seven are, or have been, members of social organizations and clubs for the handicapped. The fact that they continue to proclaim their handicaps as salient features of their self-perceptions may be due in part to their extensive involvement with, as well as their comfortable dependence on, these agencies.

Many qualifiers have developed a core of mildly retarded friends from their associations with these service agencies, which again furthers their commitment to accepting handicapped social identities. These relationships, with individuals they perceive to be comparable to themselves in ability, provide companionship, opportunities for having a good time, and, in some cases, sources of support. One woman, for example, increasingly turns to her best friend for advice on small matters now that her father is less accessible. Most qualifiers, however, actively reject close associations with persons they judge to be below their levels of skill and competence. Several associates have developed a hierarchical taxonomy for viewing handicaps that formalizes for them their dissimilarities to the severely handicapped. For them, "normals" are anchored at the top, followed by epileptics and schizophrenics, then slow learners like themselves, the physically handicapped next, and "babies" (workshop clients) at the bottom. They assert that associates should be on the same level because "having friends with severe problems brings you down."

Vacillators

Ten sample members are vacillators (see Table 2). These individuals, in comparison to the qualifiers, appear to feel more tension and anxiety when they acknowledge having problems and when they attempt to distinguish their problems from those experienced by severely disabled individuals. They are somewhat reluctant to discuss their handicaps and, unless probed, rarely if ever bring them up during casual conversation. When reference is made, the vacillators describe their problems as minimal (e.g., "can't read, write, or do math," "a little slower in some things," "I wasn't an 'A' student, I was about a 'C' student.") in order to dissociate what they experience from what they believe to be a "real" handicapping condition. One man stated, "A handicap is like, you know, Porterville . . . go there and see the wards and you tell me what is a handicap . . . they're the ones with the big heads, the ones that don't know how to talk (makes apelike sounds), that's all they do all day . . . my handicap, I try to help myself." Another sample member, outraged by her mother's lamenting about having a mentally retarded daughter, insisted, "They can't read, can't hear well, can't see well. I can talk, I can read." A third sample member, upon overhearing his minister refer to him as mentally retarded, retorted, "I'm not you know, I mean I'm slow and everything, but not that goddamned dumb, you know." He was so offended by this offhand remark that he refused to return to church, his major source of social support at the time, for several months.

Most of these individuals are extremely sensitive to the negative attitudes others display toward mentally retarded persons, and all report having personally experienced such discrimination in one form or another. One woman described the way neighborhood kids yelled, "Retarded, Retarded" as she walked home from school and how she snapped back, "I wouldn't be in high school if I was retarded." A man complained that he and his mentally retarded friend were not encouraged to participate during weekly church meetings because their comments were considered "too inconsequential." Another man revealed that he hides his illiteracy from co-workers because "people think you're nuts if you can't read or write." Other sample members noted that employers will not hire you if they learn you are mentally retarded. Some complained that their parents treated them differently from their siblings.

As was true of the qualifiers, the vacillators are not only aware of the stigma associated with being considered mentally retarded, they are also cognizant of how their lives have been affected. Because they use every opportunity to downplay their handicaps, the effects on their lives are pervasive. They resent their "exceptional" statuses. As one sample member noted, "you know, everything is special, everything has to be the opposite of what other people do, but I ain't like that." They are frustrated by their lack of achievements, comparing themselves unfavorably to their siblings who have professional careers, nice homes with pools, take nice vacations, and so forth. They find themselves accepting a considerable amount of parental involvement in their lives and relying extensively on service agencies (i.e., nine are Regional Center clients, eight receive SSI, six have been enrolled in independent living training programs), but they feel stigmatized by such dependency. One woman, for example, a self-proclaimed victim of dependency addiction, blames her mother for insisting she apply for SSI and Medi-Cal and claims that she herself had no say in the matter. She complains that she would like to live without these benefits, but she is so used to them that she is afraid to try to manage on her own.

Although vacillators seek to project nonretarded public images, they also struggle with the realization that their limitations make them dependent on more competent others. This ambivalence has salient consequences for self-esteem, and all vacillators invoke one of the following coping tactics to maintain a sense of self-worth.

Development of personas to project self-reliance. Four vacillators, whose goal is to conceal their frailties, invoke strategic self-presentation to project images of normalcy that are supported by fabrication of accomplishments and other forms of self-aggrandizement. One sample member insisted, "I showed 'em," with respect to his family who, he claimed, "thought I'd be a burden all my life." Another man claimed to be an electrician, veterinarian, and ex-Hell's Angel member, identities tailored to the set of listeners he was trying to impress. A third bragged to an ex-schoolmate he ran into, "I work six jobs a week." All feign understanding and competence rather than admit that they do not know something, and all have excuses readily available when their claims are challenged or proved false. For example, one man, after losing at bowling (a game at which he had boasted he was a champion), contended he didn't have his good ball that day. When perceived as less than capable and unable to protect their vulnerable self-identities (e.g., the minister's assertion that his church member was mentally retarded and unable to think for himself), these individuals abandon their supporters or walk away from friendships rather than tolerate breaches in their public facades.

Participation in on-going battles to discredit their supporters. Four other vacillators are engaged in a dependency/autonomy struggle with their supporters. These individuals express their wish to be independent. As one sample member stated, "Parents are there to help you but basically should let you do as you please when you're grown." However, the actions of individuals in this group reveal a lack of desire to sever their dependency ties. One man continually demands help from his parents to extricate himself from the many difficulties he gets himself into (e.g., making a bad deal with a used-car salesman, initiating and canceling divorce proceedings from his schizophrenic wife, being evicted from his apartment because of noisy arguments with his wife) but resents it when they try to exert any control over his activities. For example, after his eviction, he thought he should be able to live in his parent's house (with a wife they disapprove of) but that they had no right to tell him what to do or how to behave in their home. He says he will be glad when they die because "then they won't bug me anymore." Another sample member sees her mother's intervention as an invasion of privacy. She recounts bitterly how she relented under parental pressure to have a tubal ligation, whereas her sister who was pregnant "got to keep it . . . my mother doesn't think I can handle a child. She doesn't think I can do a thing. She can't accept me the way I am which I don't think is that bad off." At the same time, she expects her mother to respond to her daily phone calls and to provide reassurance about all kinds of things (e.g., she called one night at midnight, concerned whether the oven cleaner would asphyxiate her, her husband, and their rabbit).

Establishment of terms for continuing their willing dependence on parents and others. The two remaining vacillators have accepted their dependence on family members but insist that they themselves set the terms of the help they receive. One sample member, although grateful to her mother for the assistance she provides (e.g., she straightens out incorrect phone bills, fills out forms for

SSI renewal, explains letters which are not readily understood), nonetheless prefers to conceal some things, such as the extent to which she and her live-in boyfriend smoke marijuana or the adventures they have with people they pick up in bars. Her mother, in turn, has learned to be non-judgmental about her daughter's life "in order to keep the door to communication open between us." For example, she no longer nags her about getting a job and she refrained from lecturing after her daughter's jaw was broken by her boyfriend.

Consistent with the vacillators' struggle to reconcile their desires for normalcy with their dependent status is their view of increased dependency as deplorable. At least three individuals have actively fought to prevent greater enmeshment. After much deliberation, one woman rejected her mother's offer to subsidize her rent if she moved closer to the family home. She was convinced that acceptance of this offer would result in a decrease in the control she exerts over her own life. One man, with the support of his father-in-law, refused to accompany his mother and step-father in their move to another state. He feared, were he to do so, that they would try to take control of his money. After receiving an eviction notice, another sample member was concerned that he would have to move in with his married brother and his family. He called upon all available resources until a new apartment was found.

Like the qualifiers, the vacillators pursue associations with individuals judged to be at least comparable to themselves in ability and actively avoid contact with lower functioning persons. In most cases, these associations involve mildly retarded peers that they have met through various agency affiliations. However, some vacillators regard their non-reciprocal, situation-specific relationships with nonretarded persons (e.g., co-workers, busdrivers) to be their most important friendships. In general, their relations with both retarded and nonretarded acquaintances can best be characterized as shallow and unstable with relatively little satisfaction being derived from them.

Background information from the families of six of these vacillators indicates that their parents practiced well-intentioned dishonesty to insulate their children from the harsh realities of mental retardation, as well as to mollify their own needs to de-emphasize their children's imperfections. Although these parents were knowledgeable of both mental retardation and the consequences of that handicap on their sons' or daughters' lives, they avoided engaging in explanatory discussions with their chldren as they were growing up. It was not until the parents were faced with questions, such as "Why am I like this?" "Why can't something be done about it?" "Why did God make me like this?" that they were forced to deal with the issue, and even then, most deliberately chose to ignore the obvious implications. Despite this ambivalence, they were concerned that development be fostered. Toward this goal, they searched for special schools, training programs, and social organizations which were available at the time; they participated in the day-to-day training of their children, and, in some instances, even lobbied legislators for new programs and facilities for mildly retarded children.

Although the parents of both the qualifiers and the vacillators acted in what each believed to be the best interests of their children, the parents of qualifiers coupled words of explanation with words of encouragement to emphasize that their children could and would accomplish. In contrast, parents of the vacillators typically tried to downplay their children's handicaps and, in doing so, offered misleading hope to their children. Even now that their children have reached the adult stage of life, the parents of the vacillators continue to send ambiguous messages. Although they would like to see their grown sons or daughters more self-reliant and are disappointed at their lack of independence thus far, they are responsible for creating the same cushioned lifestyles they criticize. One mother, for example, can't understand why her son refuses to take responsibility for his actions and yet is always coming to his rescue before he is confronted by the consequences of those actions. Another mother threatens time and time again to cut her son off from herself and the family house, but continues to prepare lunch and dinner for him daily (he lives a few blocks away), to drive him grocery shopping and to the laundry, to give him large sums of money, and so on.

In many respects, the vacillators' lives appear similar to those of the qualifiers. They are of comparable age, heavily involved in delivery system services, still very much dependent on their parents, and they tend to associate primarily with mentally retarded peers. Unlike the qualifiers, however, their handicaps remain prominent concerns, and they are highly ambivalent towards those features of everyday life which emphasize their mentally retarded statuses.

Deniers

Thirteen sample members refuse to acknowledge being mentally slow or retarded (see Table 2). Six deny outright having ever experienced any personal incompetence; for example, one man, when asked what he considers his handicap to be responded, "Nuttin', I don't have one," and one woman insisted, "I'm normal." Two sample members admit to having been identified as slow learners during their school years but argue that their ability to manage their own apartments and to work confirms that they have outgrown their conditions ("When you grow you change."). The five remaining sample members redefine their problems in terms of some relevant physical or emotional problem and remain steadfast in their denial of any mental handicap. One man, for example, contends that his mind and memory are okay, and he is "smart like everybody else," he just has a "coordination problem."

All 13 deniers have consistently shown a reluctance to discuss the topic of handicap and, when questioned, either responded, "I don't know" and then tried to change the subject or flatly stated, "I don't want to go into all of it." Even efforts to ease them into conversations were unsuccessful. For example, one man, when questioned as to why he is able to purchase a reduced-fare bus pass (for which a doctor must certify a handicap exists), avoided answering directly and responded with nervous laughter. When another sample member, who insists she is normal, was asked whether it would bother her if a stranger touring her sheltered workshop assumed she was just another handicapped client, she denied such an assumption would ever be made. Only 5 of the 13 deniers have made even passing reference to mentally retarded or handicapped persons, and, in all instances, implied that those persons were very different from themselves. For example, 2 individuals who spent a number of years in institutions described the other patients there as mentally retarded or paralyzed but indicated that their reasons for hospitalization were different (i.e., a seizure condition in one case and a volatile temper and school truancy in the other).

Another sample member noted of her co-workers at the workshop, "I've gotten so used to those handicapped people, if I ever left that workshop I would miss them. I would miss their hollering and their jumping and their this and their that, I've gotten used to it already."

For the most part, these sample members tend to back away from any meaningful self-disclosures and prefer to report that they have few problems and lead trouble-free existences; for example, none has ever admitted to being the victim of teasing or discrimination even though reports from their parents reveal the opposite to be true. One mother described how her son was so cruelly taunted by neighborhood children that she took to "watching over him like a hawk." On a few occasions, however, there have been instances of rare personal disclosure. One woman, who had admitted to being slow as a child, recounted that at the time she felt "different" and it bothered her. Another woman, who concedes to having a crippled arm and "nervous spells" (i.e., seizures), revealed her resentment toward both her father, who never seemed to listen to her or value her thoughts, and her sister, who seemed to be considered more worthwhile and credible than she. Admissions such as these occur infrequently, however, especially when compared to the amount of time these individuals spend covering up their feelings or simply refusing to respond to queries about their backgrounds or concerns. Therefore, it is very difficult to estimate the extent of their denial to themselves or their sensitivity to the stigma associated with being considered mentally retarded. There is only indirect evidence, most obviously their refusals to admit to personal incompetence or their redefinition of their disabilities in terms of some less stigmatizing medical condition, which suggests a concern about having mentally retarded social identities and the pejorative connotations attached to such a status.

Their life careers have been significantly altered by the presence of their disabilities; for example, four individuals spent a number of years as patients in a state hospital, three were sent to live with grandparents or other family members during their childhoods, and two were kept as recluses in their parents' homes. Nevertheless, these deniers are similar to the acceptors in that they do not dwell on their pasts but rather accept their lives as "that's the way it's supposed to be." Most seem to feel they lead good lives and are secure and satisfied in the niches they inhabit. They have internalized the view that they are like everybody else and so dismiss any inadequacies as insignificant. For example, one man noted, "Everybody makes mistakes, we're not perfect," and another remarked, "We all have our limitations, I'm not worried about it." They emphasize the ability to live on their own, competence in coping with the demands of everyday life, and, for those who work, their work statuses, accomplishments they are committed to maintaining. For example, the employed deniers are industrious and conscientious workers. They rarely miss a day of work, refuse to call in sick unnecessarily, and are always concerned about getting to work on time. One man, who has worked at the same workshop for over 20 years, spent 3 hours walking to and from work during a 2-week-long bus strike so he would not miss a day. Another sample member, who was fearful of riding the bus alone and who had always traveled to work with her co-worker husband, had him accompany her on the bus even when he was on sick leave.

As in the case of the other sample members, these individuals' attitudes toward their disabilities appears to be largely a function of parental influences and practices. Reports from family members of 11 deniers indicate that their parents either avoided or delayed explanatory discussions of the children's handicaps or redefined the conditions in terms of less stigmatizing afflictions. A number of parents referred to the physical aspects of their children's disabilities—polio, "nervous spells," coordination difficulties, cerebral palsy—labels they believed were easier for their children to accept. Other parents tried to conceal the handicaps. One mother made both her daughters wear corrective shoes so as not to bring attention to the disabled daughter's crippled leg. Another parent responded to her son's questions concerning why he couldn't do things by placing the onus on an earlier speech problem, "You got behind in those early years when you weren't able to speak, but now you can, so go ahead and do it."

These parents' desire to act in the best interests of their children, in most cases, resulted in rearing practices which were characteristically overprotective. Two sample members, one at age 6, after being denied admission to a number of schools because of a severe seizure condition, and the other at age 12, after her mother learned her daughter's class had been assigned the responsibility of cleaning the cafeteria, were confined in their parents' homes where they spent their time in virtual isolation, listening to music or watching television. Little opportunity was provided for them to leave the house, to interact with other children, or to assume responsibility; everything was done for them. Independent living, marriage, or having children were considered out of the question, and, in both cases, it was not until their parents' deaths that opportunities for self-development (e.g., independent living training) were made available.

In other cases, parents provided so much warmth and care that they inadvertently socialized their children into dependency, compliance, and incompetence. Rather than stand by and watch their children fail, they discouraged risk-taking and spontaneity; they made all decisions for their sons or daughters, convinced that they were too reticent, didn't speak their own minds, or went along with others to avoid confrontation, and they encouraged extensive reliance on family members for advice in all matters. These parents acknowledge that they were "somewhat overprotective." For example, one parent admitted that family members had warned her and her husband that they were babying their son too much; others were confronted by agency counselors who blamed them for not adequately preparing their children for the outside community. In one case, the family was forced to refrain from contacting their son for the first 6 weeks of an independent living training program to reduce their mutual dependence.

Other parents have continually mixed overprotectiveness with denial. One mother noted that she always emphasized wanting her daughter to act normal and to be with normal people. She blames the recent regression she sees in her daughter's behavior on the influence of her two mentally retarded roommates and a handicapped boyfriend, and, therefore, has been insisting that her daughter return home where she can supervise her more closely. Another parent had her son transferred out of the special education program because she felt there was not enough emphasis on academics; in later years, she enrolled him in classes in junior college and law school. In contrast, she discouraged his desire to move out of the home, and it was not until age 36 that he was prevailed upon by an uncle to do so.

These parents, or in some cases siblings who have become caretakers, continue to keep abreast of the goings on in the lives of their mentally retarded family members. Although they claim to hold back from making decisions in order to encourage self-reliance, they are disturbed when decisions are made without their counsel. For example, one sample member's parents were furious when they learned that their son, although living on his own and competitively employed, had purchased a moped without consulting them first. These sample members, however, have been so patterned in their dependency that they generally defer any decisions or problems to their parents or other authority figures and rarely look to themselves as potential decision makers or problem solvers.

All of these individuals accept their families' overprotection and the concomitant value of compliance/dependency as being what is best for them. They seem unconcerned with the relative lack of control they have over their lives, nor are they struggling with issues of self-identity. Rather, they project an image of naiveté and, in some cases, obliviousness. More than sample members from the other groups, they appear to be plodding through life, unquestioning and committed to the status quo. For example, many are unrealistic in assessing their attractiveness and the depth of their relationships with members of the opposite sex. They are quick to identify those who pay any kind of attention to them as their boyfriends or girlfriends and to say, "They love me." Similarly, they seem unaware of their unkempt appearance, their overweight bodies, and their "eccentric" or slovenly dress, and they appear unmindful of the stares of people passing by or the nagging pleas of family members to clean themselves up.

Most deniers live highly routinized lifestyles and are comfortable with the few demands and the diminished risk-taking of such a narrow and defined mode of existence. For example, many do their laundry, grocery shopping, and banking on the same day each week, are regular customers at the same restaurants, spend each night vigilantly glued to the television set, and have set times when they telephone or visit family members. One sample member consistently refused promotions on his job, maintaining he likes to handle his world, to know what to expect. Another man makes out a weekly and then monthly schedule of activities for himself so he is left with little free time to fill. One woman is so comfortable with the life she and her husband have carved for themselves that when questioned as to what she would do if her husband was no longer around, she replied, "I guess I'll have to die too."

Most of these individuals have few close relationships with peers and are content to rely on their families for social eventfulness. Their families, in turn, always welcome them in their homes and include them in all family functions and social gatherings. Only 4 of the 13 deniers have a group of friends they consistently see, and, in each case, they are mildly mentally retarded individuals whom they met while participating in programs for the handicapped. Discussions about their disabilities or their concerns do not generally occur; instead, these relationships provide opportunities for enjoying conventional pastimes.

The deniers are the oldest of the four categories (i.e., mean age 41 years) and are thus less accustomed to relying on the delivery system services that have relatively recently become available to them. Those sample members who utilize services or programs designated specifically for the handicapped seem to do so without understanding what the implications are for their social identities. For example, one woman has enlisted the services of the Department of Rehabilitation and has signed up for Medi-Cal, services she believes are available to her because she makes so little money. Another woman connects her "employment" at a sheltered workshop to her lack of job skills; if she "knew more," she could get another job. When problems arise, such as marital conflicts, difficulties with roommates, appliance malfunctions, or SSI or Medi-Cal tangles, these individuals tend to seek help from family members rather than Regional Center counselors or other delivery system contacts. When family members are unavailable, extensive dependence has developed with agency counselors. For example, one man had to be returned to trainee status at the workshop after his promotion to "employee" did not work out. He was apparently so accustomed to relying on work counselors at the first sign of trouble (support which was available for trainees only) that the loss affected his ability to remain calm and function most effectively.

Conclusion

Bearing in mind that the main criterion for sample selection was independent living status, which implies relatively good personal and social adjustment, we began with a research cohort in which it was unlikely that great differences in adjustment would be found. Analysis of the ethnographic and background data has, however, revealed what appear to be four differing types of people characterized by variations in their self-perceptions as mentally retarded persons, their focal concerns with respect to their self-definitions, the forms of strategic self-presentation they invoke to cope with social reality, their socialization histories, and the quality of relationships they maintain with family members, peers, and agents of the delivery system.

It now remains to identify the factors responsible for the self-perspectives developed by our sample members with regard to their disabilities and their lives as adults. The primary pattern that emerges is the influence that parental practices and expectations have had on both the attitudes that these handicapped individuals bear toward their conditions and their adult adjustment. The parents of the acceptors and the qualifiers believed that their sons or daughters were capable of accomplishments, and, therefore, actively promoted growth. They encouraged normal activities and risk-taking, set realistic goals for their children, and pushed until a reasonable degree of self-sufficiency had been reached. Their sons or daughters have, in turn, accepted their limitations and sought normative accomplishments—which for the acceptors, confirm their success as adults, and for the qualifiers, reassure them that they are on the path to success. Those parents who had difficulty adapting to their mentally retarded children and the associated stigma either communicated their views to their children and inadvertently encouraged their sons or daughters to set unrealistic expectations for themselves (as in the case of the parents of the vacillators) or tended to be over-protective and over-regulating and restricted the life experiences available to their children (as was true of the parents of the deniers). In both cases, what resulted were individuals who do not strive for normative accomplishments or growth and who are rendered less capable of being all that they could be. Instead, the vacillators continue struggling to reconcile their handicaps with their desires for normalcy and derive little satisfaction from the quality of their lives; the deniers strive for routinization and continuation of the status quo, thus permitting themselves to continue the self-deception of accomplishment and self-maintenance.

The second most important factor related to self-acceptance appears to be years of independent living, which for these sample members is significantly correlated with age (r = .76). The acceptors and deniers are older than the qualifiers and vacillators and have lived independently for a greater number of years. The acceptors and deniers, like Edgerton and Bercovici's (1976) subjects, have successfully adapted to the demands of community living with the passage of time, and they have eventually come to perceive their handicaps as insignificant. They appear satisfied with their current lifestyles which confirm for them their success as adults—for the acceptors, their normative accomplishments, and, for the deniers, their very circumscribed, well-ordered existences. They place more importance on their status as successful adults than on any personal incompetence they may experience. Both the acceptors and the deniers refer to normal adults for social comparison and, in doing so, have established for themselves a positive reference group.

The qualifiers and vacillators are younger and just starting out in independent living. They are not yet settled into characteristic lifestyles but instead depict themselves as enroute to achieving their strategic goals—for the qualifiers, increased self-reliance, and, for the vacillators, deviance disavowal. Members of both groups are still somewhat uneasy with their identities as mentally retarded persons (the qualifiers to a lesser extent than the vacillators) and see projecting favorable images of themselves as important. They do so, in part, by using available opportunities to deny any association with the more severely impaired members of the mentally retarded population. Whereas the acceptors and deniers compare themselves to normals, which allows them to arrive at stable and coherent images of themselves, the qualifiers and vacillators emphasize their "differentness" from the more severely disabled. Their use of a negative reference group does not provide any basis for a healthy sense of self because it offers no positive standards with which to define the self. It is an adaptive technique which permits them to establish for others what they are not and is useful only if it is shortlived (Carver & Scheier, 1981).

A third relevant factor to emerge is reliance on support services offered by community care agencies, the availability of which was a function of the era in which the sample member grew up. The acceptors and deniers, being the oldest sample members, grew up during a time when little was known about the development of the mentally retarded child. Most parents were encouraged by doctors to institutionalize their children and then to forget about them. Those parents who chose to ignore such advice found few community services available and either resourcefully developed their own home skills training programs (as did the parents of the acceptors) or provided a restrictive life experience to insulate their children (as was true of the parents of the deniers). In contrast, when the qualifiers and vacillators were younger, professionals were more optimistic about the potential of disabled children and community care services had been established for their use. Their parents, whether they accepted or were ambivalent toward their children's exceptionality, actively sought available programs for their sons or daughters and, by doing so, began their children's reliance on support agencies.

Because they are less accustomed to relying on the delivery system, the acceptors and deniers see the services offered as less significantly related to their ability to maintain themselves in the community. Although they may be the recipients of such services, the acceptors more or less keep them in reserve for difficult-to-handle problems, and the deniers view their use as unrelated to any personal incompetence. The qualifiers and vacillators, on the other hand, have been more involved with community care agencies since childhood and even now, as independent adults, continue their heavy reliance on such services. The dependence does not present a problem for the qualifiers who (like the acceptors) are more casual about their need for support and make it less of an issue; however, dependence only aggravates the vacillators' quest for normalcy. They are unable to deny that their reliance on such services provides a mean to offset their own inadequacies and so remain forced to publicly subscribe to mentally retarded social identities.

These data demonstrate the plausible link between past environment and circumstances and characteristic attitudes and ways of thinking about oneself. These modal attitudes can be reliably identified, and, for the most part, appear to be stable patterns (i.e., even marriage to or friendship with individuals with different attitudes did not affect a change in the sample members' own attitudes). Nevertheless, a cautionary note is in order. Under certain defined conditions, sample members may switch the ways they portray themselves. First, those sample members who are most concerned with their public images, the vacillators (and, to a lesser extent, the qualifiers), possess repertoires of situational identities which are invoked depending on the audience, setting, or circumstance. One vacillator, for example, who generally claims he is like everyone else, willingly admitted that he was mentally disabled when he began to comprehend how he had been cheated by a used car salesman and was expected to pay exorbitant monthly installments. Another sample member, a qualifier, laughed as he described how he had presented himself to the judge as mentally retarded so as to be excused from fines or penalties for the traffic violations he had committed. The strength of these sample members' situational switching, as well as the specific circumstances under which switching is triggered, is in need of further examination.

Second, there are changes as some individuals mature and gain confidence through their experiences and/or achievements. A small number of sample members, who struggled with their "exceptionality" as children, became acceptors or qualifiers as adults. Others, who had perceived themselves as impaired when they were younger, assumed that their adult achievements meant their handicaps were no longer relevant to their lives. One acceptor, for example, has recently begun to deny his mental retardation as he becomes increasingly enmeshed in a social network of nonretarded acquaintances who share his interest in model trains. He will no longer admit to having attended special classes, he has decreased the amount of contact he has with his long-time mentally retarded associates, and he will only discuss his handicap in terms of his most salient problem, his inability to read, which he now blames on a lack of concentration.

Lastly, as rapport develops with the passage of time, changes in the way sample members talk about and portray themselves to their confidants occur. In general, the basic strategy for most of these individuals is to initially avoid discussion of their handicaps and, in doing so, give the outward impression that they are deniers. This initial reluctance to disclose their mentally retarded statuses is a sign of their awareness of the associated stigma and their fear of rejection by the nonretarded world. Their silence provides a means to manage information about their social identities so as to keep secret a potentially discrediting fact (i.e., that they are mentally retarded) and to maintain desirable public selves (Edgerton, in press; Goffman, 1963). However, as Goffman (1963) notes, as people come to be on closer terms with each other and as stigma is replaced by understanding, there is less need to invoke self-protective adaptive actions to conceal one's "spoiled" identity. Such was our experience; once intimacy with field researchers had developed and researchers came to be perceived as nonthreatening, many sample members became more open and casual about referring to their limitations and feelings.

That long-term relationships were required before sample members would allow researchers to enter their circle of confidants to whom sensitive information would be revealed may explain why few studies have been able to demonstrate the effect of stigma in the lives of mentally retarded persons. Most studies reported in the literature (Corman & Gottlieb, 1978; Guskin, 1978; MacMillan, Jones, & Aloia, 1974) contrast the responses of retarded and nonretarded individuals on standard paper and pencil measures of self-concept or to structured questions administered by unfamiliar examiners to determine their attitude toward stigma. Given the pervasive use of adaptive self-presentational strategies to protect their vulnerable sense of self (e.g., information management, self-aggrandizement) as indicated by our data, the validity of their responses under such conditions must be questioned.

In a society which places such high regard on mental ability and competence, it is difficult to imagine that an individual can be personally aware of his or her status as mentally deficient and yet remain immune to the associated stigma. It is more likely that individuals so labeled acquire identity standards which they apply to themselves (in spite of failing to conform to them) and which inevitably lead them to feel some ambivalence about themselves (Goffman, 1963). Our data attest to the fact that stigma is indeed recognized and subsequently coped with through a process of reconciliation that involves both the parents and the mentally retarded individual. Within our select cohort of sample members, four types of individuals were identified who differed in their socialization histories and their consequent personal and social adjustment as adults. Two of the composite groups developed lifestyles which accommodate to their handicaps and from which they report satisfaction, members of the third group are absorbed in conflict and are discontented, and members of the fourth are content with the benefits to be had from accepting dependency and restriction.

The adult adjustments of these individuals reflect the attitudes and practices adopted by their parents, which supports the argument that factors important in the determination of socioemotional adjustment and societal adaptation are responsive to the influence of the family (Edgerton, in press; Zigler & Harter, 1969). The question posed by Zigler and Harter (1969) over 10 years ago, and which still remains unanswered, centers on the issue of how socialization potential can best be developed to maximize the personal and social adjustment of the mentally retarded individual. Our data indicate that a better understanding of how to guide parents of handicapped children is needed (e.g., parents may need to focus more on the most productive way for the family to relate to their child's handicap and to talk with the child about his or her disability) as well as information on how the delivery system can best be used to support the family's efforts. Finally, the lives of members of the youngest groups, the qualifiers and vacillators, have been the most affected by recent societal changes in practices and expectations for the disabled. Unknown to us, however, is what the adjustment outcomes will be, in light of these changes, as these individuals, like the acceptors and deniers, mature and settle down. Continued research is in order to follow this research cohort, or another like it, as they proceed through the various stages of life.

References

Bogdan, R., & Taylor, S. J. (1976). The judged, not the judges: An insider's view of mental retardation. *American Psychologist, 31,* 47–52.

Bogdan, R., & Taylor, S. J. (1982). *Inside out: Two first-person accounts of what it means to be labeled 'mentally retarded'.* Toronto: University of Toronto Press.

Carver, C. S., & Scheier, M. F. (1981). *Attention and self-regulation: A control-theory approach to human behavior.* New York: Springer-Verlag, Inc.

Corman, L., & Gottlieb, J. (1978). Mainstreaming mentally retarded children: A review of research. In N. R. Ellis (Ed.), *International review of research in mental retardation* (Vol. 9, pp. 251–275). New York: Academic Press.

Dexter, L. A. (1964). On the politics and sociology of stupidity in our society. In H. S. Becker (Ed.), *The other side: Perspectives on deviance* (pp. 37–49). New York: Free Press.

Edgerton, R. B. (1967). *The cloak of competence: Stigma in the lives of the mentally retarded.* Berkeley: University of California Press.

Edgerton, R. B. (in press). Mental retardation: An anthropologist's changing view. In B. Blatt & R. Morris (Eds.), *Perspectives in special education: Personal orientations.* New York: Scott-Foresman.

Edgerton, R. B., & Bercovici, S. M. (1976). The cloak of competence: Years later. *American Journal of Mental Deficiency, 80,* 485–497.

Edgerton, R. B., & Sabagh, G. (1962). From mortification to aggrandizement: Changing self conceptions in the careers of the mentally retarded. *Psychiatry, 25,* 263–272.

Farber, B. (1968). *Mental retardation: Its social context and social consequences.* Boston: Houghton Mifflin.

Goffman, E. (1963). *Stigma: Notes on the management of spoiled identity.* Englewood Cliffs, NJ: Prentice-Hall.

Gozali, J. (1972). Perception of the EMR special class by former students. *Mental Retardation, 10,* 34–35.

Guskin, S. L. (1978). Theoretical and empirical strategies for the study of the labeling of mentally retarded persons. In N. R. Ellis (Ed.), *International review of research in mental retardation* (Vol. 9, pp. 127–158). New York: Academic Press.

Guskin, S. L., Bartel, N. R., & MacMillan, D. L. (1975). Perspective of the labeled child. In N. Hobbs (Ed.), *Issues in the classification of children* (Vol. 2, pp. 189–212). San Francisco: Jossey-Bass Publishers.

Hobbs, N. (Ed.) (1975). *Issues in the classification of children* (Vols. 1 & 2). San Francisco: Jossey-Bass Publishers.

Jones, R. L. (1972). Labels and stigma in special education. *Exceptional Children, 38,* 553–564.

MacMillan, D. L. (1977). *Mental retardation in school and society.* Boston: Little, Brown and Company.

MacMillan, D. L., Jones, R. L., & Aloia, G. F. (1974). The mentally retarded label: A theoretical analysis and review of research. *American Journal of Mental Deficiency, 79,* 241–261.

Mercer, J. R. (1973). *Labelling the mentally retarded.* Berkeley: University of California Press.

Turner, J. L. (1983). Workshop society: Ethnographic observations in a work setting for retarded adults. In K. Kernan, M. Begab, & R. Edgerton (Eds.), *Environments and behavior: The adaptation of mentally retarded persons* (pp. 147–171). Baltimore: University Park Press.

Turner, J. L., & Gallimore, R. (1979, May). *Being retarded as a social identity: Self-presentation and coping tactics of mildly retarded adults in the community.* Paper presented at the 103rd Annual Convention of the American Association on Mental Deficiency, Miami Beach.

Valpey, D. D. (1982). The psychological impact of 18 years in a board and care home. *Journal of Community Psychology, 10,* 95–97.

Wright, B. A. (1960). *Physical disability: A psychological approach.* New York: Harper and Row.

Zigler, E. F., & Harter, S. (1969). The socialization of the mentally retarded. In D. A. Goslin (Ed.), *Handbook of socialization theory and research* (pp. 1065–1102). Chicago: Rand McNally and Company.

The authors are affiliated with the Socio-Behavioral Group, Mental Retardation Research Center (Neuropsychiatric Institute), UCLA. This research was supported by NICHD Grant HD 11944–03. We gratefully acknowledge the contributions of Tom Brauner, Marsha Bollinger, Melody Davidson, Pauline Hayashigawa, Sandra Kaufman, Dave Tillipman, and Lesley Winik to the collection of data and the helpful comments of Dr. Ron Gallimore and Dr. Bob Edgerton during the writing of this chapter.

Escape from Boredom: The Meaning of Eventfulness in the Lives of Clients at a Sheltered Workshop

Joseph Graffam and Jim L. Turner

For the most part, attention to the socioemotional adjustment of mentally retarded persons has focused on post-institutional community and vocational adjustment (Baller, Charles, & Miller, 1967; Clark, Kivitz, & Rosen, 1968; Cobb, 1972; Edgerton, 1967; Fernald, 1919; Floor, Daxter, Rosen, & Zisfein, 1975; Hegge, 1944; Henschel, 1972; Mattinson, 1970; Windle, 1962; Wolfson, 1956). Such studies are consistent in reporting generally favorable results. However, researchers usually have attended to the question of how well people adjust, rather than focusing on the adjustment process *per se*. In contrast, Edgerton and Sabagh (1962), Edgerton (1967), and Bogdan and Taylor (1982) have examined feelings of mortification and self-aggrandizement within institutions and the stigmatizing effects of an institutional history on post-institutional living. Edgerton (1982) has also suggested that evaluation of "success" in adjustment is often, in itself, value-laden, and seldom takes into account the values and concerns of the mentally retarded persons themselves. Rosen, Clark, and Kivitz (1977) have supported the idea that future research should take a more comprehensive perspective, focusing on "daily personal situations . . . the intensive study of smaller numbers of persons, rather than more superficial nose-counting with larger populations" (p.149). These suggestions have been taken into account in addressing the question of how members of a "sheltered workshop" population adjust to the ramifications of what might politely be termed a "sheltered" existence, one characterized by relatively heightened dependency and restricted mobility.

In working with members of a particular sheltered workshop population, *boredom* has emerged as a major expressed concern of the clients in general. These individuals are engaged to a large extent with the perceived lack of eventfulness in their lives and with their concern over boredom. For many individuals within the workshop client population, the maintenance of self-esteem and the presentation of a positive social identity are related to the relative degrees of boredom and eventfulness that one experiences. This chapter describes eight separate informal means available for raising the level of eventfulness in one's life, provides examples of each, and demonstrates how these various means have been employed not only in making life more eventful but in the maintenance of self-esteem and presentation of a social identity by individual members of a workshop society.

Within the total set of behaviors exhibited by workshop clients relevant to their concern over boredom and the lack of eventfulness, the common and accepted presence of grandiose claims of personal achievements or exploits, highly dramatized or emotional responses to apparently mundane events, and sometimes quite intense involvements in a fantasy life have all been observed. On the basis of initial impressions or in a clinical setting, one might be tempted to view such responses as pathological; in terms of the goals of normalization, such responses might be considered maladaptive. However, after prolonged and direct involvement in the lives of workshop clients, the possibility of an alternate interpretation has presented itself. The social environment of workshop clients, in general, is one which affords little opportunity for a truly active social life. Workshop clients view "normal" adults as independent and highly active socially. Given the limitations of social resources available to workshop clients and their perceptions of what it means to be "normal" or "grown up", it is not surprising that individuals may go to rather extreme lengths in an attempt to make their lives more eventful. When taken in context, such responses no longer appear as pathological or maladaptive. Instead, the workshop emerges as a subculture which provides means for individuals to raise the level of eventfulness in their lives, enhance their self-esteem, and make positive presentations of a social identity within the boundaries of implicitly agreed upon propriety.

Methods

The research reported here was carried out over a period of 2 years, during which weekly or twice weekly visits were made to a sheltered workshop for mildly and moderately mentally retarded adults. The primary methodology employed was participant-observation in a natural setting. More specifically, data were gathered from observations, audio-taped group peer-counseling meetings, audio-taped informal interviews with individual workshop clients, and conversations held at lunch, during "break" times, or while clients were at work on one of the several assembly lines. Additional data were derived from structured periods of behavior observation, both in the workshop and on the lunchyard, during which social interactions and various other relevant behaviors were recorded. In addition to the research carried out among the workshop client population as a whole, several individual clients were followed more intensively for periods ranging from 12 to 16 months. Bio-demographic profiles were prepared from information obtained from workshop personnel files and "life history" accounts given by the clients themselves. In each case, individuals were met with on a regular basis (generally weekly) at which time they discussed their current emotional state, any recent events or problems, and their outlook for the future (anticipated outcomes or future plans). Four such "case histories" are included here. These four individuals are all male Caucasians ranging in age from 29 to 31 years. All have been classified as mildly mentally retarded (IQ 55–70), although they range between the upper and lower limits of that classification. During the study, all four lived in parental homes which were, in each case, of middle-class socioeconomic status. One individual is also physically handicapped and one has Down's Syndrome. The case histories provide insight into how specific individuals have attempted to make their lives more eventful by employing means available within the workshop society; they also provide insight into the importance of eventfulness in self-esteem maintenance and self-presentation. Further, inclusion of the case histories allows a measure of insight into the operation of the informal sociocultural system within the workshop.

The Workshop and Its Clients

Establishing the parameters of the social world which the workshop clients inhabit is a fundamental first step in the discussion of socioemotional adjustment to conditions of daily life. For these individuals, social ecology can be roughly segmented into workshop and external social environments. The workshop employs 220 clients, most of whom are in the mild to moderate ranges of mental retardation. The workshop is located in suburban Los Angeles, and most of the clients come from middle-class backgrounds. There are also, currently, seven group homes affiliated with the workshop, each housing six clients.

The workshop provides various work programs in which clients might be engaged. Most clients are employed on the several small assembly lines. Contracts include packaging record albums, skateboard and motorcycle parts, stationery, exercise pads, make-up kits, and surgical equipment. Disassembly of telephone parts and the assembly of bath article gift sets and parts for airplane seats are also common tasks. Some clients are responsible for handling heated sealing machines, drill presses, or small spot welders. Clients in the role of "leadworker" or "assistant lead" assist production supervisors by counting work and providing materials for other clients as needed. These roles are prestigious and eagerly sought after by the general client population. In addition to employment on the assembly lines, there are 10 full time and 9 part time client positions on the grounds-maintenance crew and 12 clients are employed in the kitchen, in food preparation and service. Finally, there is a ceramics room which employs 15 clients in the production of planters, windchimes, ashtrays, and various other decorative items.

In addition to these work programs, the workshop provides habilitation services as well. During the research period, there were five counselors, each with individual clients assigned to them. In accordance with federal law, each client must be provided with an Individual Program Plan (IPP) aimed at meeting his or her particular habilitation needs. The counselors are charged with development and implementation of these IPPs. Clients may be concurrently enrolled in a social skills group, a speech class, a recreation class and/or a diet class. Counselors are also available if a client has a personal or interpersonal problem. However, clients are more likely to approach a counselor for rather mundane interpersonal problems (e.g., "Jane is bugging me!") than for more pronounced socioemotional problems. More pronounced problems, afterall, occur less frequently, and there is also some reluctance on the part of many clients to divulge personal information to the counselors, apparently due to an association that clients make between counseling staff and an authority structure. There is a well-articulated, informal network of peer-counseling which clients employ quite frequently for more pronounced problems.

Workshop Rounds

The workday begins at 8:30 a.m. Prior to this, clients circulate on the lunchyard, drinking coffee and/or socializing. Work continues until the morning 10-minute break period at 10:00 a.m. The lunch period runs from 11:15 a.m. until 12:00 p.m., and there is an afternoon break from 1:50–2:00 p.m. The workday ends at 3:30 p.m., at which time the clients promptly leave for home. Over half of the clients ride to and from work on "workshop buses," 61 ride the RTD (Los Angeles city bus line), and 40 use private transport. That the bus rides provide an opportunity for additional social interaction is evident from the innumerable "bus incidents" reported either informally or in group meetings. The various habilitative services mentioned are generally interspersed throughout the workday and staggered across the work week so as to minimize disruption of job performance. One additional main feature of the work routine is rotation. Every 6 weeks, clients are rotated from one "line" to another. Thus, one's immediate workmates are regularly changed. One may also request being rotated at any time if interpersonal problems are severe.

Social Roles

For many clients, work is the primary motivation for attending the workshop. These clients develop a social identity as "workers," and the main focus of their attention and conversation is on the performance of their assigned tasks. Their self descriptions are filled with references to their respective roles within "the shop" and many such clients stylistically resemble the stereotypical "workingman." For example, Stan approached and was greeted by the researcher. He responded, "Hey, how the hell are you? How's your wife been treating you, Joe. Man, I'm so busy! We got a lot of work in! Gotta get it out of the shop today!" Clients may, of course, shift personae trans-situationally, and often do, but for many clients, the preferred identification is as a worker. For at least as many others, however, job performance as a form of identification is secondary to its value to social interaction. These clients have been described as "socialites" (Turner, 1983). The workshop provides an arena for positive comparisons with fellow clients, a high degree of social stimulation, and the development and maintenance of peer relations. Many clients enjoy a stable, long-term relationship with a member of the opposite sex, maintain same-sex friendships, and are members of one of several "small circles" of friends. Some clients, of course, are relative social isolates who socialize little, and still others move from one rather temporary relationship to another. Sustaining one's peer relations during a 45-minute lunch period and two 10-minute breaks is quite a challenge. However, much socializing is carried on during the workday as well. Structured behavior observations conducted in the workshop proper indicate that clients spend approximately half of their time either engaged in social interaction or in "monitoring" workshop activity while they are performing their assigned tasks. The work-related aspects of the workshop clearly do not preclude social stimulation.

Home Life

In general, the social environment outside the workshop is quite different. Approximately 70% of all clients live in a parental or familial home, with most of the remainder living in "family care" facilities that house six or fewer individuals. After workshop hours, contact with one's peers is often limited to occasional and regulated telephone conversations. Clients commute to the workshop from numerous communities spread throughout the northern Los Angeles area. Few clients have the opportunity to visit one another during the evenings or on weekends, and much time is spent in one's room watching television or listening to a radio or stereo. These observations are based in part on data obtained from 48 clients on their respective leisure and recreational activities and in part on numerous informal comments made by various workshop clients during the course of this research. Individuals averaged approximately 7 hours of television viewing per weekday, and it is not uncommon for clients to have virtually the entire weekly television schedule memorized. It is apparent, and not at all surprising, that television viewing occupies a significant portion of the leisure time of many workshop clients. Weekends provide little relief from this solitary existence. As one woman remarked, "That's the part I don't like. I'm always alone, both ways, and weekends and holidays too." Another woman who is very active socially within the workshop complained, "Oh God, just don't let the weekends come!"

Many clients identify strongly with and imitate characters and celebrities from television and films. It is common for individuals to name such luminaries among a list of their friends or to claim associations with them. Many clients aspire to such a career and lifestyle themselves. In some cases, identification is more direct or overt. A number of male clients actually claim to *be* "the Fonz," affecting a syncopated gait, snapping their fingers, using stock phrases, and insisting that they are the *real* Fonz. Other popular characters and shows receive similar treatment. The fact that the primary figures with which many clients identify are from cancelled shows or shows no longer popular with the wider viewing audience is a notable characteristic of this phenomenon. It is, in part, explained by the popularity of late afternoon television, which features various recycled series. An equally plausible, noncontradictory explanation is that those perhaps outdated figures often demonstrate "super powers" of strength, magic, or romance (i.e., Wonder Woman or the Incredible Hulk).

Among groups of friends at the workshop, television serves as a lively topic of conversation as well. Groups of clients have been observed discussing the current ratings of certain TV shows, changes in the TV schedule and the inevitable reruns with the advent of summer, plot development of various serials, and their support of opposition to television violence and sex. A number of individuals fill their lunch and break periods with discussions of recent developments in their favorite shows or reenactments of episodes as characters themselves. Certain individuals have, at times, registered extreme distress over the injury or misfortune of a "friend" or favorite character. Many have reported dreams which included such celebrities or characters. In short, television occupies an important place in the social lives of many workshop clients, especially those who are more socially isolated when away from the workshop.

Social Activities

The degree of social activity outside of the workshop is highly variable from client to client. Many are members of various bowling leagues, social clubs, and church groups. Many attend bi-weekly dances at a local park recreational center. For a number of clients, however, there is no involvement with peers outside of the workshop. For these clients, the workshop is an even more important source of social stimulation. Even the socially active clients have relatively little external social life. Bowling leagues meet once a week, social clubs sponsor periodic bus trips, church groups meet once a week and dances are held two Fridays per month. Even so, 32 of the 48 clients sampled reported that they "go out more and do more things than most people." The social activities reported by those "busy" clients were primarily events highly novel and relatively low in frequency, such as trips to Disneyland, Magic Mountain, camping trips, and the like. Trips to see movies were also typically reported, but few clients could claim to have been to a movie within the recent past; many did not remember the last picture they had seen. What might seem on the surface to be rich and varied is, in fact, rather sparse compared to the social lives of most single adults in Southern California. One may say with some assurance that the life of the workshop client is one of relatively restricted mobility and heightened dependency. Much leisure time is spent isolated from one's peers and engaged in solitary entertainment; available social activities are, for the most part, organized, run on a schedule, and supervised. Most individuals are allowed to make few major decisions and, in general, life affords little spontaneous activity. Break periods at the workshop are an exception, although these too are scheduled and supervised. Social stimulation is low if all spheres of life are taken into account.

Boredom and Relief

Boredom is a subjective state and is not necessarily related to the level of actual eventfulness in one's life. The critical and unavoidable fact is that with prolonged and direct involvement with member of the workshop client population, boredom has emerged as a major expressed concern of the clients themselves. In informal conversations, in group peer-counseling meetings, and in the administration of measures of emotional state, the subject of boredom was repeatedly brought up. Further, despite widespread claims of an event-filled existence, clients have often equated their boredom with a lack of eventfulness. As one man put it, "If you got nothing to do, what can I do?" Individuals' expectations of the degree of eventfulness which is desirable and attainable are to some extent influenced by the group or persons with which comparisons are made. It is likely that for many clients, notions of an "optimal level" (Berlyne, 1960) of eventfulness are based on the frenetic and idealized encapsulations of life presented on the television screen, whereas other clients are more likely to utilize normal adults as a reference group in assessing an optimal level of eventfulness. "Grown-ups" are described as being very "busy," having tremendous responsibilities both at work and at home, and as being highly active socially, having both a vast network of social relationships and an endless flow of social activities. Adults are also described as independent, having the freedom "to to anywhere you want, anytime," and as being self-satisfied and fulfilled. Clearly, such conditions do not describe the lives of workshop clients.

Nevertheless, for many of the less socially isolated clients, who have a greater opportunity to interact with normal adults in a wider range of settings, those adults serve as a primary reference group against which comparisons are made and upon which aspirations are based.

The restricted mobility and heightened dependency that characterizes the lives of workshop clients precludes, to a large extent, the possibility of increased social activity. Given the limitation of social resources, it does not seem surprising that workshop clients might attempt to construct an event-filled life from the resources that *are* available by maximizing the eventfulness potential of seemingly commonplace occurrences or other events of apparently little significance. Thus, a fundamental aspect of the socioemotional adjustment process of workshop clients is concerned with raising the level of eventfulness in life. This involves redefining the nature of certain events to make them more personal, more timely, more intense, or more "real" relative to what is perceived as normal. To consider this "artificial eventfulness" is not accurate, because the phenomena that emerge as patterned group responses to the perceived lack of eventfulness are not merely reported but are more or less emphatically claimed as experience. In a certain sense, life actually does become more eventful through the process of redefining it, reporting it, and reacting to it as such.

Beyond alleviating boredom by providing an adequate degree of social stimulation, eventfulness-raising displays often function in the maintenance of self-esteem and social identity as well. Clients asked to provide self descriptions commonly responded with a list of activities, for example, "Let's see, I'm a good bowler, I go places a lot, I'm always busy, I got friends all over." A number of clients made statements indicating low self-esteem, such as, "I don't want to say in front of my friends. I don't think much of myself, I'll say that!" Generally those respondents were clients who led more restricted and limited social lives. Client perceptions of normal adulthood can be adequately represented by the equation "Grown-up = Busy." There is an obvious desirability to having a social identity or *persona* which includes a complex network of both relations and activities. Whether normal adults or television and film personalities serve as an individual's primary reference group, being "busy" is perceived as most attractive to oneself and to others. Although it may often remain unclear whether such eventfulness-raising displays are more strongly related to the maintenance of self-esteem or to the formulation of a self-concept or social identity, it does seem obvious that eventfulness and meaningfulness are not mutually exclusive.

However, raising the level of eventfulness in life by redefinition is, to some extent, contingent on both a shared set of assumptions about the plasticity of social reality and on the consent or collusion of one's peers in the act of eventfulness-raising. At the very least, implicit agreement as to the appropriateness of eventfulness-raising displays is necessary. It is not enough for an individual to make claims of an eventful life; those claims must be believable and valuable in the eyes of one's peers, otherwise one runs the risk of having those claims negated and one's reputation diminished. In short, it is not advisable to make claims on too grandiose a scale; it is helpful to provide some sort of substantiation with even the most circumstantial or fabricated evidence. It is not acceptable to claim eventfulness at the expense of another; instead, the event should be generalizable so the audience may share involvement, and one must acknowledge the reciprocity inherent in the mutual acceptance of such behavior. In studying the socioemotional adjustment process of workshop clients with respect to the concern with boredom and eventfulness, a number of informally constructed means of raising the level of eventfulness in life have been identified, and, in each case, redefinition of "events" is based both on the plasticity or malleability of certain aspects of social reality and on the implicit agreement among workshop clients regarding the appropriateness or acceptability of certain behaviors which contribute to raising eventfulness. By providing descriptions and examples of each of the various means available to workshop clients for making life more eventful and more meaningful and by providing an explanation of how this system is internally regulated, an answer is supplied to the question raised earlier, "If you got nothing to do, what can I do?"

Vicarious Eventfulness

Vicarious eventfulness entails taking part, or exaggerating one's part, in the events in the life of a meaningful other person. Generally, this "other" is a close friend, co-worker, or relative. However, one's favorite celebrity is also occasionally the object. A commonly witnessed example of vicarious eventfulness is: "My sister's gonna have a baby; (then more emphatically) *I'm* gonna be an *Uncle!*" Another common example is the very excited, sometimes proud reporting of a family member's birthday. One woman, whose father had taken a trip to Europe, provided a weekly update on his itinerary (in detail); when he returned, she brought a pile of photos to the workshop, proudly showing them and passing them around to friends while she described each. The vicarious experiencing of an event in another person's life is not limited solely to positively valued experiences. For example, one man stated, "I have a problem. Jim and Don had a fight last night and they got in trouble with Fanny (the resident caretaker)." One woman, Deanna, reported for 3 consecutive weeks that she was distressed over "Tattoo's" (a character in a popular television show) supposed real-life marital problems. By de-emphasizing the distinction between self and other and personalizing events occurring in another person's life, individuals are able to raise the level of eventfulness in their own lives and, perhaps, enhance their feelings of self-worth as well.

Prolonged Eventfulness

Prolonged eventfulness is achieved when an individual attaches immediate significance to an event somewhat removed from the present (either past or future). The event in question is part of the individual's own life-experience, only it occurred some time ago or has yet to occur. Shortly after this researcher started visiting the workshop, I was asked very excitedly if I was going to attend "the Bazaar." I responded in the affirmative and asked when it was being held. I was told, "October something." The conversation took place in early August of that year. Perhaps the most graphic example came from a woman who excitedly volunteered, "My hair's gonna be soooo blond!" When asked why, she responded, "The sun's gonna bleach it when I get out in that sun." An ensuing conversation clarified her reference to a trip to Hawaii which was planned for 8 months into the future. Prolonged eventfulness is not restricted to positively valued events. Frequently, Paula has approached me sobbing. When I ask what is troubling her, she responds, "I miss my mother." Then I tell her that I am sorry, and she smiles. "That's okay, she's been gone a long time," she adds and walks away. John has been brought to tears on a number of occasions by the mention of his long-deceased parents. Prolonged eventfulness is marked by the conveyance of a sense of immediacy in relating an event from one's own life, but one somewhat removed from the present. By temporarily relaxing the temporal distinctions of past, present, and future, individuals are able to make the "here and now" considerably more event-filled.

Exaggerated Eventfulness

To make life more eventful and to gain and hold the valuable attention of one's peers, "events" are often generated by the exaggeration of relatively routine or mundane happenings. Examples include highly dramatic statements, such as, "I had pot roast last night!" or "'Dallas' is on tonight!" or "I lost 2 pounds!" Seemingly invented or exaggerated "problems" are likewise often reported. One woman claimed that her mother was going to make her quit the workshop and that they were going away because she (the client) had said "Shit!" Another woman stated that she couldn't live at home anymore; her mother was making her leave because of arguments that she was constantly having with her mother about cleaning her room. Each of these women was able to gain attention and verbal support from peers, and neither woman actually had to move. Many clients seem to change their problems as often as they change socks. Sam lost his girlfriend to Dale a number of years ago. Yet, on a regular basis, Sam has presented continued, yet distinctly varied complaints about Dale. Dale has supposedly followed him around, fought with him, picked on him, told him to "shut up," and refused to leave him alone at various times; in reality, Dale has never been observed in direct interaction with Sam. Paula has reported a number of problems with anonymous "boys" who have picked on her, teased her, laughed at and bothered her, either on the lunch line or on the bus. When asked who they are, she has routinely responded with "Oh, never mind, they're alright." By elevating mundane events to a more profound level of experience and by generating or exaggerating personal problems from events in the daily routine, individuals may win immediate attention and support from peers, as well as gaining a sense of having an event-filled existence. One then appears loved or successful, as well as "busy," all of which are considered characteristics of the ideal normal adult.

Actual Problems

Often, actual personal problems, albeit generally those of smaller significance, can provide access to attention and support and can apparently be rewarding in themselves. In one group peer counseling meeting, Tim began to talk about a problem that Susy was having. "Hey, that's supposed to be *my* story!" she said (and took over from there). Jilly was relating problems that she was having with some male clients who rode on her bus. Her boyfriend Phil kept interrupting her in order to reassure her that everything was alright. Jilly became increasingly frustrated and finally threw up her hands and said, "Okay, I guess I don't have any problem!" She began to sulk, but Phil finally kissed her into better spirits. Two clients, each in response to a death in their respective families, exhibited quite similar behavior. Each man would approach an individual, solemnly inform the listener of the death, and then smile broadly, presumably in anticipation of condolences. One of these men received so much attention over the death of his brother that he spent a preponderance of his time walking around the workshop soliciting sympathetic responses. Finally, he was given a job working outside on the grounds-maintenance crew. These latter examples indicate how even rather profound personal problems with presumably negative value may be somewhat rewarding to a client, providing attention and support from others, both of which are positively valued. Further, personal problems are recognized as part of the lives of normal adults. Thus, actual personal problems may raise the level of eventfulness in one's life in a positive way and have a positive effect on one's self-esteem.

Normalcy Fabrications

Normalcy fabrications entail assertions, and perhaps elaborations, of a presumably "normal" existence outside of the workshop (Turner, 1983). Some of the more elaborate versions persist over time, seemingly indefinitely, despite obviously contradictory information about the client's life. Normalcy fabrications no doubt contribute to the maintenance of self-esteem, and they also provide a certain amount of excitement or meaningfulness for the client. For example, "I got a new job!" (outside of the workshop) is frequently reported. One woman insisted that she had been hired to work as a mathematics professor at UCLA, then proceeded to demonstrate her expertise to her peers by adding up a column of numbers incorrectly. The same woman, some months later, claimed to have been hired as a parks maintenance person, also at UCLA. One man routinely insists that he has been hired either to manage the workshop in some capacity, to manage a television station, or to work as TV actor. Reports of verifiably fictitious trips to Paris and beyond are relatively common as well. Other fabrications include the development of an entire family structure, complete with detailed life histories of spouse and children. One man, aged 49, asserts that he lives in Beverly Hills, that his wife works at "The Brown Derby," and that he has two children. He produces photographs from his wallet to substantiate their existence. In fact, the man lives with his brother and sister-in-law. Assertions of a normal existence outside of the workshop are routinely met with acceptance or compliance on the part of one's peers. The fabrication of what are perceived as normal experiences entails a disavowal or denial of the distinction between "handicapped" and "normal," and de-emphasizes the distinction between "real" and "imaginary." Normalcy fabrications may enhance one's self-esteem and provide a certain amount of heightened eventfulness and meaningfulness in the lives of some of the workshop clients.

Fantasy Identification

Fantasy identification involves taking on the identity of various movie or television actors or characters, with no admission of pretense. Occasionally, this identification is with an anonymous "Wells Fargo Agent," policeman, or even security guard; in these cases, badges and/or nametags are generally offered in support of one's claims. The actors who most commonly serve as the objects of fantasy identification are Olivia Newton-John, John Travolta, Lee Majors, and Henry Winkler. The characters that clients most often claim to be are "The Fonz," "The Bionic Man" or "The Bionic Woman," "James Bond," "The Incredible Hulk," and "Wonderwoman." Acting out one's fantasies is also acceptable, short of adamant insistence on the reality of the identity. If one becomes too vocal or aggressive about these claims, explicit, yet informal constraints are placed on the individual by his or her peers, and the perpetrator is forced to renege. Generally, one assumes the demeanor and distinctive mannerisms of one's hero, makes repeated references to working at a "studio" or on a particular show, and alludes to intimate social relationships with other celebrities mentioned by name. This identification with the "larger than life" figures from television and film undoubtedly enhances self-esteem and provides a measure of excitement to individuals who otherwise fill roles not unlike those of any other factory worker. Much like Walter Mitty, the distinction between reality and imagination is reduced or eliminated and life becomes immediately more fulfilling. That other workshop clients comply with the acting out of fantasies by those who indulge is of special significance. Without compliance, fantasies would perforce remain internalized. Instead, they become part of the self-presentations of a number of clients.

Fantasy Entertainment

Fantasy entertainment is differentiated from fantasy identification primarily by the lack of identification with any specific character and by the recognition of the fantastic quality of one's endeavor. In fantasy entertainment, the fact that one is "pretending" is generally clearly stated. Despite the recognition that the events are imaginary, there is no apparent attempt at excluding the *act* of "imagining" from consideration as valid and valuable activity in everyday life. This form of entertainment is engaged in by either individuals or small groups. Most commonly, individuals admit to the existence of a fictive home, family, and perhaps a network of social relations. One man has stated, "I like to pretend that I'm a woman. I pretend to fix up my hair and talk to my girlfriends; I just like to see what it feels like." There has been no indication, either by observation or reputation, that this man is either homosexual or bisexual. In the group peer-counseling meetings, discussion occasionally evolves into a group construction of a "dream" narrative in which individual group members take on various active roles in the supposed dream. Common themes include a wedding and honeymoon and an adventure in a haunted house. On the lunchyard, small groups occasionally act out brief scenarios from either "Grease" or "Saturday Night Fever." Although there is some measure of identification with the stars, the actors are admittedly "only pretending," and thus this activity is considered as entertainment. In short, fantasy entertainment provides yet another means for workshop clients to make life more eventful, and often more nearly normal, by temporarily relaxing the boundary between reality and fiction.

Idealistic Expectations

Finally, there are idealistic expectations, which can be described as a belief in a more normal existence in the future. Often, elaborate planning goes into what are quite unrealistic expectations for the future. Most of the workshop clients will undoubtedly remain in sheltered employment throughout the course of their adult lives, and only 3 of the 220 clients are married. For most of the remaining clients, prospects are low. However, a number of individuals (and couples) claim that they want to "settle down" someday, to get married and have children. One man has stated that he wouldn't like to remain a bachelor for his entire life, but wants to get married and buy a farm in Iowa. A number of women have reported making regular trips to a local bakery to look at wedding cakes and admit to perusing bridal magazines in their leisure time. For many individuals, their expectations for the future include getting a more prestigious job once they "get out of the workshop." For others, the goal is heightened independence: to "get out on my own" and have an apartment, a car, and control over one's finances. Despite the improbability of such outcomes, idealistic expectations make a very real contribution to the maintenance of self-esteem and the presentation of a more normal social identity. The difference between what has been termed "prolonged eventfulness" and these idealistic expectations is that these expectations are not related to actual events designated for the future but, rather, refer to hoped-for, yet presumably unattainable goals. For most of the workshop clients, the likelihood of attaining these goals may not be great, but such expectations provide the excitement and hope of planning for the future and add direction and meaning to the present.

Internal Regulation of the System

At the heart of this informal social system is an inherent reciprocity in the acceptance of eventfulness-raising behavior. In allowing an individual to make certain claims of eventfulness, there is an implicit expectation that similar "indulgences" will be granted the other participants at some later point in time. As social harmony is highly valued among workshop clients (Turner, 1983), peer interactions tend to be nonconfrontive and the acceptance of such displays is encouraged indirectly by the wider social milieu. Even so, there appears to be a set of specific, yet unspecified, principles which keeps the system in operation. The generalizability of one's eventfulness-raising displays is often a key factor: To what extent does the event of one client become an event in the lives of those around him or her? The more generalizable the event reported, the more likely it is to be accepted. Likewise, the question of whether one's report reflects positively or negatively on the quality of the lives of those around him or her is a key factor in determining the acceptability of a claim. If one's report of eventfulness indirectly implies that members of the audience are in some way depressed or deprived, that claim is apt to be challenged. Thus, reporting the death of a loved one, for example, might allow others present to participate in that "event" vicariously and, at the same time, allow those others to make a positive valuation of their own life situations. Moderation is a third key factor in deciding the acceptability of individual claims of eventfulness. Reported events ought not to contradict either the unspoken social "rules" of the workshop or the workshop social order. Accounts that are too emotionalized or too grandiose are also apt to be challenged by one's peers and subverted. During the course of this research, the monitoring and modification of eventfulness-raising displays was observed as continuously as the displays themselves. Examples of the most common types of "offense," or recognized breach of conduct, and the nature of group responses will undoubtedly make the system and its regulation more understandable.

Grandiose Claims

Grandiose claims of eventfulness have perhaps been most commonly observed. Generally, such claims undergo a process of mediation, whereby one is forced to settle on a more realistic, yet suitable compromise. Tim claimed to be an actor who had won an "Oscar." This claim was challenged, and, following a brief group debate, he grudgingly settled on having been the winner of a local talent show. After this, everyone present agreed that Tim was a "very talented guy." In one instance, cited earlier, a woman claimed to have been hired as a mathematics professor at UCLA. She was asked to prove her expertise by adding up a column of three digit numbers. Although she was obviously inept, in that some of her peers could and did point out her mistake, she was spared further embarrassment by creating an atmosphere of entertainment which left the listeners satisfied that she was *perhaps* pretending. She was not forced to renege however. Many of the eventfulness-raising displays which have been characterized by the term "normalcy fabrications" are grandiose in scale. It is not surprising that, for the most part, such fabricated alternate lives remain private and are admitted more in confidence than among larger groups of peers.

Gross Repetition

A number of clients have been designated by their peers as "broken records" because of their propensity to fixate on either one event or one person and continually bring up what is considered "old news" *ad nauseum*. Kenny is such an individual. He would routinely complain of Sully barging into his room at home and of Sully's problems with the housemother. His only other topic of interest was repeated with equal frequency: Lisa was jealous of his spending time with other female clients and would hit him. Whenever Kenny would attempt to explain his "problems," a chorus of his peers would echo: "Oh no, not again!" Matt's persistent reporting of recurrent dreams about his dead grandparents and problems at home with his teenage sister would elicit more coercive responses. "Sit down and shut up, Matt!" or some variation thereof, was a common group refrain. Such highly repetitive displays provide nothing for the listeners, except perhaps a reminder that life is, in reality, just that monotonous.

Norm violations

Claims that violate workshop social norms have generally been reacted to with immediacy and force. A number of clients have, at various times, reported either "going out with" a supervisor or being awarded a job as supervisor or counselor. The distinction between staff and clients is inviolate however. Tim, on one occasion, boasted of having been appointed as head of the maintenance division, "manager of the shop." Phil challenged him and suggested that he just might ask the authentic supervisor of maintenance about that. Phil did not relent in this threat until Tim had begged, in tears and humiliation, that Phil forgive him. Even then, his assurance was only tentative. Claims of having argued with or "told off" members of staff have also been common. In general, clients are not willing to listen to the intricacies of such accounts, but instead issue stiff reprimands to the claimant. Highly unpopular staff members may be open to criticism. However, such individuals have usually not remained at the workshop for very long either. Reports of events that contain threats of violence against any member of the workshop population, staff or client, are generally strictly censured. Although one might claim, "He better watch out for me, I'm dangerous, I could kill somebody!" it appears strictly unacceptable to make a direct threat. On occasions when such threats were made, those present protested vigorously in all cases.

Labeling: A Last Resort

Beyond the undesirable possibility of having one's claims challenged if they do not satisfy these informal criteria, persistent offenders are faced with the added incriminations of a labeling process. Aside from the label "broken record," there is a series of other descriptive terms which may be applied to those who do not conform to the behavior norms of the workshop client population. Individuals who persist in reporting interpersonal problems with staff or peers and do so in an agitated state, those who make threats of physical violence, or even those who persist in verbal aggression are likely to be added to the list of recognized workshop "troublemakers." Those who are given to highly emotional reactions, either people who act "silly" by laughing nervously while they attempt to provide some reported event or those who routinely resort to tears as a form of communication, are apt to be labeled a "baby" by their peers. The term "crazy" is reserved for those individuals whose fantasies get the best of them and are unable to face the mediation process.

In short, this informal system for raising the level of eventfulness in one's life does not simply exist unconstrained by sensibilities. Behavior is monitored from within, and, in many cases, behavior is regulated by peer intervention. Those individuals who unremittingly exceed the boundaries of accepted workshop propriety are subjected to the labeling process described. Thus, extreme behavior that might be described as either social disruptive or self-destructive is discouraged by the system itself.

Beyond examination of the system as such, an attempt has also been made to document the system in action, as it is utilized by individual clients. Several individuals were followed intensively in order to determine the extent of their social lives outside of the workshop and the relative salience of boredom as an expressed concern in their lives. Case histories were accumulated documenting how this informal system has been employed by individuals over time for the relief of boredom and the role that the creation of a more event-filled existence may have played in the maintenance of their self-esteem and social identity. Four such case histories are presented as an illustration of how the system has been utilized by specific individuals.

Case #1 Mitch

Mitch is 29 years old and lives at home with his parents. He has an older brother (married) and attests to having had a twin brother who died in childhood, although there is no record of this in his file. Mitch is mildly retarded with a history of psychiatric disturbances, including a "nervous breakdown" 3 years ago. Other than this, he has no medical problems. Prior to his employment at the workshop, Mitch attended special classes at a regular high school and then worked for a time as an orderly in a local hospital. He either quit or was fired because of "problems with the patients." For the past 8 years, he has been at the workshop where he resists attempts by his social worker and his counselor to place him in more habilitative work settings. Outside of the workshop, Mitch sees little of his peers. He is not involved in any organized social activities. He used to see his girlfriend on intermittent weekends and for special occasions like birthdays, holidays, or for infrequent "double dates" with his girlfriend's sister and her boyfriend. However, they broke up altogether towards the end of the research period. Mitch attends church regularly and often goes camping with his family. At the workshop, he is a "socialite," well-liked by most clients, and, when observed, he spent most of his free time with his girlfriend. Mitch does not belong to any of the smaller circles of friends; he is somewhat introverted much of the time. However, he is easily upset and becomes quite animated when faced with perceived threats to his self-esteem.

Over the course of the 16-month period during which he was studied intensively, Mitch was continually and actively involved in raising the level of eventfulness in his life. At two separate times, first early in the research period and then again about midway through, Mitch became quite distraught about his brother's marital problems. Each time, Mitch spent weeks going over the "facts" of the separation, the possibilities for divorce, and his brother's irresponsibility. He claimed involvement as a confidant and advisor, asking, "What should I do? I don't know what to tell them." Each time the couple was reconciled, much to Mitch's relief. Also, early in the research period, Mitch's girlfriend's parents were divorced and he got quite upset about the matter. He was concerned with the possible effects of the divorce on his girlfriend, Dee. Again, he cited his role as confidant and suggested that Dee's adjustment to the divorce was dependent on his ability to minister to her needs. In each of these instances, Mitch became emotionally involved in events in the lives of persons close to him. He characterized his role in these events as that of a quite competent lay counselor, thus enhancing his own self-image at the same time that his life was made more eventful.

Much more important in Mitch's life were his idealistic expectations for his relationship with Dee. For almost 6 years, they had planned to be married on Valentine's Day, 1982, although both remain highly dependent on their respective parents. Their plans included looking at wedding invitations, attempting to find an apartment, working on a "budget," and the wedding itself. "We gotta get photo books, I gotta furnish the flowers, get a tuxedo, buy the ring, and her parents do the rest." Their plans also included outside employment, "In about two or three months, I'm gonna be working in a hospital. I already got an arrangement with (a counselor) and everybody. I'll have a white uniform, maybe I can buy a stethoscope. I should do down and get a doctor's Ph.D. in school, but I already know it, I already learned it." Sometime later, he claimed that he was going to work at a local university in the cafeteria, but neither job materialized, and they "split up" two months prior to the proposed marriage date.

Mitch also presented exaggerated problems throughout the research period. These accounts became more frequent and more demonstrative following his breakup with Dee. In August, Mitch said that Dee had returned from her vacation, and when she returned to the workshop, she'd be in a "bad mood" because of a crisis in her family. He was afraid that she would take her anger out on him. "If you see her, don't tell her I'm here." He added, "She's out for blood!" When Dee announced in December that she would move away with her reunited parents, Mitch was upset. However, when asked if he was hurt by the cancelled marriage plans, he said, "Well, ya, but she's sensitive. If I get upset, then she'll cry and go tell her mother, and she'll tell her brother, 'Put him in the grave'. Then my dad will get mad and go beat up her dad. Then you'll have a feud, like the Hatfields and the McCoys."

Shortly after this incident, Mitch's family had a reported dispute with a neighbor. Mitch claimed to have threatened first the wife and then the husband. He said that the man had squirted him with a garden hose, that he had taken the hose away, and had said, "I'm gonna stick that hose right up your fucking asshole." He continued the account with the threat of slashing their tires and the eventual possibility of another family feud. This outburst was precipitated by the neighbors' request that Mitch's family park their camper in another place. At this time, Mitch claimed to have had 50 girlfriends before Dee, and that one had wanted to have his baby. Finally, when Mitch's transistor radio was supposedly stolen, he insisted, "I'm gonna get the cops in on this." His plan involved getting fingerprints and then having his father beat the culprit soundly.

Throughout the course of this research project, Mitch was able to generate a consistent flow of events in his life. He involved himself in the affairs of other persons and exaggerated his role in the resolution of their problems. Also, by holding elaborate and unrealistic expectations for his marriage to Dee, and, when those began to fade, by generating a series of new and equally exaggerated problems, Mitch succeeded in maintaining an event-filled existence. To a large extent, his self-esteem had been dependent on his relationship with Dee, and, when she terminated the relationship, Mitch's self-description changed from that of a devoted and tender mate and friend to that of a dangerous and volatile "tough guy." His aggression remained verbal and appeared to shore up an otherwise damaged self-image. Once Mitch found a new girlfriend, his threats and gestures subsided almost immediately.

Throughout the course of the research, Mitch's behavior was subject to modification by his peers on only two observed occasions. When he first claimed that he was going to receive outside employment, he was ambiguous but made his supposed position at the hospital sound as though he would be more important than the doctors. This provoked a series of pointed questions from his peers, and he became more explicit and considerably more moderate in his assertions. Later, when his radio was stolen, Mitch initially made a direct threat to assault a suspected client. When it was suggested that he would be suspended from the workshop for fighting, Mitch decided to have his father exact retribution. The threats he made against his neighbors remained unchallenged by his peers, possibly due to the presence of those situations outside of the shared reality of the workshop. In short, by creating an event-filled existence, and even by weaving his incredible "tales of power," Mitch was attempting to present an impression of himself which was more self-reliant, more active, more assertive, and, indeed, more nearly normal than was the case.

Case #2   Greg

Greg is 31 years old, is mildly mentally retarded, and lives in a mobile home with his elderly mother, a 53-year-old sister, and a 32-year-old Down's Syndrome brother, Buddy, who is also a workshop client. Greg was born with multiple birth defects, including kidney problems, a blocked urinary tract, "club" feet, spina bifida, a hole in his heart, and a slight case of microcephaly. His medical history is long; he has undergone three heart operations, corrective surgery on his urinary tract and on his feet, and hospitalization for numerous kidney infections. Greg is incontinent and must wear a clamp to control urine flow. He has only been employed at the workshop since 1979, when he moved to Los Angeles from New York with his mother and brother. Prior to moving, Greg attended a special school, but he did not begin his formal education until age 12, having been kept at home for "medical reasons." Even so, Greg works as a leadworker and is highly valued by his supervisor.

Greg's social life outside of the workshop is confined to playing pool at the recreation center in the mobile home park and going on family outings. He does not engage in any of the organized activities that many clients do, instead he spends most of his leisure time doing macramé, building models, and playing cards with his mother, sister, and a neighbor. Greg's family still indulges in a regular "Sunday drive." Greg has voiced a desire to "get out more" on his own and feels that his mother restricts him too much. At the workshop, Greg is a "loner," with a strong work orientation and no solid friendships. He is no social isolate, however; during breaks, he generally circulates and socializes with various people for short periods. In the course of this research, he had two relationships with female clients, but each of these was rather superficial, sporadic, and short-lived.

Greg often attempts to raise the level of eventfulness in his life. Throughout the 12 months that he was followed, he maintained a consistent preoccupation with money that he would receive at Christmas time from a Christmas Club that he belonged to. When the holiday season passed, he began looking ahead to the next year's windfall. He also attempted to prolong the excitement of getting new models to work on. Often he would carry a catalogue around with him and point out various models that he intended to purchase at some later date. He had an extended list of his proposed purchases and would call local hobby shops on a regular basis to verify the availability of the desired models. Over a 12-month period, Greg reported only two purchases. At the same time, he regularly volunteered progress reports on various macramé and needlepoint projects that he had started, and he occasionally brought his pieces to the workshop to show to his supervisor, other staff members, and peers. Greg's handiwork remained a tremendous source of pride to him, representing a certain competency and a high degree of work activity away from the workshop. He often speculated freely on the potential fortunes to be made in handicrafts.

Greg also presented a number of accounts of problems that he was having, during which he appeared very angry and suggested rather extreme solutions to what seemed to be far less extreme circumstances. Complaints of disputes over household chores and threats of running away were intermittent throughout the research period. On one such occasion, Greg said that he had had an argument with his sister Betty over his assigned chore of "feeding her damn cat." He said, "We don't get along too good under one roof, we just get on each other's nerves." Greg then suggested that he would have to move away from his family because of his differences with Betty over the cat. On a later date, Greg said that he was worried about what he would do to Roddy, who had "stolen" his former girlfriend, Pam, from him. Greg said, "When I get mad, I'm dangerous. I might really hurt him if I get in a fight with him. One time I punched a hole right through a solid oak door." In Greg's eyes, his problem was not only how to win Pam back but how to control his rage and professed awesome strength. Greg has never been observed in any altercation, disagreement, or insubordination. Further, his relationship with Pam had been virtually non-existent at the best of times. She had courted a series of boyfriends during the same period of time that Greg claimed they were "going together." His assessment of the relationship and his assertions of incredible strength, which were more or less regularly repeated, appear to be attempts at protecting his self-esteem in the face of what he described as a humiliating experience. Over the entire 12-month period of involvement with Greg, he regularly reported break-ups and reunions with both Pam and Sara, his other, mostly mythical girlfriend. Both of these women meanwhile carried on obvious and apparently rather serious relationships with other men and spent little, if any, break time with Greg.

One of Greg's principal concerns was the lack of independence that he experienced. He complained that his mother would not let him take his brother to the zoo on the public bus. In fact, he simply was not allowed to ride on the municipal bus lines at all. Further, he claimed that she restricted him too much by controlling his finances and keeping his money from him. He said that he would have to give up his SSI check, take off on an airplane for Texas, and, after visiting some relatives, live on his own and work in a factory. This final incident provides insight into Greg's expectations (or at least hopes) for the future. He has repeatedly stated that, when his mother dies, he would like to move into his own apartment, live independently, manage his own money and life, and take care of Buddy. Although such developments are highly unlikely, Greg holds them to be possible. "If everything works out okay. I don't know what's in her, you know, her will." Somewhat exaggerated problems and this rather idealistic view of the future provide Greg with a measure of relief from the boredom that he repeatedly cited.

Greg's various recurrent problems were generally interrelated. His complaints about the restrictedness of his social life and the supposedly authoritarian rule of his mother and sister were almost always made as a prelude to a statement of his competency. The implication was that the situation at home was unwarranted. Likewise, the repeated assertions of his physical prowess may be a reaction to his medical condition and the resultant forced constraints on physical and social activities. His continued yet confidential complaints allowed him to vent some of his frustrations as well. Most importantly perhaps, his success as a worker at "the shop" and his "artistic" successes at home contributed significantly to his self-image as competent and independent. His complaints themselves were statements of that competency and self-sufficiency.

Case #3   Don

Don, at age 29, lives with his parents and younger brother in an isolated house on L.A. County reservoir property. At separate times, Don has been classified as either "borderline" or mildly mentally retarded, although he was apparently normal at birth. Don contracted spinal meningitis at the age of 10 months, subsequently suffering cerebral palsy, spastic quadriplegia, blindness in his left eye, and a prognosis that he would be "subnormal" by the time he reached school age. Apparently he progressed well until the age of 14, when he began to develop scoliosis. By the age of 17, Don had to have a brain shunt implanted. A few years later, he began to grow weak and had to start using a wheelchair; by age 27, the shunt malfunctioned, and he lapsed into a coma. The shunt was replaced, and doctors predicted that he would recover and again become ambulatory. However, he still remains confined to a wheelchair and continues to degenerate.

Despite all of his medical problems, Don attended a high school for handicapped students, graduating prior to his coming to the workshop. Aside from an occasional family outing and sporadic church attendance, Don has no social activities outside of the workshop. He spends most of his time at home in his recliner, watching television or listening to the radio. He is an avid sports fan. At the workshop, Don is a "loner"; he is generally liked, but has no enduring friendships. He did have one friend who helped him get his lunch daily, but this man died during the course of this project. Understandably, over the course of the research period, Don's complaint of boredom became an almost constant refrain.

During 13 months of study, Don utilized various means of raising the level of eventfulness in his life. During the research period, both of Don's brothers had marriages planned for more than a year into the future. Don was excited about both of the weddings, although in all likelihood he would be unable to attend either and recognized this fact openly. Early in the research period, Don's parents were involved in a bowling league. Don provided regular updates on how well each was bowling, what the team standings were, and what the chances were for the team winning a trophy. When his parents' team won the league championship, Don was elated although he was unable to attend the awards dinner.

Throughout this period, Don reported several problems related to his condition. Each of these problems was brought up repeatedly, but, in each case, Don resisted advice offered on what he might do to resolve the dilemma. Apparently, he was satisfied with the attention and support derived merely from reporting them. Perhaps Don's most frequently reported problem is the inevitability of his having to move into a "home": "Over and over and over, I do not, simple fact, I do not want to end up in a home. But if it has to come to that, then that's what they're going to do, that's where they're going to put me." Don often complained of his increasing weakness, how it interferes with his work, and how his parents sometimes have to feed him because he is so tired. Even so, he was not involved in any physical therapy or in any regular exercise program. Don has complained of being "teased" by clients who pull his cap over his eyes or laugh at his legs when they "jump around." But he would not tell people to stop because "they don't mean any harm, sometimes I laugh too."

Frequently, Don engaged in fantasy entertainment either by making up poems or by having "dreams," such as pretending that he can walk, that he is married with a lovely wife and child, that he lives in "a real nice condo," or that he is in some idyllic wildlife refuge. Often, such fantasies color Don's perceptions of the present and his expectations for the future. Although Don had not seen his "girlfriend" in almost a year, he said, "Now that she lives just a hop, step and a jump away, I see her every chance I get." As Christmas approached, Don was excited about seeing her at the workshop Christmas party. At the party, this woman spent little time with Don and instead socialized with a number of other workshop clients. Nevertheless, Don continued to proclaim their mutual love. Don's hope for the future is that something will happen to change his predicament, "I like to have fantasies, maybe they might come true, maybe one of these days. Who knows, some miracle might happen." Such comments are not made off-handedly but are prominent and integral to Don's "getting along day by day, stride by stride."

It is evident that every domain of Don's life is affected by his condition. His job performance, his lack of social activities, the taking in of food and drink, even his imagination, flooded with thoughts of another existence, virtually all of his life is defined by his physical condition. Despite Don's outspoken complaint over boredom and his hope for a cure that will allow him a normal and active existence, he actually avoided medical treatment on at least one occasion. For 4 weeks, he had been complaining about his failing health and his parent's failure to make an appointment for him to see a doctor (he had not been to see a doctor since 1979). When, during a group meeting, his counselor, social worker, and peers applied pressure on Don to take the initiative, he responded with: "Hey, I've got great news. I'm fantastic. I'm gettin' so strong, I don't even need the doctor." Evidently his concern with upsetting his parents was greater than his desire to see the doctor. He definitely did *not* want to risk having them move him to the "home" where he had been "bored to death." Instead, he utilized his problems to garner attention and support from those around him.

Don's highly active imagination not only provided him with a means of creating an event-filled life but played an explicit role in his self-esteem maintenance as well. He described the post-operative recovery from his first brain surgery as miraculous, with the nurse running down the hospital corridor shouting. He explained his parent's refusal to allow any future surgery on the grounds of a poor prognosis: "I might come out looking like a vegetable." He repeatedly asserted that although he is physically handicapped, he has a perfectly sound mind: "The doctor said the brain damage didn't do no effect to my thinking, I mean, I can think of a million things."

Case #4   Hal

Hal, 30, lives with his mother, who manages their apartment complex. He has a sister and brother-in-law who live near to him and with whom he is actively involved. Hal is mildly mentally retarded (IQ 59), has Down's syndrome, and is somewhat overweight. He has no additional medical problems. Hal attended special schools for the handicapped prior to his employment at the workshop. He is an active member of the Mormon Church and is involved to some extent in church activities. He is also member of "Diamond Days," a social organization for the handicapped. Family, church, and this social club comprise the entirety of his social activity outside of the workshop. Within the workshop, Hal is a "socialite." Although not integral to any of the smaller circles of friends, he considers himself, and is considered, a friend to all, moving freely from circle to circle. Hal presents himself as being infinitely happy, perfectly socialized, and very much a "Good Samaritan." He is also quite a comedian and commands a great deal of attention from peers when he is "on."

Over the course of a 16-month period of research, Hal utilized several available means for raising the level of eventfulness in his life. Early in our involvement, Hal very excitedly reported that his brother-in-law had made a trip to Utah. He implied that this trip had enhanced his family's standing in the church, and he was quite proud of the accomplishment. As Hal recounted the trip, the listener was made to feel very much as though Hal had had a part in it. On two separate occasions, Hal presented an identical "normalcy fabrication," claiming to be a virtuoso performer on a number of musical instruments including piano, guitar, violin, and accordian. On two other occasions, Hal claimed to be a character on the television series "Barney Miller" and once claimed Robert Redford as a friend. More frequently, Hal employed fantasy for entertainment's sake. He was a regular contributor to the group-constructed "dream" narratives which were occasionally part of group peer-counseling meetings. He also sometimes presented "pretend dreams" of his own, seemingly spontaneously generated, yet fantastic monologues. These comic monologues provided Hal with much attention, as well as his own enjoyment which he shared with the audience. One example of such a monologue involved a description of kissing practices viewed cross-culturally, with "Romanian" nose-kissing, Alaskan body-kissing, and Indian kissing (where the woman grabs the man's "utters" and the man sends "worms" into the woman) were all highlighted. Such performances provide a definite relief from boredom for Hal and all those around him. They also support Hal's self-image as "witty, charming, debonair—everybody likes me. I'm a lovable cuss."

Over the 16-month period, Hal experienced one real expressed problem, which persisted for over 6 months and which Hal increasingly exaggerated. Hal's girlfriend, Perla (a recent emigre from Iran), had been terminated from the workshop for continually attempting to leave the premises during working hours. Hal thought she had left the workshop building in search of her wallet, which he had found on the ground outside, and he felt responsible for her termination. His counselor, Netta, assured him that he was not at fault, that Perla had problems because she couldn't speak English and was frustrated in relationships with other clients. Hal reported, "See, one counselor told her, she told me she won't be in for a while, and I don't believe that. I believe that's a rumour because you hear rumours going around about that. Like one counselor says the next thing, one person says the same thing, and that can lead to the next thing. I told you, everything points to Netta." When Hal learned that Perla's supervisor, Shelley, had reprimanded her for leaving the workroom without permission, Hal asserted that she must have been looking from him because he had learned her language ("Salaam") from her brother. Two weeks later, Perlas's brother had become somewhat less than an ally. "My mother told me not to trust him or anything." Over time, Hal's preoccupation with her brother reached monumental proportions, and Hal finally accused him of having raped a woman at gunpoint outside of Hal's bedroom window.

Shortly after Hal's "problem" had reached this point in its evolution, he began to downplay the entire incident. He said, "Ya, I been talking to her. She's been pretty good. I been helping her a little." Hal insisted that she would come to the next Christmas party and "many other functions and events." He claimed to have seen her in a market and that she was "getting along just fine now." As for her brother, "I thought I saw her brother, 'til I turned on the television. They caught the guy who was doing all the rapings; it was a guy who sounded like him." This exaggerated problem had been a tremendous source of stimulation to Hal for 6 months. Yet, despite the attention and peer-support that he derived from it, he eventually moved rather decisively to reduce its effects on his life. Originally, Hal had felt responsible for Perla's dismissal. He then came to describe himself as a somewhat helpless victim in what became a bizarre scenario. Finally, Hal reaffirmed his persona as the quintessential Good Samaritan who helps people with their problems and brings happiness along his way. He began to present himself again as brimming with self-confidence and blessed with a privileged existence: "Ya, I'm simply adorable. No problems. I never have any problems. Everything's just great!" He had apparently found the social stimulation which he continued to enjoy from his fantasy-oriented entertainment to be more rewarding than the attention that his personal "tragedy" had afforded.

Conclusion

A system of informally constructed means by which members of a sheltered workshop for retarded adults can alleviate boredom and make their lives more eventful and more meaningful has been described. The lives of these individuals are characterized by relatively restricted mobility, heightened dependency, and a relative lack of spontaneous activities. Outside the workshop, many clients experience very little social stimulation. Through prolonged and direct interaction with members of the client population, boredom and the perceived lack of eventfulness have emerged as major expressed concerns of the group. As an adaptive response to conditions in the social environment, an informal system for raising the level of eventfulness has emerged. The system is employed by a large proportion of the workshop clients who differ in many respects. Yet the system is *comprehensive* enough to meet the needs of this varied population. The system is also *flexible*, taking advantage of the plasticity of the boundaries of social reality. To a large extent, the system neutralizes very real differences between what might be termed "event-rich" and "event-poor" clients, allowing anyone who is sufficiently motivated to create a rich and varied existence. Further, this informal system for raising the level of eventfulness in one's life is *socially regulated*. Behavior is monitored by others who may reject certain claims as improper and modify certain other claims. Individuals are characterized by relatively restricted mobility, heightened dependency, and a relative lack of spontaneous activities. Outside the workshop, Finally, this system provides for the socioemotional needs of clients as well. For many clients, self-esteem maintenance and maintaining a healthy social identity are integrally related to the maintenance of an acceptable level of perceived eventfulness.

Individuals quite often have employed a number of techniques and have been both more active or more adamant about claims at some times than others. The extent to which an individual employs eventfulness-raising techniques, and the specific types which he or she employs, relates to a complex of variables. Put simply, boredom and the lack of eventfulness are of more prominent socioemotional relevance for some clients than for others. Individual differences may exist in what might be termed an "optimal level of arousal" (Berlyne, 1960) as well as in the amount and kind of regular and unregulated social activity. Likewise, clients vary greatly with respect to their primary reference group; some primarily make comparisons with peers, others with normal adults, and still others with celebrities and characters from television and movies. For many clients, the relative salience of each reference group has varied across contexts and over time as well. Satisfaction or dissatisfaction with the eventfulness in one's life appears to be related, to some extent, to the identity of the reference group on which such comparisons are based. The social identity of the client as "elite," "socialite," "loner," or "nonconformist" (Turner, 1981), as well as individual personality attributes and stylistic differences in performances, are also relevant factors contributing to group heterogeneity. However, as a set of patterned group responses, the eventfulness-raising techniques of workshop clients suggest that coping with the concerns of day-to-day living fundamentally includes attempts at making life more eventful by redefining the nature of various "events" in terms that make them more personal, more timely, more intense, and more "real." Clients are thereby provided with a richer and more varied existence which alleviates boredom and may also enhance one's self-esteem and social identity or persona.

Given a strict clinical interpretation, this informal system and a good deal of the total set of behaviors that it condones could be considered pathological. Indeed, in terms of the goals of normalization (Wolfensberger, 1980), such responses could also be considered maladaptive. However, when considered in its full context, this elaborate pattern of responses appears to be highly adaptive. The suggestion here is that all analyses involving the imputation of evaluative terms, such as "pathological" or "maladaptive," must be seen as setting-specific. Although attempts by workshop clients to adjust emotionally to conditions in the immediate social environment can be viewed as primarily culturally appropriate, a potential for conflict exists in the discrepancy between values of the workshop culture and larger societal values which place a premium on "realism" and resolution of problems rather than on fantasy and the extenuation, and sometimes positive valuation, of "problems." Sensitivity to this problem of potentially conflicting values is necessary to effective intervention or habilitation (Edgerton, 1982). Professionals charged with the implementation of programs geared toward normalization goals are urged to consider the saliency of the client's concerns with boredom and eventfulness in developing such programs.

References

Baller, W. R., Charles, D. C., & Miller, E. L. (1967). Mid-life attainment of the mentally retarded: A longitudinal study. *Genetic Psychology Monographs, 75,* 235–329.

Berlyne, D. E. (1960). *Conflict, arousal and curiosity.* New York: McGraw-Hill.

Bogdan, R., & Taylor, S. J. (1982). *Inside out: Two first person accounts of what it means to be labeled 'mentally retarded.'* Toronto: University of Toronto Press.

Clark, G. R., Kivitz, M. S., & Rosen, M. (1968). *A transitional program for institutionalized adult retarded.* (Project No. RD 1275–P). Washington, D.C.: Vocational Rehabilitation Administration.

Cobb, H. (1972). *The forecast of fulfillment: A review of research on predictive assessment of the adult retarded for social and vocational adjustment.* New York: Teachers College Press.

Edgerton, R. B. (1967). *The cloak of competence: Stigma in the lives of the mentally retarded.* Berkeley: University of California Press.

Edgerton, R. B. (1982). Deinstitutionalizing the mentally retarded: An example of values in conflict. In A. W. Johnson, O. Grusky, & B. H. Raven (Eds.), *Contemporary health services: Social science perspectives* (pp. 221–235). Boston: Auburn House Publishing Co.

Edgerton, R. B., & Sabagh, G. (1962). From mortification to aggrandizement: Changing self-concepts in the careers of the mentally retarded. *Psychiatry, 25,* 263–272.

Fernald, W. E. (1919). After-care study of the patients discharged from Waverly for a period of 25 years. *Ungraded, 5,* 25–31.

Fiske, D. W., & Maddi, S. R. (1961). *Functions of varied experience.* Homewood, IL: Dorsey Press.

Floor, L., Daxter, D., Rosen, M., & Zisfein, L. (1975). A survey of marriages. *Mental Retardation, 13,* 33–37.

Hegge, T. G. (1944). The occupational status of higher grade mental defectives in the present emergency. *American Journal of Mental Deficiency, 49,* 86–98.

Henschel, A. M. (1972). *The forgotten ones: A sociological study of Anglo and Chicano retardates.* Austin: University of Texas Press.

Mattinson, J. (1970). *Marriage and mental handicap.* London: Duckworth.

Rosen, M., Clark, G., & Kivitz, M. (1977). *Handbook of habilitation: New dimensions in programs for the developmentally disabled.* Baltimore: University Park Press.

Turner, J. L. (1983). Workshop society: Ethnographic observations in a work setting for retarded adults. In K. T. Kernan, M. J. Begab, & R. B. Edgerton (Eds.), *Environments and behavior: The adaptation of mentally retarded persons* (pp. 147–171). Baltimore: University Park Press.

Windle, C. (1962). Prognosis of mental subnormals. *American Journal of Mental Deficiency, 66,* 23–25.

Wolfensberger, W. (1980). A brief overview of the principle of normalization. In R. J. Flynn, & K. E. Nitsch (Eds.), *Normalization, social integration and community services* (pp. 7–30). Baltimore: University Park Press.

Wolfson, I. N. (1956). Follow-up studies of 92 male and 131 female patients who were discharged from the Newark State School in 1946. *American Journal of Mental Deficiency, 61,* 224–238.

The authors are affiliated with the Socio-Behavioral Group, Mental Retardation Research Center (Neuropsychiatric Institute), UCLA. We gratefully acknowledge support for this research from NICHD Grant No. HD 04612, the Mental Retardation Research Center, UCLA, and NICHD Program Project Grant No. HD 11944–02, The Community Adaptation of Mildly Retarded Persons. Special thanks are offered to Dr. Robert Edgerton for his guidance and encouragement and for his patience and assistance in preparing the various forms of revision.

Black "Six-Hour Retarded Children" As Young Adults

Paul Koegel and Robert B. Edgerton

The concept of the six-hour retarded child—retarded from 9 a.m. to 3 p.m., 5 days a week, solely on the basis of performance within the classroom, without regard to adaptive behavior outside the classroom—has been widely influential since its formal introduction over a decade ago (President's Committee on Mental Retardation, 1969). The concept has helped to reduce inequities in labeling based on the criteria of academic failure and IQ, especially when these are not fully appropriate as is often the case with children from isolated rural areas or from low-income ethnic minority neighborhoods. There can be no doubt that six-hour retarded children do exist, not only in Appalachia (Gazaway, 1969) and the inner-city, but throughout the nation (Mercer, 1973). It is also apparent that some persons with IQs below 70 can live more or less normal and unlabeled lives as members of the general population, whether that population is school children in Scotland (Birch, Richardson, Baird, Horobin & Illsley, 1970) or the Swedish Army (Granat & Granat, 1973). Other research suggests that many graduates of educable mentally retarded (EMR) classes more or less "disappear" into the normal population after they leave school (Cobb, 1972; Gruenberg, 1964; MacMillan, 1977).

Although it is commonly acknowledged that inner-city Black children are particularly vulnerable to the six-hour retarded child phenomenon and generally assumed that the majority of Black children who are placed in EMR classes go on to lead largely normal lives after leaving school, there is virtually no relevant detail regarding the lives of previously labeled Black adults in their communities with which to support or reject these assumptions. Mercer's data (1973), often cited in support of the six-hour retarded child concept (or "situationally retarded," in her terms) are suggestive but fail to provide any ethnographic detail concerning non-school environments and behavior. Kernan and Walker (1981), discussing factors affecting the under-utilization of services by Black families from low-income, "inner-city" neighborhoods in Los Angeles, include some data collected through long-term observations of and interviews with a small sample of mildly retarded adults. By and large, however, little is known about the quality of the lives of Black EMR students after they have graduated. Even less is known about the extent to which they identify themselves or are identified by others as being handicapped and their relative success or failure in meeting the demands of daily life.

We previously discussed (Koegel & Edgerton, 1982) various aspects of labeling, perception of handicap, and adaptive behavior among an inner-city population of 45 Black EMR class graduates. Here we look in some detail at the lives of 12 persons in this sample who displayed such apparent social competence that our Black ethnographic field researchers returned from their first visits with each of these persons convinced that they could not be mentally retarded. At first glance, the self-presentation and life circumstances of these 12 individuals were such that they did indeed appear to have blended into their communities-at-large, confirming the popular conception of the six-hour retarded child turned adult. Observations of these individuals over time and in varied settings, however, as well as interviews with them and those who were close to them, revealed a more complex picture. Without calling into question the normal appearances that led field researchers to doubt the appropriateness of the label "mental retardation" in the first place, a more intimate understanding of these individuals challenges the assumption that Black EMR students go on to lead adult lives which cannot be distinguished from those of their non-labeled peers in their inner-city neighborhoods.

Methods

Sample

The larger sample from which these 12 were selected consists of 45 Black adults, all of whom had IQs below 70 and/or had attended EMR classes. Rather than being a probability sample, this group of 45 consisted of individuals chosen because they represented the broad range of competencies and lifestyles found among mildly retarded adults in the Black community (see Koegel & Edgerton, 1982, for a detailed discussion of sample selection and sample demographics). It included individuals who continued to receive services on the basis of being labeled mildly retarded even after completion of formal education. It also included individuals who had attended EMR classes but were no longer receiving services from any agency. This last group was more difficult to locate; however, they were identified with the help of individuals and their parents from the first group, who were more easily located due to their continued agency contact.

The subsample of 12 was selected on one criterion: Ethnographic field researchers, during the course of their first visits with these individuals, expressed serious doubts that they were, in fact, retarded. These 12 individuals, when compared with the larger sample, clearly led more normal lives. As Table 1 reveals, they were more often living on their own or in independent living training programs; were more likely to be competitively employed, or if not competitively employed, to be unemployed (as opposed to working in a sheltered workshop); and were more often married.

Procedure

For 1 year, beginning in September 1980, a staff of Black ethnographic field researchers maintained regular contact with research participants, visiting them for periods of 1 to 4 hours on an average of 12 separate occasions, and speaking with them regularly on the telephone between visits. Field visits took place in a broad range of settings that had significance in the lives of these individuals; they were visited in their homes, at their work sites and schools, accompanied on leisure activities, shopping expeditions, job searches, and so forth. Continuous observations and informal interaction with participants in all of the above settings and activities further contributed to an understanding of

TABLE 1
SAMPLE VS SUB-SAMPLE DEMOGRAPHICS

	Independent	Residence Independent living training	Parents	Board and care
Sample	24%	12%	51%	18%
Subsample	66%	17%	17%	0

	Competitively employed	Employment Workshop/work training	Unemployed
Sample	20%	31%	49%
Subsample	42%	0	58%

	Sex Male	Female	IQ Mean
Sample	47%	53%	58
Subsample	33%	67%	62

	Marital Status Married	Single	Divorced
Sample	16%	77%	7%
Subsample	33%	58%	8%

their relationships, their abilities, and their general adaptation. In addition, interviews with family members and caretakers yielded information on the ways in which significant others have viewed them.

To supplement the general ethnographic data provided by on-going contact, more focused but open-ended interviews aimed at eliciting specific information relevant to labeling issues were conducted as well. Natural opportunities were sought to raise the topics of handicap and limitations (e.g., mention of a handicapped bus pass, Supplemental Security Income [SSI], a problem with reading a job application, attending a job fair for the disabled) and were used as a springboard from which to discuss how participants labeled their "problems," if at all, and what they saw their limitations as being. Where such opportunities did not arise, researchers questioned participants about their school memories, leading them obliquely and carefully to the subject of handicap. Where possible, the issue was discussed in depth, covering such questions as how a participant's life has differed from the lives of other people, how they defined the terms they use to describe themselves, how they defined such words as "retarded," their experiences with teasing, their perceptions of how others see them, and so forth.

Although most parents and caretakers were willing to discuss their perceptions of their children's (or charge's) handicaps and limitations, here too the need for caution and sensitivity was ever-present because it was rarely clear what labels, if any, parents accepted and used comfortably. Parents were asked to talk about their children's early years and to comment on any special problems that were noticed, as well as ways in which the participant might have differed from other children in the family and neighborhood. School and special education were also discussed as a way of introducing the issue of handicap. In most cases, these discussions made it clear whether and how parents labeled their sons and daughters. In addition, questions were asked regarding whether the parents saw the participant as being handicapped, the ways in which he or she was handicapped, the ways in which his or her life would have differed had he or she not been handicapped, the ways in which the participant's life and opportunities differed from those of his or her siblings, the issue of whether other people in the neighborhood considered the participant to be different, the circumstances surrounding the first recognition of a problem, and so forth. Questions were also asked regarding what parents foresaw in the future and what they felt their sons and daughters would be capable of accomplishing. Parents were available for interviews in the case of 10 out of 12 subsample members. In the remaining two cases, parents were deceased and close family members unavailable. Instead, independent living training program directors were questioned on both their knowledge of the individual's background and their current assessment of the individual's abilities.

Results

In what follows, we describe each of these 12 individuals in terms of their current life circumstances, their own perceptions of their handicaps, their strengths and limitations, and their roles within their families and communities. For convenience the ethnographic present tense will be used.

Dora Mitchell

Dora Mitchell looks like a normal 21-year-old woman. Very pretty, well-dressed, and well-groomed, she has an engaging smile and a cheerful sparkling disposition. She is so normal in appearance that our field researcher initially mistook Dora for her normal sibling. However, Dora cannot count well enough to make change, nor can she read or write. Her most recent IQ score was 58.

Dora and her three normal siblings were raised in a run-down, low-income, Black neighborhood in the inner-city. Dora's parents both worked to earn a barely adequate income but were determined that their four children would graduate from high school. The first two children, a boy and a girl, enjoyed school, did well, and graduated. Dora seemed normal as a small child, but as she grew older, her parents noticed that she was slow to learn. When she started school and could not learn, her parents took her to an evaluation center where she was found to be "2 years behind her age level." School officials repeated the psychometric evaluation, found that Dora was mildly retarded, and placed her in special classes for the EMR. Throughout her elementary school years, Dora was tested often. Sometimes her IQ was found to be above 70, and she was placed in regular classes. Other times it was lower, and she was returned to EMR classes. When she reached high school, there were no EMR classes, so she remained in regular classes, graduating with a regular diploma.

After graduation, Dora did not disappear from the roles of agencies, nor did she become "normal," either in her own eyes or those of others. She remained a client of a Regional Center, became a recipient of SSI, and received services from Vocational Rehabilitation. In the 3 years since her graduation, Dora has remained at home. Every morning, she takes the bus to an adult school where she is learning to sew and make leather purses. She returns early each afternoon and spends the remainder of the day watching TV and helping out around the family apartment. She almost never leaves the apartment without her mother or sister. She made no friends in school and has no friends now except for one or two whom she has met at adult school and sometimes talks to on the telephone. She has never dated nor been a member of a recreational group.

Dora's mother openly refers to her as "slow" and "retarded." Her father is more reluctant to use these terms, but he is acutely aware of her limitations. For one thing, Dora was able to progress through school only because her parents did all her homework. Dora's parents also doubt her ability to cope with the ordinary problems of everyday life. They say that she would be exploited or victimized. As her mother put it, "I worry about how she'd do when people find out she can't click her brain that fast."

Dora seems to accept her social isolation and her parents' protectiveness. She displays no rebelliousness and even her few complaints are mild and qualified with doubts about her abilities. Dora admits that she cannot read or "do math" and sometimes does not understand what people are talking about. She also reluctantly admits that she is "slow," adding that only her family knows "for sure" that she is slow. She says that she can get along with other people "as long as they don't know that I'm slow, which I don't want them to know." Even her occasional efforts to assert her normality are tremulously made, as when she was asked by the field researcher what it meant to be slow. Dora said, "I don't know, really, 'cause I can do anything anybody else can do . . . up to a limit . . . I think."

Willa MacDonald

Willa MacDonald is a short, heavy, but completely normal-looking 25-year-old woman who lives in a dilapidated three room apartment in the South Central area of Los Angeles. Her living quarters typify extreme poverty. Situated at the end of a dark hallway in a run-down, two-story building, her apartment features a door that does not lock from the outside; soot- covered, smoke-scarred walls (the aftermath of a recent electrical fire); rotten and broken floors; paint peeling in sheets; faucets gushing continuously, overflowing onto the floor from stopped sinks; a bare mattress on a broken frame; dirt, brazen cockroaches, and endless spider webs. At times, she shares this apartment with Panther, her boyfriend, whose wife (an erstwhile friend of Willa's) lives down the street. Panther is always around when Willa's SSI check arrives. He drives her to a place where she can cash it and then relieves her of the lion's share, admonishing her that she is asking for trouble if she walks around with a lot of money. Willa is thus chronically short of funds after her $50 rent is paid.

Her expenses are minimal, however. Her days are spent hanging out on the front porch with the residents of her building—middle-aged and older men and women in equally dire straits—passing the time by passing a bottle and shooting the breeze. Willa claims that these are her associates, reserving the term "friend" for non-existent social acquaintances who, to earn the name, would have to meet her impossibly high expectations. But she enjoys their company, in spite of her complaints, and does have warm and caring relationships with many of the women in the neighborhood (a surprising fact given her brusque, hostile, slightly paranoid, and "I-don't-care-about-anyone-but-myself" attitude). At a glance, her life is not different from theirs: She depends on a monthly check for her livelihood, is not seeking gainful employment, struggles with the challenges of her marginal existence, copes with Panther's threats to beat her if she does not turn over her money, and devotes each day to easy social interaction with others in her immediate neighborhood.

Though it might be said that Willa is indistinguishable from her neighborhood peers, she is not viewed as being normal by her parents and is recognized as being different by many of those in her immediate social milieu as well. Willa's father and step-mother (who raised her), both migrants from the rural South, are quite aware that Willa is "slow." "She doesn't learn how to do things, like cook, and wash and iron, and sew. She just never could learn to do that," they point out. She can't manage her money either, and is easily taken advantage of, they feel. However, in their eyes, Willa's primary disability is that she is "emotional," a "defect" with which they believe she was born and which she shares with many of her siblings, half-siblings, and step-siblings. Although Willa's emotional nature did not start manifesting itself until she was 6 or 7, her parents report that it has gotten progressively worse through the years and is largely responsible (in their minds) for her current life-style. They feel she is paranoid—convinced that anyone who is trying to help her is actually taking advantage of her—and tends to distort reality to substantiate her impression that she is constantly being victimized. Moreover, they feel her "slowness" and her "emotional" character render her incapable of caring for the 10-year-old daughter (Phyllis) she gave birth to at the age of 15, and for whom the MacDonald's have always been responsible. For the MacDonald's, the thought of ever entrusting the care of Phyllis to Willa is out of the question. It is their belief that Phyllis is mentally older than Willa.

Willa's neighbors have confirmed the MacDonald's feeling that other people are aware that something is different about Willa. Doris, for instance, an older, alcoholic woman who has lived in the building for 20 years and who plays the role of mother to many of its tenants, has taken Willa under her wing. "I try to talk to her," she remarked to the researcher on one occasion. "I know she don't understand. You know what I mean. She's mentally ill. You know that—her and her brother [who is also retarded] and all of them." When asked to elaborate on the extent to which Willa was mentally ill, as opposed to "slow," Doris revealed that she was not sure and was using the term "mentally ill" merely to indicate that *something* about Willa's mind prevented her from understanding things. "It's one of the two," she concluded, "I don't know really exactly what it is."

Willa herself adamantly denies any implication that she might be mentally handicapped, in spite of the fact that she was placed in special classes in high school and, on the basis of her measured IQ of 69, has been a Regional Center client, a board and care resident, a sheltered workshop employee, and a student at an exceptional adult school. She is very sensitive to the mention of special education classes and openly defensive about her tenure in them, denying that she is slow. Her care in distinguishing "retarded" people from "slow" people, however, calls into question her insistence that she does not fall into the latter category. "A retarded person," she explains, "is deformed. Something's wrong with their body inside of them. A slow learner is just, they just slow catchin' on to their work and stuff, catchin' on to what they supposed to do. They behind in their work. That's what slow is." For her, a retarded person is one who is unilaterally slow: "You can grow up slow. Just like a retarded person. They growin' up slow in life. I feels sorry for 'em. I thank God that I'm not like that, that He didn't make me that way." Willa maintains that her only disability is her poor eyesight, and that it is for this reason that she receives SSI.

Superficially, then, Willa does not appear to be very different from her neighborhood peers. Although she has difficulty reading, so do many of the residents in the building, who often call upon the researcher to read and explain letters from agencies or to fill out forms for them. However, Willa is not seen as being competent either by her parents, who point to her lifestyle as *prima facie* evidence of her handicap, or more importantly by the neighbors who share that life style. She is accepted, tolerated, and included—afterall, each of them has problems of their own. She has not, however, been able to participate in this marginal community without her limitations being recognized.

Kathy Stone

Kathy Stone was labeled mentally retarded during her first year of elementary school. She is now 23 years old and is currently a resident in an independent living training program for developmentally disabled persons. Her most recent IQ test, a WAIS administered 3 years ago, yielded a full-scale score of 60. But Kathy is so articulate, so attuned to innuendo, and so normal in appearance—even though she is overweight and gives the impression of being a teenager—that it is difficult for anyone who does not know her well to think of her as anything other than a "cool," "streetwise" young Black woman. This is Kathy's public self—wisecracking, hip, even bullying. However, Kathy knows that she has been labeled mentally retarded, realizes that she has intellectual limitations, and suffers acutely as a result.

Kathy had such difficulty learning in the first grade of her all-Black, inner-city elementary school that she was sent to a prestigious evaluation center where she was diagnosed as "border-line mentally retarded." When her father, who works as an airline skycap, heard this report, he dismissed Kathy as hopeless, saying to his wife, "There's nothing you can do about it, so why bother?" Soon after, he left the house for good. Kathy's mother was shocked by Kathy's diagnosed retardation. She had worried about Kathy's slow development (she was slow to walk and to talk), but relatives and neighbors had told her there was no reason for concern because children developed at different rates.

Kathy's mother accepted her daughter's "handicap," which became increasingly apparent as her younger brother, born 4 years after her, grew up as a bright, normal child, and as Kathy continued to do poorly in school.

Kathy was placed in special classes, where she learned little and was the victim of merciless abuse by other children who stood outside the special classroom door and called the children "dummies." Also, Kathy was often followed all the way home by taunting, teasing children; her mother vividly remembers Kathy returning home in tears. It is not surprising that she made no friends in school or that she remembers school with anguish and anger. She says that her teachers in special classes always treated the students "like we were in kindergarten and couldn't understand anything. You know, they'd repeat everything a thousand times." Her mother tried to tutor her at home, but Kathy did not learn to read or do mathematics beyond a rudimentary level. Kathy now says, "I can read some, but I can't read the hard words." Kathy's mother adds that Kathy's inability to read embarrasses her tremendously; for example, sometimes when she is with people who don't know her, Kathy will pick up a book and pretend to read it. She also recalls a time when she was trying to teach Kathy how to make change, and Kathy was frustrated by the difficulty she was having in understanding. Finally, Kathy slammed her fist on the table and screamed that she hated herself.

It was not until Kathy left high school that she made her first friends. Through various vocational and recreational activities made available by the Regional Center, Kathy met her boyfriend (at a camp for developmentally disabled teenagers); she also participated in weekly bowling, the Special Olympics, and other social activities. The Regional Center also arranged several volunteer jobs involving child care, something Kathy still wants to do, but she lost each job for one reason or another. A year ago, she entered a training program designed to prepare her for independent living; her mother supports Kathy's wishes to live on her own, saying that while Kathy "has limitations," in time, "she will be just fine."

At the age of 23, Kathy's life is almost entirely involved with developmentally disabled persons. When she ventures into the social world of normal people, she usually "passes" well enough. Her brash and articulate banter both creates a veneer of normal appearance and keeps people at a distance. If people press her too closely or raise potentially discrediting topics, she "clams up," refusing to speak or respond further. Yet her self-esteem and self-confidence are low. She fears that her inability to read will prevent her from getting a "paying job," and although she badly wants to drive a car, she has failed the test on three occasions. Kathy's program director, like her mother, has confidence that Kathy will "make it on her own" some day, but everyone, Kathy included, realizes that the deficiencies in academic skills that led her to be labeled in the first grade still exist, and they now impair her ability to adapt to the demands of everyday life.

Reggie Willet

When Reggie Willet, 23, attended a party in commemoration of his older brother's graduation from law school, he had no trouble fitting in with a crowd of educated strangers. He interacted easily with the other guests and danced with as many of the young ladies as he could (much to their delight as Reggie is quite good-looking and an excellent dancer). Whereas his mother often felt paralyzed by the thought that those to whom she was speaking were far beyond her educational level and intellectual ability, Reggie confidently approached everybody. Ruminating on his social ease, Reggie's mother offered, "Reggie doesn't have any problem talking. And he doesn't see himself as having any kind of handicap. To him, he's fine. So he doesn't have any fear. He's not worried about being able to speak on another person's level. He's just thinking, 'Well, that's a person. I can talk to him.' He just go ahead and talk to him."

Reggie does, in fact, have a rather relaxed attitude toward his abilities and disabilities. He speaks comfortably about his days in special education classes, indicating his belief that he belonged there because he was "messing up—not really concentrating on doin' work." He remembers being teased about being "in that retarded class" but he asserts, in a believable manner, that he simply "overlooked" the taunts. He takes full responsibility for not being able to read ("I don't know. I guess I never put my mind on readin' a lot and stuff like most of my brothers did.") but in no way punishes himself for his inability. He recognizes that it gets in the way—most notably when it comes to filling out job applications and passing city job exams—but feels in general that his life is not very different because of his reading problems. He has his fair share of friends—"home boys" in the neighborhood, his brothers, their friends. He also has a girlfriend (who he indicates is "kinda slow"), takes responsibility for himself, is sure that his current unemployment is temporary, and has every intention of eventually living "the good life." He becomes somewhat defensive when the issue of being handicapped is pursued. Although he recognizes that not being able to read can be a handicap, in his mind "a handicapped person can't do anything," and he does not see that description as being appropriate for himself.

Mrs. Willet is not nearly as cavalier in her attitude toward Reggie's problems. To her, Reggie is clearly handicapped, and his limitations are all the more obvious and painful when juxtaposed against the accomplishments of his four older brothers, all of whom have graduated from college. Reggie's problems first became obvious at the age of 2 when he reacted traumatically to the birth of his younger brother. An EEG proved to be normal, and doctors assured Mrs. Willet that he would outgrow his problems. But Reggie was labeled EMR "from day one" and remained in special classes until he graduated. Mrs. Willet accepted his placement in special classes but felt frustrated by the fact that he was not getting the attention he deserved. Unfortunately, she, a divorced woman struggling to raise six sons alone in Watts, did not have the time or resources to find special programs. A counselor at school was able to get Reggie on SSI and did direct him to a sheltered workshop where he remained for a summer and, later, to a custodial/maintenance training program. His involvement with the delivery system ended at that point (with the exception of his SSI), although Mrs. Willet feels that he is currently in desperate need of some kind of structured activity and would welcome any services for which he is eligible.

Mrs. Willet sees Reggie's current problem as "reading," but she also worries that "he doesn't have the ability to keep his mind on one thing that long.

He doesn't have a very long attention span. It's very short. There are some things that he doesn't forget and then there are others—they just don't stay with him." In addition, she questions his ability to order his financial priorities. She is pleased with his friends and thankful that his brothers and their friends accept him ("They know him and they know he has a problem so they just include him, you know, just like the other guys.") However, in her mind, he is handicapped. "Not being able to read," she notes, "has prevented him from being an all-around, normal functioning man, like all of his brothers." She realizes that it is easy for Reggie to pass but feels that this at times works toward his disadvantage:

> Most people don't see Reggie as being handicapped. Because he can camouflage it too well. He doesn't look like he has a problem. He looks perfectly normal when you look at him. And he can camouflage it with the talking. That's where, you know, you would never know. You could say, 'Well, he's lazy, he's stupid, he just doesn't want to do it.' And you don't realize that this kid really *does* have a problem.

The future is a source of concern, but not worry, for Mrs. Willet. "I know one thing," she says, "I *know* Reggie will always be able to survive out there." However, she is less confident that Reggie will be able to live the "good life" that he wants for himself. No one, she has learned, is willing to hire someone who cannot fill out an application, cannot read, and whose mind wanders after a short time.

Allen Stanton

Though appearing younger than his 24 years, Allen Stanton is pleasant-looking man whose engaging personality and social competence easily enable him to shine in most of the social situations into which he places himself. Despite periods of moodiness, he is a highly gregarious individual with a sizeable social network consisting exclusively of nonretarded friends, co-workers, and acquaintances. One is likely to find him breezing through the department store where he works as a cafeteria busboy, greeting and being greeted by employee after employee. His animated style of communication is a natural complement to his outgoing manner; his narratives are rendered with great drama, he gestures extravagantly as he speaks, and he alternately adopts and drops a lisp and decidedly effeminate mannerisms. He is, in fact, homosexual, a side of his life which he only obliquely alluded to at first but which later became a more comfortable and acceptable topic of conversation as a relationship of trust slowly developed between him and his field researcher. Though gregarious, Allen is suspicious, guarded, and artfully manipulative—he chooses carefully what he will reveal of himself, sharing his private side only with those who have proven themselves to him.

His normal appearance and social skills notwithstanding, Allen continues to have a great deal of contact with agencies who provide him with services on the basis of his having been labeled retarded (IQ 64). He was first placed in special classes around the age of 6, when his learning problems became apparent. He subsequently became a client of a Regional Center and remained so even after frustrations over not learning and anxiety over gang fights led him to leave high school in the beginning of the 11th grade. The Regional Center was instrumental in getting him into a sheltered workshop, where he remained for 3 years until workshop counselors found him his job as a busboy, and currently funds his participation in a supervised independent living training program. Allen himself continues to depend on his Regional Center and workshop counselors for vocational guidance and has recently enlisted their aid in finding a new job.

This dependence on the Regional Center or another agency is something which Allen's mother feels will exist for the duration of his life. Although she is as guarded, suspicious, and slow to trust as her son, Mrs. Stanton clearly revealed that in her mind Allen will always be handicapped and in need of services. She herself was slow to recognize Allen's problems. She confesses to vague suspicions that something might have been wrong with Allen during his pre-school years but notes that it "really didn't focus in (her) mind until he started going to school. With his reading you know, and his schooling—it seemed like he was a slow learner, like in reading and math and all the things they have in school." He was tested, and she was told that he was, in fact, "slow, you know, in learning different things." As much as it hurt, Mrs. Stanton accepted the diagnosis. She has continued to view Allen as handicapped since then, although she recognizes that most people who know him socially are now aware of this. She was quite apprehensive about Allen moving out of the house, believes that Allen is limited by his inability to read and handle money, and continues to feel that he will always need help and counseling.

Allen himself only reluctantly discusses his handicap and tries to carefully screen who will see him in situations where his limitations are sure to manifest themselves. Almost a full year of research contact had taken place before he introduced the idea that he was handicapped by mentioning his attendance at a job fair for the disabled—he revealed that he had told the people there that he was a "slow learner." Once he had made this admission, he began requesting that the field researcher accompany him on job interviews in order both to minimize the possibility of his being taken advantage of and to ensure the presence of someone who, on the basis of the information he would verbally provide, would write out an application. For in spite of the social competence which led one interviewer to suggest training in office work as being appropriate, Allen could not spell his middle name or his current occupation, did not know the meaning of the word "veteran" when it was read to him by the field researcher, and ultimately conceded that left to his own devices, he would be unable to make sense of the vast majority of the application form.

Although realizing that he is, in fact, a slow learner, Allen is loathe to admit this to his friends and takes care to hide from them his involvement with agencies or programs for the retarded. They do not know he attended a sheltered workshop, that he was in special classes, or that he is a slow learner. "They don't look at me different," he says, "If they do, they never mention it to me. They don't know as far as my reading and spelling—they don't know about that."

Allen himself tries to discount the importance of his being a slow learner.

He asserts that his reading problem results from his lack of patience—he hasn't the attention span to sit down and read a book. He counters the admission that he has problems managing his money with the assertion that he has no problems actually counting change. He carefully distinguishes himself from the other clients at the sheltered workshop he attended, noting that his problems were less severe than theirs. In the end, however, Allen indicates that he does, in fact, believe that he is slow, as much as he hates to admit it. During a conversation on the difference between being slow and being retarded, he offered, "I don't consider myself to be slow, but I am. I definitely don't consider myself to be retarded, and I ain't." Pressed to explain the first statement, he ultimately acknowledged, "I know that I'm slow, but I don't want to believe that I am . . . And maybe I won't be someday."

Alene Brant

At age 33, Alene Brant leads a very settled existence, dividing her attention between her job in the mail room of a life insurance company and the care of her 14-year-old daughter, with whom she shares an apartment in an ethnically-mixed seaside community. She is a plain and somewhat matronly looking woman—slightly overweight, with wan skin and a tired look to her face—who dresses in the same cautious, conservative style that characterizes her approach to life. Although completely normal in appearance, her manner is overwhelmingly slow; she speaks slowly and deliberately, as if carefully considering each thought before verbalizing it, and her gestures and physical movements seem to take place in slow motion. She is not without her dignity, however. Her pride in being a responsible, independent, and self-sufficient adult is always apparent, and her determination to continue "making it" on her own is a repeated theme.

Alene and her fraternal twin sister, Irene, were the second and third of seven children. They were raised, along with their siblings, in a small, worn house in a fairly rundown, violence-plagued Black section of Venice. Born prematurely, she and her sister had birth weights of 2 pounds, 10 ounces and 4 pounds, 3 ounces respectively and remained in incubators for several weeks before being brought home. Their mother remembers their early childhood development as being normal, unlike her youngest son, who was clearly recognized as being "real slow" from a very early age. Alene's mother did become somewhat concerned about the girls when they seemed unable to learn their alphabet and their numbers before entering school in the way that her two older children had. Her suspicions were confirmed when both girls were placed in special classes in the first grade, remaining in EMR classes until their graduation from high school. Although initially upset by the realization that the twins were "slow," Alene's mother learned to accept it and looks back on special education as having been a positive experience for her children.

As a child and adolescent, Alene was quiet and somewhat passive, content to remain in the shadow of her more aggressive and socially active twin. It thus came as a complete surprise to everyone except Alene when she became pregnant during her last year of high school. The pregnancy was not accidental; Alene's younger sister had just had a child, and Alene was determined to have one as well. Unlike her younger sister, however, she took responsibility for the care and upbringing of her daughter, proving to be an attentive and competent mother. She left home a few years later when she married a man other than the one who had fathered her child. He, unfortunately, "liked his liquor," according to Alene, "but didn't know how to handle it." Her trials in dealing with his irresponsibility ended when he "upped and a left" after 2 years, leaving her with his debts for which she had co-signed. She and her daughter returned to her mother's home but subsequently moved out when an apartment became available in a building owned by her cousin.

Alene availed herself of the service delivery system throughout this time. Upon graduating from high school, she was referred to Vocational Rehabilitation, which placed her in a sheltered workshop so that she could "get acquainted with work and with people." Subsequently, she was trained in housekeeping and worked at a convalescent hospital until she was fired for being "slow"; she later received training as a file clerk and worked at a university in that role for a few years. She ultimately turned to the Department of Rehabilitation for help in securing her current position with the life insurance company, and she admits that she would contact the Regional Center or the Department of Rehabilitation for help should she ever lose this job. In addition, she briefly received SSI when her husband left and she was out of work, a fact she only admits with shame and embarrassment.

Although Alene has turned to the service delivery system for the retarded at critical times, it is her family on which she has depended for day-to-day help and support. She relies heavily on her mother (whom she sees every day) and other family members for both company (her social life is largely restricted to Church activities) and aid with practical tasks. The family, especially her mother, keep a watchful eye on Alene, recognizing that because she is "slow," she needs help in handling her finances and in solving a variety of other problems. There is some concern as well over Alene's judgment when it comes to men; Alene's mother asserts that she is too trusting as a rule and worries that she will be taken advantage of.

Alene is proud of her accomplishments, but she continues to view herself as being "slow" and realizes that others recognize this as well. At times, she feels the need to let other people know she has problems, as in the case of work, where she worried that she wasn't adequately meeting the expectations of her employer. "Sometimes you have to tell people," she says. "You can't just hide it. Because, like if you do, they won't try and help you." She expresses the belief that she can do practically anything, if given the opportunity and enough time, but acknowledges a number of limitations nevertheless. She realizes that she works slower than her co-workers. She has problems reading and admits that she "doesn't understand some things" that other people say. She is frustrated by an inability to "put things into words" and, at times, to make people understand her. She questions whether she will ever learn to drive car. She confesses to being vulnerable to being "conned" and is wary of relationships because of this.

However, there is much that Alene finds to feel good about. She compares herself to her more severely handicapped brother and notes that at least she can "half-way cope with certain things and do certain things." She feels "blessed" that she has the ability to help herself. She points to the crucial support she has lent other family members in need, such as providing a temporary home for her alcoholic sister and being a constant source of strength to her cancer-ridden mother. In the end, she strongly proclaims that in spite of her limitations and the world's impatience with slower people, she has, by her own standards, achieved a success of which she can feel proud.

Irene Tucker

By her own admission, Irene Tucker (Alene's sister) is often envied by other people. In addition to being an attractive woman whose stylish dress and carefully applied make-up augment her natural good looks, she is vivacious and articulate, capable of charming a table out of a reluctant restaurant host or playing Pied Piper to the neighboring children. Married to a film technician for 14 years, she owns, along with her husband, a small house in a suburban neighborhood and is active in her neighborhood block association. Her job as a meat wrapper in a supermarket pays quite well and has allowed her such luxuries as a smart sports car and a weekly cleaning woman. Vacations are spent in such places as Hawaii, and she and her husband recently joined a golf club in which they are the only Black members; Irene reluctantly hobnobs with the "snooty" White women while her husband plays golf with his co-workers.

However, Irene is confused by the envy she excites in other people. She realizes that the grass is always greener on the other side, but is acutely conscious of how "rough it is on (her) side of the fence." The major reason for this negative perception of her life is the fact that Irene cannot read at all. Although she skillfully hides her limitations from others, she is painfully aware of them. Life, for her, is a constant struggle to overcome the obstacles presented by her handicap and to come to grips with a highly stigmatized identity. As she poignantly says:

It can be really rough. Like my reading ability. Look at this—voting is coming up. I want to be able to go through this whole ballot and read the whole thing and vote for who I want, but I can't read. Or like in Bible class. I worship at one church and I go to another for studies because I'm not put on the spot there. Maybe I want to change to another job. I mean, there's a position open now. I could work down in the office, you know—dress up like the office girls and secretaries—but that means taking a lot of orders on the phone. I've had to memorize the things that I do, you know, and it's hard to change. Too many things are happening now that could help me better myself, but I can't do them because I don't read well. It just tears me up sometimes. And I'm a loner. Like I said, I want to go socialize more with the girls down there at the church. I don't do it because I don't want them to know. They, they only know the outside of me. So you can really ask somebody, 'What is Irene about? Well, she's here and five minutes later she's gone.'

Because of her sophistication and the highly normal cast to her life, Irene's conviction that she is "slow" stands out in vivid relief. Allowed to "let her hair down" in front of a non-judgmental field researcher, she discussed in a moving way how life has been different for her because she is handicapped. In addition to speaking of feeling trapped in a menial, even if well paying, job, being fearful of becoming intimate with others who might discover her problems, and believing at times that she is the "only dummy out there," Irene addressed issues such as having children. She loves children and admits that she envies her sister Alene for her daughter. However, even were Irene's husband able to have children, she is not sure that she would have them.

> "First thing I would think of if I got pregnant would be, 'Would I have a handicapped child? Or would my child be slow? Would it take an educated man's sperm to have a decent child?' I've heard about artificial insemination on talk shows, you know, and have thought, 'First thing I would pick would be a professor or something.' Because I wouldn't want no dumb child. There's too many dumb kids. Yeah, I would be scared to have a child."

Despite her moments of despair, Irene is determined to succeed and recognizes that her determination is responsible for the success she has already achieved in life. Aggressive and dynamic where her twin is passive and retiring, she was active socially during her school years, spending most of her time with students from regular classes with whom she shared interests in dance and modeling. She defied her parents' injunction against learning to drive, stole their car keys in the dead of the night, and taught herself to operate a vehicle. "I was determined to drive," she said, "I think I tore up two cars in the process of learning, plus getting a beating and having to get a job to help pay for the damage. But I was determined to drive. My mother and father wasn't going to let either of us girls drive because of our handicap. But I knew that had nothing to do with my mobility, you know, my functioning." This same spark led Irene to leave home at the age of 17 to live with the man she later married.

> It was rough in my parent's neighborhood. My father, he drank, and my mother was doing day work, and there were seven or eight of us. I just wanted to get away, so I left. I knew if I stayed there I wouldn't have been able to experience the things that I've gone through. Alene will never experience the things that I've gone through because she's down there with my mom. My mom takes care of a lot of her business that I take care of myself—you know, her checking and utilities. Her reading abilities are probably better than mine. But then, her common sense and her reasoning aren't like mine. That's the difference that I can see. She finds it hard to talk to people too. I don't. And my character has gotten me into a lot of things I do.

Irene's initiative has kept her independent of any service delivery agency. She frowns on public aid, commenting, "I'd go nuts if I had to wait for the first and fifteenth of the month for some money. I don't know how people do it." Where Alene turned to workshops and the Department of Rehabilitation to obtain job-training, Irene jumped in and trained herself, first at an electronics plant and then at a meat counter. Her resourcefulness in obtaining her present job stands as a testament to her strength of character and drive to succeed. Upon learning about meat wrapping and how well it paid, she went to the library, had the librarian show her a chart, and began, with help, to identify various cuts of meat. She then began hanging around meat counters, talking to the supervisors, until one of them gave her a break—he offered to train her without pay. For 3 months, she labored at memorizing all she had to know and eventually got a job when another wrapper quit. It was a hard struggle, she recalls, and there were times when she almost quit, but her determination pulled her through.

Irene wonders, however, whether determination can take her any farther; she fears that she will never be more than a meat wrapper. She blames this, in part, on her schooling, noting that her diploma was merely a token.

> They didn't care if I learned anything or not. I didn't learn anything, really. All I had to do was smile or strike up a good conversation. They could have spent a little more time with me, given me more homework. And instead of pushing me into those courses like homemaking, cooking—I mean, that's all going to fall into place, you know. If you have a mother and father you can see it around you every day. I wanted typing. I wanted English. I wanted to go further in history. I wanted algebra. But they just got me through the basics. I wanted more, but the time just ran out. That's why I hate to see handicapped kids get out of high school. Because if they don't have nobody to help them, they're lost. You're out here, you know, and you're lost, you can't go back. 'Cause you're going to have to live— you're going to have to provide food for yourself. How can you do that and go back to school? I wish they had pushed me a little farther. I think I would have been more than a meat wrapper. I really do. I would have like to have taught school. Being a slow learner myself, I would have opened a school for the handicapped or something like that. And I probably would have gotten real involved with the kids— let them know, 'I'm 33 years old and I can't read real good, so don't feel bad,' you know. 'So here we are. Let's do it together and try to better ourselves.' That would have been a dream come true for me.

For Irene, very real competence and an enviable life style exist concurrently with the carefully guarded secret that she is, in fact, handicapped and limited in what she will be able to achieve. Although overtly an ideal example of a six-hour retarded child turned adult, her inner struggle identifies her as a woman who, in her own mind, has not blended neatly into the community at large.

Tim Alton

In many respects, Tim Alton's story differs dramatically from those reported thus far, both in terms of his background and the life he currently leads. His childhood was a stormy one, its rhythm set by the erratic, inexplicable, and often abusive behavior of his schizophrenic mother who moved continuously from place to place and man to man with her seven children, each the product of a different relationship. His life became no more stable when his mother was hospitalized after she severely assaulted them while she was "sick." Tim was 11 when this occurred. He spent a number of difficult years in juvenile halls and foster homes during this period, being transferred from one place to another because of this "wild" behavior. Part of this time was spent in an "MR" home where "the other kids had to be washed and fed." Tim attributes his placement in this facility to the fact that he was wild, "not acting like a normal kid," and the authorities could not find an alternative living arrangement for him.

Tim eventually spent two satisfying years in Utah in the Job Corps, returning to Los Angeles at age 18 when his stint was over. By this time, the family had largely disintegrated, and all but one brother had disappeared. He took a room in a local YMCA and lived there alone on his SSI until advised by Regional Center counselor of an independent living training program for which he was eligible. Because the YMCA was scheduled for demolition, Tim took advantage of this offer and entered a very different world—a world set in a White community and peopled, largely, by White faces. He arranged for himself a hectic schedule of program classes at a local city college, a schedule which he currently follows while working part time. He is almost completely isolated from the Black community and remains isolated in the White community where the primary social contacts open to him are developmentally disabled individuals whose company he shuns. By and large, he leads a solitary existence, immersed in his daily round of activities, interacting primarily with counselors and casual acquaintances.

Although Tim's life and way of looking at the world have radically changed with the passing years, he has remained steadfastly consistent in his assertion that he is not handicapped in any way. Tim recognizes the body of evidence suggesting that he is retarded—he was placed in homes for retarded children, was in special classes, receives SSI, and is currently involved in a program which serves develpmentally disabled individuals. Over time, however, he has given each of these bits of evidence careful thought and has constructed elaborate rationalizations which enable him to dismiss them. He defends his involvement in the independent living training program, for instance, by arguing that he was not told in advance that the program was for handicapped individuals; that handicapped individuals were conspicuously absent when he toured the program; that he was, in a sense, misled and tricked into entering the program; and that once involved, he realized he had no place else to go and thus decided to make the best of it.

However, Tim is most preoccupied with one particularly compelling bit of evidence: He cannot read. Not being able to read, he acknowledges, is, in fact, a serious handicap. His self-consciousness over this disability kept him from dating interested girls in the Job Corps for fear they would discover his illiteracy and think him less a man. It has placed him in awkward situations in some of his city college classes when classmates, who assume that he does not have a book because he cannot afford one, offer to share theirs or even buy him one. It inhibits his ability to achieve the goals he has set for himself, such as attaining a B.A. in psychology. Most importantly, it makes it difficult for him to think positively about himself. In his mind, his entire self-worth and future life as a normal individual hinge on the extent to which he can overcome his reading problem.

At different times, Tim has offered numerous explanations for his reading deficit: his family "messed him up," he had to change schools every time he entered a new foster home, his mother kept him out of school for a full year, she failed to impress on him how important it was to learn to read, his diet as a child was lacking in necessary vitamins, and so forth. He has begun to insist, however, that through his work at the city college he has overcome his inability to read. On one occasion, in fact, he offered to demonstrate his prowess to his field researcher as proof that this was the case. Opening up an elementary reader, he tentatively began sounding out the words in a slow, faltering manner, stumbling over the more difficult ones and abandoning those which presented too much of a challenge. His monotonic voice and erratic cadence suggested that he was understanding little, if anything, of what he read; he was merely engaging in a phonetic exercise, a largely unsuccessful one at that. Nevertheless, he was proud of his accomplishment, even while confessing that he was still working on coming to the end of a sentence and starting a new one—that still "threw him a bit." His pride only made the flimsy nature of his defense all the more heartbreaking to see.

When Tim first entered the independent living training program, his competence in most areas other than reading raised questions in the minds of his counselors as to whether or not he was actually retarded. Although they recognized that Tim had problems with academic subjects (including math) and spoke in a manner which might earmark him as being disabled (slowly, with a tendency to both divert himself with inappropriate tangents and lose his train of thought in mid-sentence), they also marveled at the fact that he entered the program with a fundamental knowledge of basic living skills. Moreover, they were impressed by his common sense, his ability to pick things up quickly, his sensitivity to others, his willingness to solve problems on his own, and their ability to converse with him without "talking down" to him. One counselor was so convinced that he was not retarded that she had him tested at a learning center. When Tim failed to demonstrate any discernible learning disorder and continued to score below 70 on IQ tests designed to compensate for cultural disadvantage, she had a complete neurological work-up arranged. The tests were also negative.

In the end, the counselors have become more comfortable with the idea that Tim is handicapped, a fact which he resents. He vividly remembers being brought to the city college and introduced as a member of an independent living program for handicapped adults. Since that time, Tim feels he is treated differently by his instructor, whom he accuses of being solicitous, almost condescending, and of treating him like he is "some kind of retarded person." "Me and the counselors don't get along so good when they say I'm a handicapped," Tim says.

Whereas Tim's counselors have no worries about his ability to survive, they are profoundly concerned over his social isolation and the extent to which his self-worth is tied to his reading prowess. They realize that the same problem which brought Tim to their program—his lack of a support system—still exists; once he leaves the program he will be virtually alone again, cut off from the Black community and unintegrated into the White. Moreover, they are pessimistic that he will ever achieve the reading competence he desperately desires. Unless he is able to build a viable social network and resolve his conflicts over his limitations, the quality of his life, they are afraid, will be significantly affected.

Linda Garvey

Linda Garvey's experience parallels that of Tim Alton's in many ways, although not to the same degree. A large woman whose only stigmatizing feature is one droopy eyelid, Linda gives every impression of being savvy about the world; she is streetwise and full of common sense. She seems older than her 21 years, partially because of her rather matronly physical appearance. Like Tim, she spent two years in, and only recently graduated from, an independent living training program consisting largely of White clients and staff in a predominantly White community. Like Tim again, she entered the program when family support waned. Her mother died in 1977, a tragedy to which Linda is still trying to reconcile herself ("She dead now. Nothin' I can do about it now."), and Linda spent two years being shuffled from one relative to another, some of whom treated her poorly, many of whom were more interested in her SSI check than in her well-being. Like Tim, she was quick to pick up household tasks within the program, leading her counselors to believe that she (in contrast to her White counterparts) had been expected to do her fair share in the homes in which she had lived. Like Tim, she is unable to read and has trouble writing and handling money. Finally, like Tim, she is caught between two worlds and has been unable to build a strong support system in either.

Linda is perhaps more fortunate than Tim in that the issue of self-concept and handicap is not an all-consuming one for her. Although recognizing that many people feel she is slow, Linda wavers between denying and accepting the idea. When explaining why she did not believe that one of the least competent residents in the independent living program was mentally retarded, for instance, she offered, "I just think she's slow at certain things, like I am. I don't think she's mentally retarded. 'Cause some people calls me that and it'll get on my nerves in a minute when they call me that. But I don't pay any attention—I been called it so many times by my brother." However, she was more reluctant to admit that she is slower at certain things when talking about her placement in special classes:

I know why I was in special classes. Well, my mother told me, and other people told me, 'Well, you's slower than other people.' And I looked at that and said, 'How am I slower than other people?' And then I thought, 'Well, some people can read and some people can't read but that doesn't mean you have to be in special classes.' I said, 'Well, I know how to read some things and I know how to do math. That's all that counts. I know how to do math and manage money and stuff, and that's all that counts.' But they said that it would be good for me to be in special classes 'cause if I was in the other classes, they said I couldn't do the work. But then I didn't know that. They never tried me at that.

Linda does see her inability to read as a handicap, although she tends to minimize the consequences it holds for day-to-day life. She admits that not being able to read has made it more difficult to pass her written test for a driver's license and has been a source of frustration when it comes to filling out job applications. (Indeed, a field researcher observed Linda's utter confusion when faced with a packet of forms covering her skills, interests, experience, and financial situation. She was required to complete these forms as part of her involvement in a job club sponsored by the Department of Rehabilitation to which her Regional Center had referred her.) She has also expressed, rather wistfully, the simple desire to read what other people read—books, magazines, and the like. On the other hand, she has noted that not being able to read does not significantly alter her ability to perform the tasks that are required to live independently. She can take the bus, she points out, and can pay her rent and other bills. She can fill out half of most applications and can usually get help on the parts that give her trouble. She has people (for example, her ex-program counselor and Regional Center counselor) to whom she can turn when she receives a confusing letter from the Social Security office regarding her SSI. In the end, she indicates that in spite of her limitations, she feels good about herself, at least most of the time.

Although it was difficult for her to break away from the security of the independent living training programs, Linda is now living on her own and working competitively in a convalescent hospital making beds. She has sustained her friendships with a few of the program's participants while at the same time keeping in touch with relatives (about whom she complains bitterly and upon whom she has learned she cannot depend) and nonretarded friends (such as the bus driver, a Black woman, who chauffeured her to and from her previous job at Goodwill). She has every intention of marrying and having a child, in spite of her grandmother's assertion that no man would marry a woman who cannot read.

Although the future, in Linda's eyes, looks promising on occasion, it just as often looks dreadfully bleak. She does have moments of loneliness, depression, and despair during which she doubts her ability to build the life she wants for herself. At such times, she worries, as do her counselors, about the absence of people in her social world, other than service delivery system personnel, upon whom she can really depend. Her dearth of stable contacts within either of the communities with which she flirts leaves her feeling alone and insecure. Without the informal support system she needs, her chances of obtaining help in compensating for her academic limitations and of feeling socially connected will both suffer.

Dan and Laura Greenwood

Dan and Laura Greenwood first met at a school for exceptional adults which they both attended after graduating from special high schools. Their 3-year-old marriage, initiated when Laura discovered she was pregnant, has been an on-again, off-again affair. They separated 6 months after their little girl was born, Dan returning to his mother's house, Laura moving with the baby to an apartment in the low-income housing project where her friends and relatives lived. They remained in touch with each other daily, however, and Dan eventually rejoined Laura and the baby until problems led to his return to his mother's house 2 months later. Shortly thereafter, they reconciled again, moved away from the housing project (one of Dan's major sources of irritation) to a new apartment, and have remained together since. Their pooled resources—each of them receives an SSI check, and Laura also receives an AFDC check for the baby, now 2½ years old—enable them to live adequately, if not comfortably. Laura is currently expecting their second child.

Dan and Laura are both completely normal in speech and appearance, indistinguishable from their nonhandicapped peers. As a couple, they project a rather Mutt and Jeff quality, differing markedly in their physical and behavioral attributes. Sam, at 28, is tall, thin, somewhat handsome, and an avid conversationalist, who evinces a quietly gracious manner while retaining a touch of naiveté. Laura, on the other hand, is 25, short, overweight, less attractive, and not nearly as voluble as her spouse, though when observed in her own milieu (the "Projects") she more readily exercised her low, husky voice in exchanges with a wide variety of individuals—family, neighbors, and local winos, who use her front door as a regular gathering place. She, more than Dan, is a guarded individual who will not hesitate to lie when it suits her purpose. She has led Dan to believe, for instance, that they are having twin boys, when she is actually aware that she is having only one baby of undetermined sex, and has withheld from him the fact that she has made arrangements to have a tubal ligation after her upcoming delivery. Their daughter, of whom they are intensely proud, is a thin, delicate, and beautiful little girl who is developing normally; Dan and Laura constantly boast about how intelligent she is.

Dan and Laura also differ markedly in the way in which they view their limitations and in the extent to which they are willing to discuss them. Dan readily admits to being "slow as far as reading" is concerned, pointing to this problem as the handicap which makes him eligible for participation in the Special Olympics. He acknowledges the difficulty he has in filling out job applications and the resistance he faces from prospective employers who feel he should be able to complete an application without another's aid. This is not to say he cannot work—he maintains that he is an excellent custodian and painter and claims proficiency in a number of manual trades (although his one competitive employment stint as an assembly worker was so stressful that he became physically ill and was advised by a doctor to quit). As far as his everyday life is concerned, potential problems are avoided by a team approach: "Well, as far as that's concerned, me and my wife works with each other. I know she reads very good, good you know. And I know she don't mind helping me and I don't mind helping her." Much of this help, in actuality, comes not from Laura but from Dan's mother.

Laura, on the other hand, tends to avoid any attempts to discuss the issue of handicap by ignoring or blatantly misinterpreting the intent of questions and denying any limitations if confronted directly, this in spite of her years in special schools for the handicapped and her participation in the Special Olympics. She claims to have no problems with either reading or math and attributes her placement in special classes to undeserved punitive action over an alleged purse stealing incident. Although Dan does not overtly challenge these statements, his comments clearly reveal his skepticism. Laura remains adamant in her denial, however, even in the face of his disbelief.

Dan's mother and Laura's mother (Mrs. Fenton) display similarly contrasting attitudes. Mrs. Fenton, a flamboyant woman (who has been accused by Dan and his mother of prostituting both herself and her daughters), acknowledges that Laura, from an early age, has been "a slow learner. You know—hard time catching on to things, slow catching on to different things." At the same time, she feels that Laura has been able to do everything she has wanted to do, believes that Laura conducts her life in a competent manner, and finds no differences in the maturity or life circumstances of Laura and her sisters. Although thankful that Laura receives a disability check (because, or so Dan and Mrs. Greenwood claim, she regularly helps herself to a portion of it), she is sincere in her assertion that neither she nor any of the other people in the neighborhood see Laura as being handicapped. Laura does have problems understanding certain things, but her situation is no worse than anyone else's. It is Mrs. Fenton's belief that her chances for a successful future are good. She is pleased that Laura is having children and feels that Laura, as she had expected, is a good parent. She voices no concerns or worries over what will become of Laura when she is gone.

Mrs. Greenwood, a hard-working, religious woman, offers a very different view, not only of Dan and his handicap, but of the problems Laura and Dan together face as a handicapped couple. She is quick to point out Dan's strong points, noting that Dan is "basically pretty bright, you know. If you really don't know him, you wouldn't know he had a problem." In many ways, she finds that he acts like the man he appears to be, in spite of his reported IQ of 60. But then, she notes, something simple comes along that one would expect him to be able to do and he is unable to handle it—"He acts like a baby." Her conclusion? "I guess if he were all the way right, he wouldn't be in that position." She realizes that "he ain't too darn handicapped" but, as she tells him when she is upset over his excessive drinking, "You already don't got what you need." In spite of his normal appearance and his ability to compete both socially and athletically with his neighborhood peers, Dan, in her mind, is definitely limited.

As far as Mrs. Greenwood is concerned, these limitations significantly affect Dan's life opportunities and his ability to handle day-to-day demands. Because he has neither the reading skills to fill out an application nor the wherewithal to hold a regular job, he has no financial security. Also, because neither he nor Laura has "too much to offer . . . I mean, in the way of thinking abilities," they are often unable to perform as she feels adults should. Mrs. Greenwood's most scathing diatribes center around two issues—their inability to handle and manage money and their inability to effectively parent; their behavior in both areas, and in a host of other ways, betray to her their complete and utter lack of responsibility. They are unable to conserve their money at the beginning of the month so that there is money for food at the end of the month—in her opinion, they spend their money frivolously on things that aren't even remotely necessary. She feels they are not consistent enough in the discipline of the baby, do not watch her carefully, and do not take the time to ensure that she is eating enough, all of which confirm her belief that Dan and Laura should not be having children ("And the babies? I hate to see them have the babies. I really do."). Lastly, she is convinced that "it would be pitiful" if she were not around to help out. It is her conviction that should she not succeed in her attempt to make the two of them more independent, Dan will "crackup or become a wino" when she is no longer around.

The question of whether Mrs. Fenton's or Mrs. Greenwood's perspective is the more accurate is difficult to assess; observations support both of these views. It is true that Dan and Laura often exhibit a misordered sense of financial priorities: Recently they spent $500 on an anniversary party, knowing full well that this money was coming from sums ear-marked for monthly expenditures. It is true that Dan has been unable to find or keep a job. It is true that their child is thin, though she is always impeccably groomed and carefully dressed. On the other hand, Mrs. Fenton may be correct in her assessment that their life is not any different from their peers in the "Projects"—there are many men who are out of work and many couples who spend large sums of money on parties knowing that the money isn't really there. It is fascinating, in and of itself, that these two women, characterized by very different value systems, observe the same couple and reach such radically different conclusions. The truth, it seems, lies somewhere in between their contrasting viewpoints: Laura and Dan are making it in a normal world, but not without the added problems caused by the fact that they are "slow catching on to things" and not without the extra help from Dan's mother.

Debbie Duvall

When Debbie Duvall's field researcher returned from her first visit to Debbie, she described an experience that in her mind significantly differed from those she had had with other prospective sample members. What had started out as an interview had quickly shifted to a conversation in which two people of relatively equal standing found common ground and began getting to know one another better. A very attractive woman, Debbie was also highly verbal, expressing herself colorfully in a drawl that betrayed her Alabama upbringing. She spoke easily and engagingly of her 10-month-old son, of her former boyfriend who refused to acknowledge him, of her plans to marry her current boyfriend, and other topics. Over an unplanned lunch at a local fast-food restaurant, she swapped stories with the field researcher on the joys and trials of motherhood and spontaneously invited her and her toddler to the baby's one-year-old birthday party. As the afternoon passed, it became increasingly difficult for the field researcher, who was unaware of Debbie's recorded IQ of 55, to believe that the 22-year-old woman whose conversation she was so enjoying could be considered retarded.

It seemed to be a somewhat different person, however, who responded to the question of how she spelled her son's unusual name. The bright, vivacious Debbie suddenly became flustered and embarrassed as she confessed that she always forgets how to spell it. Impatiently noting that it didn't make sense for her to be unable to spell her own son's name, she self-consciously initiated an effort but became confused, faltered, and finally abandoned the attempt. Ultimately she searched her wallet for a piece of paper with the correct spelling.

These two faces, the highly competent and the unexpectedly incompetent, are both part and parcel of Debbie Duvall. On the one hand, she leads a life which, in the words of her mother, "is normal. She's doin' what the other girls are doin'." She is a competent mother and a more than adequate housekeeper, bearing a large portion of the responsibility for cooking and cleaning during those times when she lives with her parents and full responsibility for domestic chores during those times when she and her husband—the boyfriend she eventually married—live together. She copes as well as she can with her rather volatile mate, alternately asserting her rights and tolerating severe physical abuse. She socializes easily on a peer level with her sisters, cousins, and casual friends (mostly old boyfriends, all of whom are nonretarded and one of whom was an A student). Her life style and general manner of interacting do nothing to suggest that she might be retarded.

On the other hand, Debbie has serious difficulty with academically-related tasks—she cannot read and has trouble with anything involving mathematical operations. Observations of her in various settings and her own comments reveal that these limitations have a profound affect on the quality of her life: They significantly affect her self-concept, they influence how other people see her, and they minimize her ability to live the life she would choose for herself.

Debbie readily identifies herself as being "slow," and indicates that she has been aware of this ever since she entered special classes in elementary school. She (as well as her mother) has given a lot of thought to why both she and a number of her siblings are slow. At times, she indicates that she really isn't sure. At other times, she blames her father, who she also describes as "slow," citing heredity and the fact that he beat whatever knowledge they were able to accumulate out of them while they were unsuccessfully struggling to learn. Although Debbie's customary attitude is "Well, I think I can do anything I want to do if I really try," she does confess to moments of pain and despair. On one occasion, she offered:

> All the kids in my family, you know, in this house, is slow. I used to always wonder why. I mean why it have to be us. I wonder if we made not to learn or . . . I don't know. I ain't dumb. But I'm slow in a lot of stuff. And like I be knowin' it and then I just cain't say it out, it don't come fast in my mind. It comes real slow . . . I mean it used to really get on me. It still do bother me at times, you know.

More than being bothered, she often fears being dependent on other people—either her parents or her husband. At one point, while feeling low, she discussed how marriage had not brought about the independence she had sought—she was now merely depending on her husband rather than her parents. In a dejected voice, she likened herself to retarded people, of whom she says:

> Most of 'em somebody helpless, you know. They got to always have somebody help them do somethin'. Most, well some of 'em, they got to depend on somebody. See most of 'em just like a little baby. And I don't wanna start dependin' on my husband to do this, or 'Michael,

sign this for me.' I wanna really try to do it all on my own. But I don't know if I'm ever gonna learn. I don't know if I'm really meant to do it, you know. I probably be just like a retarded person in this world, you know, and never would learn to do, you know, like I never would learn to read or write or whatever.

Although most people are unaware of Debbie's problems (in the words of her mother, "unless they get to know her real close and find out about her"), those close to her are certainly aware. Her husband, for one, who didn't realize her limitations when they first met, has been known to use them as a weapon. Says Debbie:

At first, I think, when he found out I was slow—I don't think he be gettin' mad, but when we used to get into it, he used to bring that up, you know, in front of me. And it used to kinda hurt. He used to always say, 'You cain't do this. You cain't do that. I bet you don't know this word. Bet you don't know that word.' It used to hurt me. It really hurt me.

Her mother is far more gentle. In front of Debbie, she speaks sincerely of Debbie's strength of will and her determination to learn. In private, she admits that Debbie "really don't understand a lot that . . . I mean she understand what's goin' on and everything but not to cope with it." Although her mother gives no indication of viewing Debbie as being seriously handicapped, she clearly views her as having limitations that leave her ill-equipped to deal fully with the demands of daily existence.

In many ways, Debbie's life is different because she is slow, and she is painfully aware of this. She is reminded of it as she makes the minor adjustments that being slow requires. On one occasion, when her husband was leaving the house and asked whether she needed anything from the store, she responded with a "No." Later, when her sister asked the same question, she thought carefully and gave her a substantial list. When asked by the researcher why she hadn't taken advantage of her husband's offer, Debbie explained that it takes her a while to decide what she needs. Michael becomes angry with her if she can't answer immediately so she simply avoids placing herself in such situations. She receives further confirmation of her limitations when she considers the opportunities that are denied her. She recognizes that her dream of becoming a nurse and working in a convalescent home is an unrealistic one. A job which involves money or math (such as a cashier position) is out of her reach. The idea of even an oral driver's test has been sufficiently threatening to keep her from attempting to get her license, although she knows how to drive. Thus, whereas Debbie's adaptation is remarkable given her areas of deficiency and given the poor quality of her educational experience, the fact remains that she and others are conscious of her problems. Although the affect they have on the overall substance of her life as compared to her peers may, at a glance, seem negligible, their affect on her self-concept is profound. Debbie is vividly aware that she lacks the intellectual acuity displayed by others, is often reminded of this in ordinary interaction, and must continually struggle to maintain the positive attitude toward overcoming her limitations that enables her to accept herself.

Conclusion

These vignettes of 12 young adults necessarily leave much unsaid, but they do document something of the variety in these lives—variety in personality, social competence, community activities and networks of friends and relatives. This individuality is marked and must be kept in mind, yet there is a common pattern underlying it and it is that pattern that we shall emphasize. First, none of these 12 persons has "disappeared" into his or her community as a normal person. All 12 are seen by others close to them as limited or handicapped, sometimes in terms of a particular skill such as reading, at other times in terms of a more fundamental deficit such as being slow to learn or possessing limited intelligence. With greater or lesser willingness, most of these 12 persons acknowledge their own limitations.

A second theme that emerges repeatedly from the experiences of these 12 individuals is that the deficiencies which troubled them in school—inabilities to read, write, and use numerical concepts—are the same deficiencies which most obviously trouble them in their everyday lives as adults. The need for at least a modicum of proficiency in these areas did not end for these individuals when they completed their formal education. They, like all members of modern society, face an endless variety of everyday tasks and situations—shopping, applying for jobs, traveling around the city, eating out in restaurants, making ends meet, obtaining driver's licenses, interpreting traffic tickets, dealing with governmental agencies, and so forth—which require basic reading, writing, and/or mathematical skills. Lacking proficiency in "academic" skills, they find themselves ill-prepared to carry out these activities without obtaining non-normative degrees of assistance. Not surprisingly, this affects the nature of their social relationships and ultimately holds consequences for the way in which they are viewed by others. In a similar fashion, it leads many of these individuals to question their own intelligence, with a corresponding reduction of self-esteem.

It is also clear, however, that the deficiencies of many of these individuals go beyond their inability to achieve even marginal competence in reading, writing, and mathematical skills. They also include limitations which reflect the more generalized and pervasive nature of their intellectual deficits. References to short attention spans, poor judgment, a vulnerability to exploitation and victimization, the need for an inordinate amount of help in rearing children, and an inability to easily and completely understand what is going on around them repeatedly appear in the accounts of those who know these individuals best. Compared to those around them and judged on the basis of the standards of their own communities, they are found lacking, not only in their academic skills but in their basic intelligence and general adaptive skills as well.

The lives and self-concepts of these 12 persons only partly fulfill the expectations one would reasonably have of "six-hour retarded children" who have become adults. Their everyday lives sometimes parallel those of nonretarded adults in their neighborhoods, but only sometimes and never completely. Regardless of whether or not they have disappeared from the official attention of the service delivery system, they continue to face the same kinds of problems which first brought them to the attention of school professionals.

References

Birch, H. G., Richardson, S. A., Baird, D., Horobin, G., & Illsley, R. (1970). *Mental subnormality in the community: A clinical and epidemiological study.* Baltimore: Williams and Wilkins.

Cobb, H. (1972). *The forecast of fulfillment: A review of research on predictive assessment of the adult retarded for social and vocational adjustment.* New York: Teachers College Press.

Gazaway, R. (1969). *The longest mile.* Garden City, New York: Doubleday.

Granat, K., & Granat, S. (1973). Below-average intelligence and mental retardation. *American Journal of Mental Deficiency, 78,* 27–32.

Gruenberg, E. M. (1964). Epidemiology. In H. A. Stevens & R. Heber (Eds.), *Mental Retardation* (pp. 259–306). Chicago: The University of Chicago Press.

Kernan, K. T., & Walker, M. W. (1981). Use of services for the mentally retarded in the African-American community. *Journal of Community Psychology, 9,* 45–52.

Koegel, P., & Edgerton, R. B. (1982). Labeling and the perception of handicap among Black mildly retarded adults. *American Journal of Mental Deficiency, 87,* 266–276.

MacMillan, D. L. (1977). *Mental retardation in school and society.* Boston: Little, Brown.

Mercer, J. R. (1973). *Labeling the mentally retarded.* Berkeley: University of California Press.

President's Committee on Mental Retardation (1970). *The six-hour retarded child: A report on a conference on problems of education of children in the inner-city.* Washington, D.C.: U.S. Government Printing Office.

The authors are affiliated with the Socio-Behavioral Group, Mental Retardation Research Center (Neuropsychiatric Institute), UCLA. We gratefully acknowledge support for this research from NICHD Grant No. HD 04612, the Mental Retardation Research Center, UCLA, and NICHD Program Project Grant No. HD 11944–02, The Community Adaptation of Mildly Retarded Persons. To the following ethnographic field workers, our indebtedness is also most gratefully acknowledged: Marsha Bollinger, Regina Love, Dara Vines, and Dr. Lance Williams. We also thank Pamela Houston and Betty Wilson for their contributions to our understanding of these research participants.

The Social Structures of Mildly Mentally Retarded Afro-Americans: Gender Comparisons

Claudia Mitchell-Kernan and M. Belinda Tucker

Knowledge about mildly mentally retarded Afro-Americans is extremely limited, despite the fact that Blacks have been the subjects of much previous empirical work. The dominant focus in such work, however, has been the retarded *state*, rather than the manner in which ethnicity colors the *experience* of retardation. The general goals of this paper are to contribute to the sparse literature on mildly retarded Afro-Americans and to explore ways in which features of culture and community affect the overall quality of their lives. Specifically, the paper examines the form and function of the primary social structures in which mentally retarded Blacks are embedded and how those structures differ with respect to gender. The direction of the present inquiry has been shaped by the social scientific literature on the Afro-American family, social networks, and social support.

Cross-ethnic comparisons are not an objective of the present paper which is focused on current interpretations of Afro-American social organization and how these analyses shed light on the social lives of Blacks who are mentally retarded. Substantive knowledge about the distinctive social structures evident in Afro-American communities forms a central background against which the adaptive experiences of mentally retarded Blacks are examined.

Studies dealing specifically with the Black family, as well as more general studies of Afro-American communities, offer strong grounds on which to expect that the kin group is likely to be a source of significant ties for Black Americans (Billingsley, 1968; Hill, 1971; MacAdoo, 1978; Manns, 1981; Martin & Martin, 1978; Stack, 1974). For this reason, kin ties and their uses form a particularly important area of inquiry in this research. A number of anthropological and sociological studies, however, also document the importance of non-kin ties as features of social organization in urban settings. Indeed, the last 2 decades have yielded a body of literature which emphasizes the importance of individual-centered interaction systems as features of urban social organization in both Western and non-Western societies (Boissevain, 1974; Bott, 1957/1971; Fischer, Baldassare, Gerson, Jackson, Jones, & Stueve, 1977; Suttles, 1972). These interaction systems are comprised of chains of people with whom an individual is in actual contact, or with whom he or she can manage to enter into contact, and have the salient property of linking the individual at the center to an ever-widening circle of ties, often conceptualized as a series of concentric zones (Boissevain, 1974; Mitchell, 1969). The most basic distinction made, and one followed in the present paper, is between the *effective* network segment (or zone)—one's most intimate and frequently seen ties—and the *extended* segment—one's most distant ties (Eames & Goode, 1977). (A further distinction between intimate and less close ties within the effective segment is often made.) Commonly referred to as social networks in anthropology and sociology and as social support systems in social psychology, these interaction system, and in particular the effective network segment, are the major foci of the present work.

Both the anthropological and social support literature point to the importance of social ties in contributing to the psychological and physical well-being of the individual because they may be used to obtain various kinds of help of both an instrumental and emotional character (Bott, 1957/1971; Cobb, 1976; House, 1980). Marital status, social disorganization, acculturation, and intimacy, among other variables, have been shown to be associated with various indicators of distress, including cardio-vascular disease, mental health, and death (Cassell, 1976; Gurin, Veroff, & Feld, 1960; Lowenthal & Haven, 1968; Moriyama, Krueger, & Stamler, 1971; Srole, Langner, Michael, Opler, & Rennie, 1962). Typically, individuals lacking in critical areas of support show greater impairment (e.g., have more heart disease, are more likely to be depressed, and are more likely to die) than those with relevant ties. Other studies have stressed the buffering or mediation properties of social support. That is, under conditions of job stress, unemployment, economic crisis, loss, bereavement, illness, and a host of other undesirable circumstances, it appears that persons who have supportive relationships exhibit less psychological and physical distress (Caplan, 1979; House, 1980).

Research Questions

In the perspective of the existing social support and social network literature, we reasoned that the formation and maintenance of significant ties might prove to be an area of difficulty for the mentally retarded individual. First, by its very nature, mental retardation imposes a dependence on others which is likely to be greater than that of the nonretarded person. Second, one who is mentally retarded may have fewer sources from which to recruit social support than the nonretarded individual, because, among other reasons, adaptation to the world of work is often problematic and because families tend to shelter mentally retarded members. Finally, the retarded individual's ability to reciprocate and thus reinforce relations is limited, thereby creating social strains likely to impair his or her ability to recruit and sustain ties.

Specific questions that guided the portion of the research reported in the following pages included:

1. What are the structural features of the social networks that surround mildly mentally retarded Afro-American adults?
2. What are the functions of specific aspects of the social networks of mildly mentally retarded Afro-American adults?
3. How do structural characteristics and uses of networks differ with respect to gender?
4. In what manner do the traditional features of Afro-American social organization find representation in the adaptive social experiences of mildly mentally retarded Afro-American adults?

Methodology

Sample

The study sample was a select subcomponent of the larger sample of 45 mildly mentally retarded adults who comprised the Afro-American component of a larger study of adaptive behavior (Edgerton, 1978; Koegel & Edgerton, 1982). Our intensive sample was chosen to represent a range of representative living circumstances and individual characteristics. The participants consisted of 24 adults, 12 females and 12 males, whose ages ranged between 21 and 37 at the time the study began. Mean age was 26.5 years for women and 26.8 years for men, with IQ scores ranging from 55 to 70. Both sexes were about evenly divided between three living arrangements: (a) with the family of origin, consisting usually of a mother, or mother-figure, and often a father and siblings; (b) in a board and care facility; and (c) in an independent living situation—that is, a conventional apartment, an apartment complex for the mentally retarded (which included a full-time, live-in counselor), or various boarding arrangements. Nearly all sample members, as well as their families of origin, were of low socioeconomic status.

Procedure

The procedures employed represented a merging of orientations—cultural anthropology and social psychology—and reflect an attempt to integrate qualitative and quantitative research styles. Two years of qualitative data collection, consisting of detailed naturalistic observations and loosely structured interviews, were followed by a 5-month period of additional observations and the administration of highly structured questionnaires, including some standardized instruments. Information gathered from a review of the field notes and through questionnaire responses included: (a) the structural characteristics of the participants' effective networks (e.g., symmetry, dispersion, dominant source, existence of intimate and critical ties); (b) whether and how ties were used as coping mechanisms (i.e., for everyday problem solving, critical incidents, child rearing); (c) the nature of transactions between study participants and ties; and (d) the qualitative (or affective) aspects of specific critical social ties.

Results

Examination of the key social structural variables (i.e., the quantitative objective dimensions), suggests that, on the surface, the retarded Black adults in our sample are not particularly distinctive. Although they are less likely to be married than one generally would expect for this age group, exactly half are currently involved in romantic relationships (see Table 1). In addition, one-third of the women and one-fourth of the men have children. They have friends, with all participants naming at least one best friend. More distinctive is their tendency to have focused rather than dispersed networks (that is, most drew upon networks that are primarily from a single source).

One very striking finding is the strong similarity between males and females (see Table 1). The two sexes are equally likely to be either married or involved in an apparently romantic relationship. They are equally likely to have children and to have friends and best friends. The distribution of kin versus non-kin ties as the dominant source of networks is not substantially different,

TABLE 1
DEMOGRAPHIC CHARACTERISTICS OF SAMPLE

	Females (n = 12)	Males (n = 12)
Age		
Mean age	26.5	26.8
Age range	21–37	22–32
Marital Status/Romantic Involvement		
Married, together	1 (N)	1 (R)
Married, separated	1 (R)	1 (R)
Divorced, uninvolved	1	0
Has romantic tie	4 (3R,1N)	4 (2R,2?)
No involvement	5	6
Parental Status		
Has children	4	3
(average number)	(2.5)	(1.3)
Does not have children	8	9
Primary Living Arrangements During Last 6 Months of Study		
With family of origin	6	4
Board & Care facility or in boarding arrangement	3	2
Independent living apartment building	0	3
In own apartment with spouse, roommate, or alone	3	3

Note: N = nonretarded, R = retarded

with women slightly more likely than men to be family focused (i.e., 9 of the 12 women primarily cited kin as network members, while 7 of the 12 men were family centered).

Differences are apparent, however, in the number of children had by parents (2.5 average for women and 1.3 for men) and in the greater tendency for men to be the sole occupant of a dwelling unit. No women had ever lived alone, whereas at least four of the men had at one time lived alone. These two results taken together represent an interesting parallel. Retarded women are undoubtedly considered to be too vulnerable (as opposed to incompetent) to live alone. Sexuality is a major factor in the reluctance of family members and institutional officials to allow retarded women that level of independence (i.e., a fear that men will take advantage of them sexually). This fear was explicitly expressed by family members of three female study participants and arose as a specific complaint of two additional women in the sample. Family efforts to discourage relations felt to be sexually exploitative did not in general seem to meet with success. The fact that women sample members with children tended to have multiple births (suggesting a lack of control over their reproductive capacity) may help fuel such beliefs.

These selected structural characteristics of the social networks of the study participants, however, provide only one angle of vision on their social lives.

Simply knowing certain demographic characteristics and how many persons of what type interact with our participants proved insufficient to understand the social environments of mentally retarded Blacks. More detailed examination of relationships between variables and the qualitative indicators suggest that the picture is far more complex.

Kinship Ties

The Role of Kinship in Afro-American Social Organization

The importance of kin ties as sources of support for both men and women in this study may be interpreted in relation to what is known about the role of kinship among Black Americans generally, as well as in light of the specific handicaps of sample members imposed by their disability. In the first connection, it is relevant to review current social science perspectives on family structure and family functioning among Black Americans.

Since the seminal work of sociologist E. Franklin Frazier (1939), a predominance of scholarly attention directed toward the Black family has been focused on a type of family documented to be disproportionately present among Black Americans. This type of family, in which a husband-father is absent and which is headed by a female, has been variously referred to in the literature as *matriarchal, matrifocal, maternal,* or *matri-centric.* Frazier linked the incidence of this type of family to other indicators of social pathology, such as delinquency and illegitimacy, and viewed the female-headed family as both a symptom and a source of family disorganization and a variety of other social ills present in Black communities.[1]

The linkage between father-absence and family disorganization and pathology which Frazier's work sought to establish was widely accepted by almost three generations of students of the Black family until it was reiterated in the widely read and discussed "Moynihan Report" (1965). Although the report sparked considerable polemical debate and was widely criticized, its appearance seems to have played no small role in the revival of empirical research on Black families. Critics of the report took issue with the implied identity between the "Black family" and the "female-headed" family, countering that the family forms which had captured so much attention were more appropriately regarded as correlates of class than culture. More importantly, the literature

---

[1]For Frazier, the female-headed family had historical origins in the slave system which disrupted family ties through sale and which essentially weakened the family as a basic institution among Black Americans. An alternative view of the roots of the matri-centric family was advanced by anthropologist Melville Herskovits (1971/1958) who regarded this social form as a retention from the West African cultures from which American Blacks were primarily derived. In this perspective, the female-headed family, of widespread distribution among western hemisphere Blacks, could be compared to the mother-child family, embedded in extended family kin structures and associated with plural marriage in West Africa. Herskovits' views did not gain wide acceptance but were revived during the 1960s and 1970s in revisionist literature on the Black family, which stressed the importance of extended kinship ties among Black Americans as a central feature of social organization. Although the origins of present day Afro-American family forms continues to be debated, recent literature has tended to follow Frazier in favoring either slavery and/or antebellum economic deprivations in explaining the incidence of maternal families among Black Americans.

began to advance the view that the very image of the female-headed family as a symptom of disorganization and pathology was rooted in Euro-centric cultural bias, which tended to identify nuclear family structure (i.e., husband-father, wife-mother, and offspring) as the "normal" condition of the family.

A redirection of interest and emphasis has been evident in studies of Black families since the early 1970s. This more recent literature has included more studies of middle-class Black families (Billingsley, 1968; MacAdoo, 1978) and work which situates the study of family and family life within the study of larger kinship systems. For example, anthropologist Carol Stack's (1980) work has undermined the conception that families without husband-fathers are per se dysfunctional. Her work, in addition, has provided empirical support for the view that kinship networks among Blacks perform many of the functions commonly associated with nuclear families. According to Stack (1974), "The material and cultural support needed to absorb, sustain, and socialize community members . . . is provided by networks of cooperating kinsmen" (p. 118). Such kin-based networks are, in fact, more stable sources of social support than marital ties, since the latter, unlike the former, can be dissolved with relative ease. Stack's findings not only suggest that a conceptual reorientation should take place in studies of the Black "family," but alerted us to the need to consider the network character of kin-ties as a methodological concern in our objective to study significant ties among the Afro-American mentally retarded. Of importance in this connection is Stack's observation that domestic networks do not have an obvious nucleus, nor are they characterized by defined boundaries. A frequent nucleus of such networks is, however, a cluster of adult females. Stack relates this empirical generalization to the importance of domestic networks in child care. Members of domestic networks are "recruited from personal kindreds and friendships, but the personnel changes with fluctuating economic needs, changing life styles and vacillating personal relationships" (p. 119).

Although this new work does not entirely refute former perspectives on the dysfunctional aspects of father-absence, it has, in our view, successfully established the limitations of attributions about family and domestic functioning based on compositional considerations alone, as well as the limited utility of viewing the Black family as a monotypal entity.

Spheres of Kinship Support

We have, in our data, found considerable confirmation of recent findings documenting the importance of networks of cooperating kin in domestic organization. With few exceptions, kinship relations constitute an important source of instrumental and emotional support for our sample members. Although the level of familial involvement may vary, most provide a range of services most easily discussed under the broad headings of: life management, housekeeping, childcare, and guidance and empathy.

Life management. Many participants have difficulty negotiating environments and handling tasks which require literacy and/or arithmetic skills. This includes many of the ordinary requirements of everyday life, such as check cashing, completing a job application, ordering food in a restaurant, reading letters, obtaining a driving license, or negotiating with institutional officials and social service agents. Overall, sample members reported reliance on relatives more often than non-kin to take care of their instrumental needs. No basic gender distinctions were apparent.

The most sensitive area of familial involvement in life management is certainly financial. Of the 24 sample members, 21 indicated that they would go to a family member if they needed money. With respect to fiscal management, whereas most of our study participants receive some form of government assistance, either SSI (Supplemental Security Income) or AFDC (Aid to Families with Dependent Children) allotments, only a very few participants received and cashed the checks themselves. Although exploitation may have existed in rare instances and occasional conflicts were apparent, overall, the assistance seemed to be genuine and responsibly motivated. Helen is a case in point:

> The oldest sample member, Helen, was 35 when the study began. She lived in a board and care facility throughout our period of contact with her and had no control over her financial affairs. Her mother is the payee for Helen's SSI benefits and makes payments directly to the board and care operator. According to Helen, the small remaining amount is used by her mother to purchase articles that she believes Helen needs. Although Helen is quite discontent with the arrangement, retardation aside, Helen's history of psychiatric problems and epileptic seizures causes her mother to doubt Helen's ability to manage such affairs on her own. Helen is permitted, however, to keep and spend as she wishes the proceeds from the sale of her artwork through the workshop she attends.

Housekeeping. Not surprisingly, women were less often the recipients of housekeeping support from family than were men. Quite to the contrary, female sample members were more likely to perform a number of basic housekeeping chores, including cooking, cleaning, washing, and ironing. This was true whether participants lived with their families of origin, in a board and care facility, or independently. Nevertheless, family members were regularly involved in seeing that the basic housekeeping needs of sample members were met.

Childcare. The care and socialization of the children of sample members was, in every case, a primary responsibility of family members. At last contact, all but one of the 14 children of our participants were living in a household that contained a grandparent (although this had not always been the case for a number of them and seemed to be the consequence of divorce, marital disputes, and housing problems). This situation was observed irrespective of gender; men with children were just as embedded in the familial support structure as were women. Families consistently provided a range of childrearing services, including childcare instructions for the new parents, babysitting, feeding, education, and, in some cases, the actual assumption of all childcare responsibilities. Examples of this latter extreme form of support ranged from the temporary practice of keeping the newborn baby in someone else's room (such as a sister or the new mother's parent) to physically removing the child from the custody of parents. These very striking patterns are illustrated by the experiences of three sample members as obtained through observation and self-report.

Carolyn, who is divorced, receives considerable support from her mother (with whom she resides) in the care and rearing of her three children through the provision of a home, money, discipline, and a host of other daily child care needs. Indeed, her mother's high level of involvement appears to be a central factor in her mother's decision to move back to their home state when it becomes financial feasible. It is there that Carolyn's mother expects to find sufficient support from her own kin group to make Carolyn's dependence less of a burden. In fact, Carolyn worries that her mother's recent increased drinking is a direct result of the strain of caring for Carolyn and her children.

Barbara, an unmarried mother of four, lives with her mother and four siblings, all of whom take an active interest in her children and their welfare. At one point, when Barbara left home temporarily to join a male friend, a sister and her mother assumed sole responsibility for the children at significant inconvenience to themselves.

Although Mitchell, a 24-year-old male, had relatively little involvement with his family, this situation changed radically after his marriage and the subsequent birth of his child. Because Mitchell's mother strongly disapproves of his wife, who is also retarded, this increased frequency of kin interaction tends to take place between Mitchell and his in-laws rather than with his own relatives. His mother's disengagement, however, is more than compensated for by his mother-in-law's involvement in his life. She invited the new couple to live with her and provides a wide variety of support for them and their baby.

These findings are consistent with Robert Hill's (Hill, 1971; Hill & Shackleford, 1975) assessments of the practice of informal adoption, considered to be a distinctive feature of Afro-American extended family arrangements. Hill has observed that the taking in of dependent children is most often performed by grandmothers (as we observe in our own data) and is due to a range of factors, including parental incapacitation, marital problems among parents, parental immaturity, and also a desire on the part of the adopter for companionship. Patterns such as these have been traced to West African family structure by Melville Herskovits (1971/1958) and Wade Nobles (1974), among others. In the case of mentally retarded parents, the grandparents have real doubts about the caretaking competence of their children, and may, in essence, be adopting the grandchildren, despite (as in our sample) the parents' physical presence.

Guidance and empathy. Whereas family members appeared to be more significantly involved in the instrumental areas of support, some participants reported reliance on relatives for other more affective needs. This includes the discussion of personal problems, feelings, the need for companionship, and general emotional support. One sample member listed her parents as her best friends. Siblings and in-laws were also occasionally mentioned as friends.

Steve, an extremely gregarious 22-year-old male who lives independently, describes his relationship with his mother:

> My mother, I would run to in a minute. I would drop like that [motion indicating speed] to run to her . . . We talk. We don't have that kind of communication as far as hanging around together. But we talk whenever I need somebody to talk to.

A case study. Although discussed above as four separate spheres of influence, the actual transmission of support is much more diffuse, with support of one kind not always clearly distinct from another. This constellation and integration of support is particularly well illustrated by the case of Deidre:

> Deidre, who was 21 years of age and single at the time data collection began, is very attractive and bears no stigmata which readily identify her as retarded. She is the second child in a family of two brothers and three sisters, ranging in age from 15 to 24. While in junior high school, Deidre left her family of origin to live with her grandmother, ostensibly to provide companionship and care. She remained there until she became pregnant and at that time moved back to her parent's home. Because she was unable to qualify for SSI, Deidre has been financially dependent on her family all of her life, except for a brief period when she had a small independent income from her job in a sheltered workshop. With the birth of her child, however, she eventually qualified for AFDC and herself became a contributor to the family budget.
>
> Following her marriage to a man who is not her son's father, Deidre's high level of involvement with her family continued and became a source of marital strain. Her nonretarded husband clearly resents her frequent visits to her parental home, a resentment Deidre attributes to jealousy because he is not fortunate enough to enjoy similar close relationships within his own family. Nevertheless, both her mother and her brother continued to make financial contributions to her support after she left the family household. These contributions were necessitated, in part, by the sporadic employment of her husband, whose frequent resorts to physical violence serve to stimulate family interventions as well. At one point in the study, much to Deidre's consternation, she was unable to satisfactorily meet the nutritional needs of her son. Turning to her brother, she received $100 to tide her over until her financial straits improved. Substantial familial involvement in the care of the son has continued after Deidre's marriage; during her honeymoon, the 1½-year-old child was the responsibility of Deidre's teenaged sister, who is also retarded. Deidre's mother also takes a very active childrearing role and occasionally intervenes in ways Deidre seems to find "meddlesome."
>
> Indeed, the involvement of Deidre's relatives in providing instrumental support is nowhere better documented than in her residential history during the period of this study. Between September 1980 and March 1981, Deidre and her young son lived with her parents in

their home. In April 1981, she moved with her son to an apartment with her husband where she remained until the end of June. In July 1981, she separated temporarily from her husband in response to his infidelity and was again living in her parental home. In September 1981, she moved in briefly with a female cousin while her husband was serving a jail sentence for burglary. By the end of October, she was back in her parental home and remained there until May 1982, at which time she moved into a rented house across the street from her parents' home. By the time of our last contact, at the end of July 1982, Deidre, her husband and child were back in her parental home, this time as the result of an eviction.

Structural Determinants of Network Linkages

In view of the recent findings of Stack and others, it comes as no surprise that, among sample members, women's ties to family are much stronger and more exclusive than those of males, leading to relatively little dependence on non-kin for either emotional or practical needs when family members are proximate. Even after leaving home, family ties were still heavily utilized by many of the women, due in part to the fact that married women with children remain very dependent on kin for childcare support.

On the other hand, male contact with and utilization of family ties decreased dramatically with attainment of independent living status—not always to the satisfaction of the study participant. Apparently, families are considerably more comfortable about loosening their ties with mentally retarded males, probably due largely to the perceived vulnerability of the women but perhaps also because males are *expected* to make it on their own.

Fred, who shares an independent living apartment with another sample member, lived in a board and care facility for 2 years prior to moving to his present residence. Although Fred is quite open about his preference to live at home and has voiced the complaint that his mother "sent him away," she is quite firm in her insistence that "he is old enough to take care of himself." Fred has also expressed a desire to move in with his brother. This, too, is a wish which seems likely to remain unfulfilled.

Mitchell (whose childcare situation was discussed earlier) was diagnosed as hydrocephalic shortly after birth and also has spina bifida with cerebral palsy. At the time data collection began, Mitchell had been living in a board and care facility for some time. His separation from his family seems to have been motivated initially by his mother's inability to find a suitable school for him in the town where she was then living. Mitchell sees his family fairly regularly at family occasions and tends to have regular telephone contact with his mother to whom he seems closest. His mother, however, clearly believes in his potential for independence and, for the most part, allows him to live his life quite free of parental interference, although she occasionally helps him out financially. Indeed, Mitchell's mother expects such considerable self reliance that when his subsequent marriage went sour, she commented: "He just had to have this girl. He didn't want

to listen to me or anyone. Then after he got into it, then he come crying on my shoulder and I told him I didn't want to hear it."

It is clear from the observations that the functions of kin ties are determined in significant ways by structural variables, primarily those of situational
context and gender. The living arrangement of the participant appears to
strongly influence the type of relationships that the retarded person enters into
(see Table 2). (While we are unable to make determinations of causality from
the data, the alternative proposition is highly implausible.) Sample members
who lived at home were thoroughly embedded in family-dominated networks.
Many had no contact with non-relatives. Once away from the family of origin,
the nature of the distinctions between socialized roles for women versus those
of men became paramount. Women in both board and care facilities and those
living independently remained in greater contact with and more dependent on
their families than did men in the same living arrangements. Evidence from our
analyses of the structure of non-kin relations among the sample members sheds
further light on this observation.

TABLE 2

RELATIONSHIP BETWEEN LIVING ARRANGEMENT, GENDER
AND DOMINANT NETWORK SOURCE

Females (n = 12)

Living Arrangement	*Dominant Network Source*		
	Family	Non-kin	Mixed
Family	6	0	0
Boarding	2	0	1
Independent	1	1	1

Males (n = 12)

Living Arrangement	*Dominant Network Source*		
	Family	Non-kin	Mixed
Family	4	0	0
Boarding	2	0	0
Independent	1	4	1

Non-kin Ties

Non-Kin Ties Among the Mentally Retarded

Although kinship networks are to some extent a function of reciprocity,
because such ties are inherited they are less dependent on individual initiative.
The cultivation of friendship or peer (i.e., non-kin) effective relationships
which lack the inherent reinforcement of "blood" requires a high degree of reciprocity. Friends simply will not tolerate the same degree of dependency that
the ethos of kinship may permit. It is in this respect that the mentally retarded
individual is handicapped. Due to constraints of resources, skills, and mobility,
he or she often has little to offer in exchange for benefits received. In addition,
the kinds of support services the mentally retarded individual is able to offer

kin, or those who share his or her household (e.g., housework, small cash offerings), differ from the kinds of exchanges that typically serve to establish and cement friendship ties.

A second area of constraints on the development of non-kin ties by retarded persons is the limited number of activity fields in which they are involved. Very few are engaged in regular competitive employment, a primary contact source among the nonretarded. Activities outside of the home are likely to be limited to workshops, the service delivery system, the neighborhood, and a very few voluntary organizations, including the church. Although the workshop environment provides access to similarly handicapped persons, limitations of transportation generally preclude contact outside of work hours. Contact within the service delivery system is usually confined to the professionals who are being paid to work with the mentally retarded person as a client. Although such relationships sometimes develop into quasi-friendships, they are usually short-lived, probably due primarily to the fact that the relationship is predicated on the mentally retarded person's dependency. The church is probably most central among the voluntary organizations where they can obtain non-kin ties. Through both institutional and individual initiative, churches have been engaged in attempts to bring mentally retarded persons "into the fold" in addition to attending to their special needs.

Observed Patterns of Non-Kin Support

Although it is rare that the networks of a sample member are devoid of non-kin ties, a more in-depth examination of patterns of interaction and the kinds of transactions that characterize the relations suggest some rather distinctive patterns. Such relationships typically involve people who are derived from a single source (workshop, high school) and consist primarily of peers and members of the service delivery system. The number of such ties vary widely, with certain sample members appearing to be virtual isolates and others listing as many as 10 friends. However, due to both the content of the relationships and the fact that they do not appear to function in the "linking" (i.e., interconnected) fashion which gives personal networks their most distinctive character, many sample members, in comparison to nonretarded persons, live quite insular lives.

As with the kinship ties, gender differences in the patterns of non-kin relations were most apparent once sample members left their families of origin. Men in our sample who were living independently or in boarding situations were fairly well imbedded in peer networks, whereas women were more likely to be either family-oriented or involved in mixed networks. Five of the eight males living away from home were significantly non-kin centered (i.e., had most contact with and sought help from friends, counselors); whereas only two of the seven women who had lived away from home for significant periods during the research had non-kin as a dominant network source.

Nevertheless, the male non-kin relations were still rather distinctive. Although their best friends were equally likely to be retarded or nonretarded, five of the eight men living away from their family of origin named *women* as best friends (including, for example, a counselor and a "girlfriend," but no wives). Men were very rarely named as best friends among women. The nature of peer relationships for the retarded men in our sample thus differs substantially from that observed with nonretarded Black men in this age range, who seem to be more socially and emotionally tied to other males (Abrahams, 1970; Liebow, 1967). Men such as these, who are particularly needy, may be better able to find the quality of support they need in women (since women are socialized to be more nurturant). Support for this notion is derived from the level of emotional support which seems to be obtained from friendships. Men living independently reported discussing deeply personal problems with friends (e.g., concerns about "not having a real family," "girl problems," sex, ability problems, and various kinds of interpersonal difficulties). They seemed to be as open as women are to seeking support for personal difficulties. We do not dismiss the possibility, however, that such open behavior is learned through participation in various programs offered by the service delivery system (e.g., rap sessions at workshops), through continuous questioning by representatives of public agencies, and simply by participating in a long-term, personally involving study conducted by investigators from the Mental Retardation Research Center at UCLA!

If the naming of women as best friends by men is related to a need for nurturance, it may be compounded by a strong tendency for families to disapprove of the romantic involvements of the mentally retarded males. Three of the six current involvements are highly disapproved of by family members, and two other recent break-ups seemed to be directly related to family pressure for disengagement. Two relatives of one participant actually went to his fiancée and urged her to break it off. Although warning their daughters of the potential dangers of sexual exploitation, families of the retarded women were much less disapproving of serious involvements, and only one such situation exists (one mother objects to the boyfriend's race). If men are therefore discouraged from forming romantic ties, female best-friend companionship may be the next best thing.

Among both male and female sample members, no clear pattern of domination by either retarded or nonretarded non-kin ties emerged, although individuals in board and care facilities only had access to other retarded persons. Higher functioning sample members (i.e., those who were literate and often competitively employed), however, clearly preferred nonretarded friendships and disdained contact with persons of lesser competence. (Sally consistently refers to lower functioning persons as "looney birds," and Steve refuses to have anything to do with fellow residents in his independent living apartment complex.)

Although gender differences in the observed patterns did not exist, the distinction between having retarded versus nonretarded social ties may have greater significance for men. We suggest this in view of the relatively greater significance attached to peer relationships among young nonretarded, low-income Black males. That is, nonretarded women of this age group are not as dependent upon the peer group for socialization of gender-specific behaviors as are men. Traditionally, female behavior, including child care, housekeeping, even seduction, can be learned through interactions with more competent female family members in domestic settings. Expected behavior for young Black males, however, is often only learned through participation in "street-corner," non-domestic type interactions. Learning, for example, to speak and walk appropriately (highly distinctive Black male behaviors), to play basketball or shoot pool, or how to approach women, requires not only regular interaction with knowledgeable individuals but also requires abilities that may be beyond the competence of one who is mentally retarded. The males in our sample have, for the most part, never become a part of such culture-specific activity.

Discussions of friendship patterns in two ethnographic treatments of Afro-Americans are of relevance in illuminating the patterns of normal males from similar backgrounds. Elliot Liebow's (1967) study of underemployed Black males in Washington, D.C. and Roger Abraham's (1970) study of Black male verbal behavior in New York City document the importance of friendship networks in the daily lives of young Black males. Liebow reported that the cultivation of friendships was a preoccupation of the men, who met as a result of their frequenting the same carry-out restaurant. For the men in his study, friendships were sought as a source of security and, it would appear, self-esteem as well because friendships figured centrally in the status arithmetic of the value system of the streets. Similarly, Abrahams notes that Black males establish a wide range of friendship ties beginning in their early years. He offers a functional interpretation of this pattern, arguing that in an environment where there is considerable uncertainty, it is advantageous to create as many links with others as possible. He also found that a very early onset of peer-group life had as a corollary the absence of the home as a focal area of activity for the young men he studied. Paralleling Liebow's findings, a wide network of friendships served to confer status on the individual in and of itself and resulted in a tendency among the men to advertise friendships.

Previous social adaptation research on gender distinctions between mentally retarded males and females focuses on the fact that the retarded male's inability to compete successfully in the work setting (as opposed to the retarded woman's ability to experience relative success in home-oriented spheres) relegates him permanently to a marginal status (Edgerton, 1967). We are suggesting, however, that for low-income Black men, the inability to fully participate in male social subculture is an additional marginalizing factor. A number of such situations were observed in our sample of males:

Carl, 22 at the study's initiation, had five siblings living in close proximity, and until the death of his mother, approximately a year before our contact with Carl ended, he lived at home. Carl's mother was the central anchor of his kindred, and family support for him seems to have deteriorated in her absence. A brief attempt to remain in the family household with another sister and a brother following his mother's death did not work out satisfactorily, and the sister who seems most interested in his welfare prefers that he live independently of her. Since leaving the family home, he has for the most part lived independently across the street from the sister to whom he is closest, but shortly before data collection ended Carl moved in with her. Both view the arrangement as temporary. Although two young men in the neighborhood are sometimes mentioned as friends, Carl's actual contact with them is minimal, and they seem more acquaintances than close ties. When asked, Carl specifically listed three of his co-workers from the sheltered workshop as friends (one simply referred to as his "Mexican friend"), but none is seen outside of the workshop

setting. Over the last year and a half, he has become increasingly isolated. He mentioned that he had broken up with his nonretarded
girlfriend because his sister felt that she was just "using Carl." Similar thoughts were expressed when family members urged Carl to stop
seeing a male acquaintance who they felt was "taking advantage of
him." It seems that Carl was arrested for shoplifting when the
"friend" slipped some stolen batteries into Carl's pocket.

Sam, 29 at first contact, is also fairly isolated. A boarder in a
private home, his caretaker (an older woman) provides for a variety
of his needs, although the relationship seems to be strictly instrumental and, in general, they go their separate ways. Sam is clearly quite
fond of a staff member at the spastic children's center where he once
lived. This individual is mentioned as his only and best friend. Unemployed, Sam's visits to the center to see his friend are an important
part of his daily routine. He has never had a girlfriend and expresses
fear of women.

Andre has four siblings living in the area, whereas his mother
(who has been hospitalized for schizophrenia) lives in northern
California and his father lives out of state. Andre is quite ambivalent
about one brother who shows an interest in him and sees him on occasion, citing a history of abusive behavior on the brother's part.
When questioned, Andre names 2 best friends and lists 18 friends (all
independent living program staff members). However, the
fieldworker who visited Andre for 3 years felt that all the friends
Andre mentioned were really only acquaintances and stated: "I really
didn't believe that _____ was that close a friend and think that
Andre just came up with a name because I had asked him a question
and he needed to give me an answer. I don't think Andre has any
close friends." Such deceptions are consistent with his past contriv-
ances to affect the appearance of "normalcy." He has in the past, for
example, claimed that two of his female counselors tried to seduce
him. He seems most dependent on a former counselor, emotionally
and instrumentally, and fantasizes about a romantic relationship with
her. Throughout the entire period of study, he has had no girlfriend.

Isolation of the sort exemplified in these three cases, was not as apparent
among the female sample members. Although this research provides no direct
test of the question, previous literature, together with these observations,
suggest that differences between the approximation of culturally normative
socialization experiences of male and female mildly retarded Afro-Americans
may account for the different relationship patterns. These low income Black
males may be less able to use a "cloak of competence" (Edgerton, 1967) to
cover their inadequacies—because they have not learned the culturally appropriate behaviors. This seems due, at least in part, to the fact that they are denied the opportunities that permit such learning to take place. Family protectiveness, separation in the school system, and lack of acceptance in the requi-
site settings (e.g., basketball court, the "corner") reinforce their marginality.

Conclusion

The activation of kin ties to provide a variety of types of support seems very much a way of life for the majority of our study participants. The cultural roots of such kinship support also find representation in evidence that the parents of sample members also receive and expect help from their relatives. Recall that Deidre lived for quite some time with her grandmother. Similarly, although our field notes do not provide complete residential histories for all sample members, a number of them have been in the primary care of relatives other than their parents for extended periods during their childhoods. Aunts, uncles, in-laws, and cousins, in addition to lineal relatives, provide some support as well. Although kin relations are not uniformly smooth, as would be expected in any group of people, relatives not only seem willing to be involved in the lives of members of the sample, some seem to derive significant satisfaction from the nurturance they offer.

There were in the data, however, a few hints about the "dark" side of the protective web of kinship. Several sample members came from families which it seems fair to depict as "problem" families with weak levels of familial integration and characterized by patterns of stressful interaction. Two sample members' mothers had histories of mental illness, and in the case of another, the sibling relationship appeared to be exploited in ways which did not serve the interests of the sample member. It may also be the case that heavy kin embeddedness may serve to accentuate the sense of dependency of some individuals, particularly those who have never successfully taken a step toward the independence typically associated with adulthood—moving away from the family home. Deidre, whose history has been detailed at length, may be such a case. For her, moving away from her family home seemed quite central to her self-definition as a responsible and competent adult. She wished to be independent of her parents residentially and financially. As she herself stated, her marriage was viewed as a fulfillment of that goal. It is notable that financial support by a husband did not similarly undermine that sense of adult independence. Time and time again, however, Deidre finds herself back under family control, most recently with her husband and child also dependent upon her family's resources.

It seems clear that degree of familial embeddedness is a primary determinant of the extent to which our sample members were able to develop non-kin ties of any nature. Such embeddedness, in turn, seems to be largely a function of residence. Most appeared to be entrenched in a greatly extended period of adolescence, continually testing and challenging parental authority in order to achieve some measure of independence but cognizant of their tremendous needs for familial support (would anyone else take care of them?). Those who were more fully enmeshed in non-kin (or mixed) networks were usually those who experienced familial loss through parental death, incapacitation, or abandonment. Others who left the family home under less traumatic circumstances, generally under the protection of independent living programs, attempted to maintain strong family ties.

Successful adaptation to independent living and a more balanced network structure also seemed related to the degree of responsibility the sample member was given in the home. It is easy to think of mentally retarded people only as recipients of aid. Our observations demonstrate, however, that many of our participants made substantial contributions to their households as well as to others. Among other tasks, they regularly engaged in child care, performed major housekeeping functions (including regular cooking of meals), one did automobile maintenance, and many made very significant financial contributions to those around them. In fact, the current extremely depressed economic climate in low-income minority communities may even make the SSI benefits a critical component of the family's economy. A number of other sample members were competitively employed and, from both a psychological and practical perspective, became significant sources of family support. The following dialogue with Steve demonstrates how intertwined and difficult, for both participant and family, the issues of reciprocity, dependency, and independence become:

> Although Steve, who was 22 when the study began, dropped out of school during the 11th grade, he held two jobs throughout most of the study period. By washing dishes in a department store cafeteria by day and cleaning a movie theatre part time at night, he provided substantial financial support for his mother and three younger siblings. He eventually moved alone into an independent living apartment complex.

> Interviewer: What kind of things do you *not* like about your mother?
>
> Steve: She likes to rely on people . . . say for instance, you're doing good, right, and she stands on your head. When you get ready to fall, she falls with you. She has nothing to back her up and I always think that a parent should not depend on a child so much. When he's doing good, they should have some kind of money stashed away or something saved away for themselves.
>
> Interviewer: Does she depend on you when you're doing well?
>
> Steve: She knows that I'm doing well. She tries not to depend on me because she doesn't want to let me know that she wants to . . . She likes to lean on people . . . wantin' someone to always do something for her.
>
> Interviewer: How would your life be different if your mother was no longer around?
>
> Steve: Oh, I don't know what I would do . . . I'd probably be on top of somebody's head and when they fall I fall with them. But I doubt it very seriously. No, I been doing good so far. This is the reason why I moved out of the house with my mother to get my own place; to see what it was like out there, to see if it was what she say it was. 'Cause she always tell me 'Steve, life is hard out there, you'll never make it.' So I'm here. And I seem to

> be doing pretty good. And the guy that's supposed
> to be working with me, I can never find him
> [reference to live-in counselor for the independent
> living apartment complex]. I can never find him
> nowhere. So you might as well say I'm doing it.

The social network thus provides contact with a range of people who not only provide assistance but who also need help. We would suggest that it is in providing this sort of help that significant training toward responsible adult roles takes place. One's self-esteem is clearly bolstered by the ability to provide assistance to others. Deidre aspires to a level of financial success that will allow her to contribute more to her mother. Similarly, Gertrude, who lives independently, expressed extreme dissatisfaction over her counselor's refusal to let Gertrude and her roommate pay for a dinner:

> Interviewer: You went out to lunch that time, didn't you, you
> and Mary [Gertrude's roommate] and Jean [Gertrude's counselor] and . . .
> Gertrude: And Valerie [friend of Jean]. But they didn't let us
> pay for the dinner.
> Interviewer: They didn't?
> Gertrude: No and that what pissed me off. And then when
> we got outside they said, "Stand with Jean. I'm
> gonna take your picture." And I stayed, but I
> didn't make no smile or nothing. She said,
> "Smile." Mary was smiling, though. I was mad
> and then . . .
> Interviewer: 'Cause they wouldn't let you pay?
> Gertrude: Uh huh. And then she said, "Stay with Valerie."
> And Valerie started tickling me and I smiled just a
> little. But I was pissed off. 'Cause they say you
> guys could pay for it, 'cause we put our money
> together. And we had enough money and then she
> say, "No you guys can't." I was pissed.

Although the design of this study has proven to be of considerable value in shedding light on the social networks of our study participants, the "social support" dimensions of these systems have not been fully illuminated. We have not, for example, explored the ways in which the outermost or "extended" network segment impinges upon the lives of our participants. How do they handle the many daily interactions with store clerks, bank officials, people on the street, and so forth, and how do such interactions affect one's sense of well being?

Despite the distinctive life history and therefore distinctive set of social relations presented by each sample member, some problematic features of their social support systems deserve highlighting. The dominance of kin in the intimate zone is one such feature. Although this may not be a problem at all points in the life cycle of the mentally retarded individual, its effects seem destined to be realized. Few networks show balance in intimate zones between kin and friends, and, whereas relatives may not actually impede the formation of emotionally and instrumentally satisfying relations with others, there seems little to propel the mentally retarded individual out of this nurturant circle so long as parents are alive and the family itself is functioning reasonably well. For most members of our sample, non-kin in the effective network segment are drawn from a limited number of activity fields. In addition, relations formed with coworkers or school mates are typically context-specific, rarely involving social interaction outside of the setting in which the relationship was formed. The service providers, who must also be considered a part of the effective segment, represent "dead ends" in terms of linking the individual to a wider network of people which might serve as a recruitment pool for friends.

The variety of adaptations evident among sample members suggests that caution should be observed in specifying what factors ultimately determine whether an individual achieves some semblance of a "normal" adult lifestyle—living independently, working, and taking care of her or his basic needs. Although it is unclear whether the individuals who achieved such stature in our sample were inherently more capable or were exposed to more adaptive socialization experiences, friendship linkages seem central to successful adaptation. Given the fact that more adult mentally retarded persons are being forced to "make it on their own" (due to deinstitutionalization) and, as we have observed in this sample, their aging parents are either dying or becoming less functional, this latter question is critical. In an age of dwindling social resources as well as ideological change, strategies to better prepare mentally retarded adults to form emotionally rewarding and socially useful non-kin ties, and to utilize existing family ties in the process, must be developed.

References

Abrahams, R. (1970). *Deep down in the jungle* (rev. ed.). Chicago: Adeline Publishing Co.

Billingsley, A. (1968). *Black families in white America*. Englewood Cliffs, NJ: Prentice-Hall.

Boissevain, J. (1974). *Friends of friends: Networks, manipulators and coalitions*. New York: St. Martin.

Bott, E. (1971). *Family and social network* (2nd ed.). New York: Free Press. (Originally published, 1957.)

Caplan, R. D. (1979). Social support, person-environment fit, and coping. In L. A. Ferman & J. P. Gordus (Eds.), *Mental health and the economy* (pp. 89–138). Kalamazoo, MI: W. E. Upjohn Institute for Employment Research.

Cassell, J. (1976). The contribution of the social environment to host resistance. *American Journal of Epidemiology, 104*, 107–123.

Cobb, S. (1976). Social support as a moderator of life stress. *Psychosomatic Medicine, 38*, 300–314.

Eames, E., & Goode, J. G. (1977). *Anthropology of the city: An introduction to urban anthropology*. Englewood Cliffs, NJ: Prentice-Hall.

Edgerton, R. (1967). *The cloak of competence: Stigma in the lives of the retarded*. Berkeley: University of California Press.

Edgerton, R. (1978). *The community adaptation of mildly retarded persons*. (Proposal submitted to The National Institute of Child Health and Human Development).

Fischer, C. S., Baldassare, K., Gerson, R. M., Jackson, R. M., Jones, L. M., & Stueve, C. A. (1977). *Networks and places: Social relations in the urban setting.* New York: Free Press.

Frazier, E. F. (1939). *The Negro family in the United States.* New York: MacMillan.

Gurin, G., Veroff, J., & Feld, S. (1960). *Americans view their mental health.* New York: Basic Books.

Herskovits, M. J. (1971). *The myth of the Negro past.* Boston: Beacon Press. (Originally published, 1958.)

Hill, R. B. (1971). *The strengths of Black families.* New York: Emerson Press.

Hill, R. B., & Shackleford, L. (1975). The Black extended family revisited. In R. Staples (Ed.), *The Black family: Essays and studies* (pp. 201–206). Belmont, CA: Wadsworth.

House, J. S. (1980). *Work stress and social support.* Reading, MA: Addison-Wesley.

Koegel, P., & Edgerton, R. B. (1982). Labeling and the perception of handicap among Black mildly retarded adults. *American Journal of Mental Deficiency, 87,* 266–276.

Liebow, E. (1967). *Tally's corner.* Boston, MA: Little, Brown, & Co.

Lowenthal, M., & Haven, C. (1968). Interaction and adaptation: Intimacy as a critical variable. *American Sociological Review, 33,* 20–30.

MacAdoo, H. (1978). Factors related to stability in upwardly mobile Black families. *Journal of Marriage and the Family, 40,* 761–776.

Manns, W. (1981). Support systems of significant others in Black families. In H. P. MacAdoo (Ed.), *Black families* (pp. 238–251). Beverly Hills, CA: Sage.

Martin, E. P., & Martin, J. M. (1978). *The Black extended family.* Chicago: University of Chicago Press.

Mitchell, J. C. (Ed.) (1969). *Social networks in urban situations.* Manchester: University of Manchester Press.

Moynihan, D. P. (1965). *The Negro family: The case for national action.* Washington, D.C.: U.S. Government Printing Office.

Moriyama, I. M., Krueger, D. E., & Stamler, J. (1971). *Cardiovascular disease in the United States.* Cambridge: Harvard University Press.

Nobles, W. (1974). African root and American fruit: The Black family. *Journal of Social and Behavioral Sciences, 20,* 66–77.

Srole, L., Langner, T. S., Michael, S. T., Opler, M. K., & Rennie, T. A. C. (1962). *Mental health in the metropolis.* New York: McGraw-Hill.

Stack, C. (1974). *All our kin: Strategies for survival in a Black community.* New York: Harper & Row.

Stack, C. (1980). Domestic networks: Those you count on. In Angeloni, E. (Ed.), *Anthropology 80/81* (pp. 117–123). Guilford, CT: Sluice Dock Press. (Reprinted from Stack, C., *All our kin: Strategies for survival in a Black community.* New York: Harper & Row, 1974.)

Suttles, G. D. (1972). *The social order of the slum: Ethnicity and territory in the inner city.* Chicago: University of Chicago Press.

The authors are affiliated with the Center for Afro-American Studies, UCLA and the Socio-Behavioral Group, Mental Retardation Research Center (Neuropsychiatric Institute), UCLA. We gratefully acknowledge support from NICHD Grant No. 04612, The Mental Retardation Research Center, UCLA; NICHD Program Project Grant No. HD 11944–02, The Community Adaptation of Mildly Retarded Persons; The National Institute of Education, Grant No. NIE–G–80–0016; and NIMH training grant No. 5F32 MHO8631.